THE TRADE TRAP

Poverty and the Global Commodity Markets

Belinda Coote

Oxfam

A catalogue record for this book is available from the British Library

Cover photo: *Shramik Abhivrudhi Sangh – powerloom weavers' co-operative,
Karnataka, India.* (RAJENDRA SHAW/OXFAM)

ISBN 0 85598 134 2
ISBN 0 85598 135 0 pbk

Published by Oxfam UK and Ireland
274 Banbury Road, Oxford OX2 7DZ
Typeset in 10 pt Palatino by Oxfam Design
Printed by the Alden Press, Oxford

OX:1036/DH/91

CONTENTS

ACKNOWLEDGEMENTS

Much of the research for this book took place overseas, with the invaluable assistance of Oxfam colleagues and project partners. First and foremost I want to thank the many people who contributed their first-hand experience of 'the trade trap', particularly those in Bangladesh, Bolivia, Chad, Chile, the Dominican Republic, the Philippines, and Tanzania.

I am indebted to my colleagues Richard Hartill, Iain Gray, and Sharon Thompson for their research on the fishing and forestry industries in Chile. My thanks also to Luz Lagarrigue for guiding me so patiently through the complexities of the Chilean economy. The work on Bolivia would have been impossible without Valerie Black and Imar Mealla, who acted as guides and interpreters during my visit, and my colleagues Juan Vargas and Ann Chaplin. Thanks also to Jim Monan for his work on the Bangladesh shrimp industry, and to Alfred Sakafu for sharing with me his expertise on the Tanzanian cotton industry and economy.

Special thanks are due to Francis Rolt, whose work in the early stages of the research helped to shape the project, and to Andrew Powell, whose input on commodity markets was invaluable. Thanks also to Duncan Brewer for his work on the tea and vegetable-oils industries, and to our volunteers, Rachel Stringfellow and Piers Cazalet, who came along just at the right moment and gave me the benefit of their time and skills. I am also grateful to my colleagues in the Public Affairs Unit, especially Dianna Melrose, Dorothy Myers, Sara Grundy, and Ann Simpson, whose help and support I have valued throughout, particularly in the final stages of the project.

Both the research and the writing of this book gained in innumerable ways from expert criticisms and suggestions. To all, especially the most critical, I am indebted, particularly Michael Barratt Brown, Alison Barrett, John Clark, Jo Feingold, Tony Hill, Ian Leggett, Neil MacDonald, Edward Millard, Catherine Robinson, Christopher Stevens, Paul Valentin, Kevin Watkins, Christine Whitehead, and Steven Wiggins.

Finally, this book would not have been written without the help with childcare given so generously by my family and friends. Many thanks to all of you.

Belinda Coote
November 1991

(Belinda Coote is a policy adviser in the Public Affairs Unit of Oxfam UK and Ireland, and the author of *The Hunger Crop: Poverty and the Sugar Industry* (Oxfam, 1987).)

GLOSSARY

ACP   African, Caribbean, and Pacific countries: 69 former colonies of European powers with which the European Community has special trade relations through the Lome Convention.

ATO   Alternative Trade Organisation, one committed to cooperation with organisations of the poor and the oppressed in Third World countries, aiming to improve living standards mainly by means of promoting trade in products from these countries.

CAP   Common Agricultural Policy, of the European Community, a system of levies and subsidies to protect European agriculture.

EC   European Community, originally six West European nation states, currently (1991) twelve, formed in 1957 under the Treaty of Rome.

ECU   European Currency Unit, the name for the common currency in which the European Community's business is increasingly often reckoned. One ecu = approximately £0.70.

EDF   European Development Fund, set up under the Treaty of Rome to provide funds from the EEC for ACP countries.

f.o.b.   free on board, the value of goods on delivery to the port of export, i.e. without insurance and freight charges.

FTA   Free Trade Agreement between the USA and Canada, signed in 1989; being extended to Mexico and possibly other countries on the American continent to provide for free movement of goods and services among these countries.

GATT   General Agreement on Tariffs and Trade, a multi-lateral trade agreement designed to negotiate rules and standards for the conduct of international trade, signed in 1947.

GDP   Gross Domestic Product, of a nation state, the value of goods and services produced in a year, i.e. including exports but excluding imports from GNP.

GNP   Gross National Product, of a nation state, the value of all goods and services produced in a year, before allowing for depreciation (capital consumption) of assets.

GSP   General System of Preferences: the system by which industrialised countries grant preferential treatment, through zero or reduced import duties, for certain products imported from developing countries; first negotiated at UNCTAD in 1986.

G77   Group of 77 Third World countries (later to become 96) which initiated the establishment of UNCTAD.

IBRD   International Bank for Reconstruction and Development

ICA   International Commodity Agreement

ICCA   International Cocoa Agreement

ICFA   International Coffee Agreement

IFAT   International Federation of Alternative Trade, founded in Amsterdam in 1989 to coordinate ATOs' activities world-wide.

IMF   International Monetary Fund, one of the institutions established by the United Nations at Bretton Woods in 1944, to provide finance for governments facing short-term deficits on their foreign balance of payments.

INRA   International Natural Rubber Agreement

IPC   Integrated Programme for Commodities, covering 18 commodities produced mainly for export by LDCs.

ISA   International Sugar Agreement

ITA   International Tin Agreement

ITO   International Trade Organisation, proposed by Keynes in 1944 at Bretton Woods but transmuted into GATT.

LDC   Less Developed Country; or more usually one of the 43 *Least* Developed Countries, so designated by the United Nations because of their low per capita incomes and little, if any, industrialisation.

MFA   Multi-Fibre Arrangement, whereby industrialised countries place quotas on imports of textiles and clothing from LDCs; one of the exceptions permitted under the GATT liberalisation process.

MFN   Most Favoured Nation, the system adopted among nation states in their foreign trade of granting to all trading partners the same treatment as accorded to a most favoured nation.

NICs   Newly Industrialising Countries

NIEO   New International Economic Order, the long-term objective of the Group of 77; the first stages were proposed at UNCTAD in 1971.

NTB   Non-tariff Barrier: any obstacle to international trade other than actual taxes (tariffs) on imports.

OECD   Organisation for Economic Cooperation and Development, whose membership includes the industrialised countries of West Europe, North America, Japan and Australasia.

OPEC   Organisation of Petroleum Exporting Countries, set up in 1973 after the Yom Kippur war between Egypt and Israel, in order to control oil production and raise oil prices; includes mainly Middle East oil producers, but also Venezuela, Mexico and Nigeria. OPEC members were responsible for about half the world's oil output in 1990.

S & D Special and Differential treatment of imports from Developing Countries, allowed after 1964 under rules of GATT, thus eliminating the requirement of reciprocity.

SDR   Special Drawing Rights, increasingly used as a unit of account by official organisations and in financial markets. They are issued by the IMF to member countries in proportion to their quotas, and represent claims or rights which are honoured by other members and by the IMF itself. Their supply, their value, and the interest payable on them are all determined by the IMF. The value of the SDR is calculated daily as a weighted average of the exchange values of five major currencies (the US dollar, the Deutschmark, the French franc, the Japanese yen, and the pound sterling). The value obtained is then expressed in dollars.

TNC   Trans-national Company, a large company operating in several countries and sometimes with owners drawn from several countries.

TRIMs   Trade Related Investment Measures, employed by governments to manage the links between their trade and the investments in their countries by foreign nationals, subject to negotiation under GATT.

TRIPs   Trade Related Intellectual Property Rights: the rights of ownership, patents etc. which go with the export of capital goods and services, subject to GATT negotiations.

UN   United Nations, international organisation established after World War Two, to maintain peace and assist economic and political development through regional Commissions in Europe, Africa, Asia and the Far East, and Latin America, and also through specialist agencies, including the World Bank, IMF, and UNCTAD.

UNCTAD   The United Nations Conference on Trade and Development

Uruguay Round   The latest round of GATT negotiations, begun in September 1986.

VER   Voluntary Export Restraint: agreement by the government of one nation state (or an industry) to limit its exports of certain products in certain markets, e.g. Japanese cars in Europe.

INTRODUCTION

In one year Kabula, a young woman farmer in Western Tanzania, earns only a little more from her cotton harvest than it takes to buy herself one kanga, the garment traditionally worn by women and men in Tanzania. Yet in any one harvest she grows enough cotton to make 720 kangas. 'Cotton is the only cash crop we grow around here, and we have to grow something for cash in order to pay local taxes, to buy books for my brothers and sister who are still at school, and to buy essentials like salt, shoes and clothes.'

Kabula is caught in the trade trap. She relies on cotton for a cash income, yet the price that she receives for it is so low that she is consigned to a life of rural poverty.

Cotton is an important export crop for Tanzania, contributing around 15 per cent of the country's export earnings, yet in recent years its price on international markets has been low. Tanzania has had to produce more cotton to keep up, but in doing so has contributed to the plunge in world market prices. Other cotton-producing countries, desperate for foreign-exchange earnings to fuel their development efforts and pay off their international debts, are doing the same, causing global supply to outstrip global demand, and international prices thus to fall still further.

Cotton is not the only product to have suffered from low prices in recent years. They have become a feature of the markets for nearly all internationally traded primary commodities, such as sugar, coffee, tin, tea, and copper. Yet these commodities are critical to the economies of most of the countries in which Oxfam works. All over the Third World there are people like Kabula struggling to survive the vicious cycle of overproduction and low prices which so fundamentally undermines their own and their countries' development efforts.

Oxfam is funding projects in more than 70 countries in the South. The main aim of its overseas programme is to alleviate poverty and suffering. The nature of poverty and its causes varies a great deal from country to country. Yet a major unifying feature is the developing world's dependence on primary commodities. *The Trade Trap* draws on

Oxfam's overseas experience to show how the terms of North/South trade disadvantage the poor and argue for structural change.

This book begins by exploring the extent to which developing countries are dependent on primary commodities, and the devastating impact that a sudden price fall on the international market can have on the lives of individual producers. It looks at the underlying causes of these price swings, and shows how efforts to stabilise them, through mechanisms such as International Commodity Agreements, have proved largely unsuccessful.

Even when prices are high, the producer receives only a fraction of the amount paid for the end-product by consumers in the rich industrialised countries. To show why this is the case, *The Trade Trap* traces two commodities, tea and coconut, on their respective journeys from the producer to the consumer. In doing so, it considers the central role played by multinational corporations in the commodity trade, and explains the workings of the futures markets.

Third World producers of primary commodities desperately need markets for their goods yet face a daunting array of trade barriers which often deny them access to rich world markets. The latest round of negotiations under the General Agreement on Trade and Tariffs – the Uruguay Round – has underlined how much the interests of the developed world predominate over those of developing countries. The growing trend towards regional trade blocs, in Europe, North America, and East Asia, could further marginalise poor producers.

The Trade Trap, which draws heavily on case studies from Oxfam's work overseas, ends by looking at some alternative models for a fairer world trading system. These are based on Oxfam's own experience of alternative trade, through Oxfam Trading. It concludes that while there is much to be learned from alternative trade, the real challenge is to move such models from the periphery of northern consumerism to the mainstream. Only then will trade become less of a trap for poor producers, and more of a means for sustainable development in the South.

1

THE TRADE TRAP

Kabula Mboje held out a piece of her brightly coloured kanga, the garment traditionally worn by women and men in Tanzania. 'Look at this', she said. 'It was a cheap one, yet it cost me 800 shillings [£4.50 sterling]; not very much less than I earned from this year's cotton harvest.' It had been a bad year for cotton, yet even so Kabula had grown enough on her two-acre plot of land to make 720 kangas.[1]

Kabula lives in the village of Mwabuzo, a scattered settlement of houses in the Shinyanga region of West Central Tanzania. The area sprawls over a vast plain, several thousand feet above sea level and 250 miles south of the equator. Until the late 1940s it had been thickly forested, but now the vegetation consists of a few baobab trees, sticking up out of the land like giants' hands, and scrubby thorn bushes. Over the years lack of ground cover has caused severe erosion, and deep gullies scar the landscape.

It was late August. The cotton harvest was over. The roadside thorns had snared the cotton from the bullock carts taking the crop to the village's storage sheds, and looked as though they had flowered bizarrely in the dry heat. Apart from the bulging walls of the village storage sheds, in some places shored up with long poles to stop them bursting, there was little evidence of farming activity. The land was grey, dusty and hard. The remains of the cotton bushes had been burnt to kill pests, while the cattle had been taken to pasture in the south.

Kabula was enjoying a well-earned rest from the hard work of cotton farming. In a few months, she and the other villagers would begin preparations for next year's crop. By law each adult member of the community is required to grow at least one acre of cotton. 'Cotton is the only cash crop we can grow around here,' she explained. 'We have to grow something for cash so that we can pay our local taxes and buy essentials such as salt, clothes and shoes.'

Kabula was disappointed with her year's cotton earnings, but relieved not to have made a loss. Some did. After they have paid to spray the crop, to hire a tractor for ploughing, and for transporting the

GEOFF SAYER/OXFAM

Tanzania, June 1990: taking cotton from the fields at Paji village, Meatu District, to the local warehouse. (In a good year, the fields yield an average of 700 kg per acre – considerably more than the figure for mechanised farms in the USA and Australia.)

cotton to the village storage sheds, there is often little or no profit to be made from the sale of the cotton.

The community of Mwabuzo is well known to Oxfam. The association between the two began in the mid-1980s, when a group of farmers asked for advice on increasing their cotton-crop yields. They had decided to farm collectively so that they could pool their resources and work more efficiently. Encouraged by the success of this group, Kabula and her friends had formed one of their own. She is now convinced that this is a better way of working: 'If we work together as a group, it's easier; we can support each other and get loans more easily. It also makes sense to grow an area of one crop all in the same place. That way you spend less on spraying than if you farm a field by yourself, away from everyone else's fields.'[2]

Oxfam has supported these initiatives in a number of ways, including help with loans for oxen, inputs, and ploughs. Oxfam's Tanzanian Country Representative feels that it is important to encourage young people to stay in the rural areas. Lack of opportunity to earn a decent living has meant that many have drifted into the cities, where they often face even worse poverty. By helping them to improve their income, there is more chance of keeping them on the land.

But despite programmes such as these, and the energy and resilience of young farmers such as Kabula, the people in Mwabuzo have become steadily poorer since the early 1980s. Like many people in the countries in which Oxfam works, they have been caught in the trade trap.

THE DANGERS OF COMMODITY DEPENDENCE

While Kabula relies on cotton for a cash income, for Tanzania cotton exports are a significant source of foreign exchange. Since the mid-1960s cotton has accounted for between 12 and 16 per cent of the country's foreign-exchange earnings.[3] The problem is that in recent years Tanzania has been earning less for its cotton exports, because of depressed cotton prices on the international markets. Cotton is produced in more than 70 countries, which include some very large producers such as the USA. Production increases in these countries resulted in a sharp fall in cotton prices in the mid-1980s, with the result that despite consistent levels of production, Tanzania's cotton earnings in 1985 were half those of 1984.[4]

While cotton is important to Tanzania, coffee is of even greater significance to its economy. Between 1982 and 1986 it accounted for 40 per of export earnings, up from 16 per cent twenty years earlier.[5] Good coffee prices could have cushioned the Tanzanian economy from its losses on cotton, and indeed did so when prices rose sharply in 1986. But apart from that one year, coffee prices were also depressed throughout the 1980s. Figure 1 plots the prices paid for Tanzania's cotton and coffee between 1972 and 1988. It shows, above all, how unstable prices have been, making it impossible for Tanzania's government to know, from one year to the next, how much it will earn from its exports.

Figure 1: Graph showing the instability of prices paid for Tanzania's cotton and coffee, 1972–1988

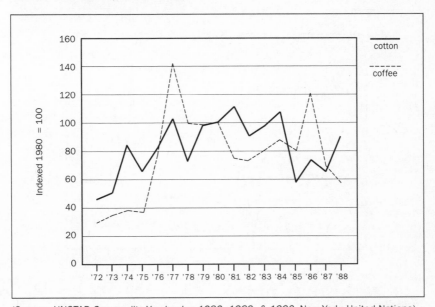

(Source: *UNCTAD Commodity Yearbooks: 1986, 1989, & 1990*, New York: United Nations)

Coffee and cotton were not the only primary commodities to suffer from unstable and generally low prices during the 1980s. It was a decade in which the average real prices of commodities fell to their lowest level recorded in the twentieth century, with the possible exception of the Great Depression of 1932. It followed a time during the 1960s and early 1970s when commodity prices were relatively stable, and then one from 1972 to 1980 when prices rose sharply and irregularly with rising oil prices (see Figure 2). For Tanzania, which relies on the export of primary commodities for more than 80 per cent of its export earnings, this meant a steady decline in income throughout the 1980s (see Figure 3).

Tanzania is one of more than 70 countries in which Oxfam works. Like Tanzania, many rely on primary commodities for most of their export earnings[6] (see Table 1). While this dependency is greatest in sub-Saharan Africa, it is also marked in the Caribbean and Latin America. Some of these countries rely on a wide range of primary commodities. Although they suffer from the general and progressive decline in prices, this diversity means that they are cushioned from the shock of a sudden price collapse in any one commodity. This is not true for many countries which rely on a very narrow range of exports. In sub-Saharan Africa, for example, ten of the countries where Oxfam works depend on one commodity for more than 50 per cent of their export earnings (see Figure 4).

Figure 2: Price of non-fuel primary commodities in relation to the US wholesale price index, 1900–1990

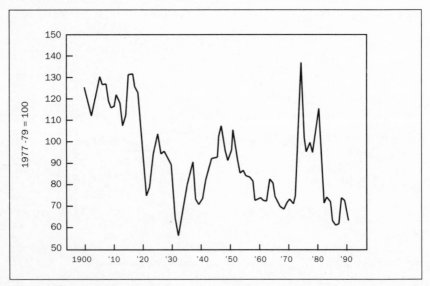

(Source: *Global Economic Prospects and the Developing Countries – 1991*, Washington: World Bank, May 1991)

Figure 3: Tanzania's export earnings from total merchandise trade from 1972 to 1990

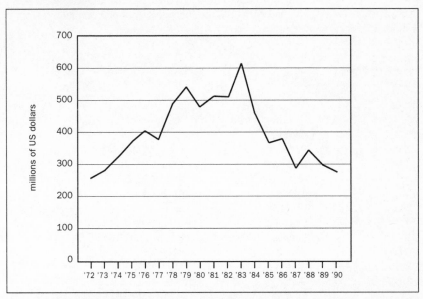

(Source: *UNCTAD Commodity Yearbooks: 1986, 1989, & 1990*, New York: United Nations)

Figure 4: Selected Oxfam countries in sub-Saharan Africa: dependence on one commodity as a percentage of total exports

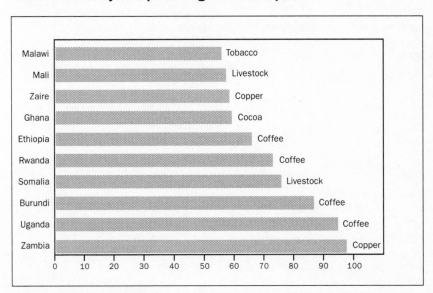

(Source: *Africa's Commodity Problems: Towards a Solution*, UNCTAD/EDM/ATF/1 – Table 2; figures for the period 1982–1986)

Table 1: Commodity dependency of individual countries in which Oxfam works (countries as listed in Oxfam Grants List 1989–90)

Primary commodities, excluding fuel, as a percentage of total exports for 1982–1986 (showing the percentage of the individual commodity where it exceeds 20 per cent of total exports)

Primary commodities as a % of total export earnings	Country	Individual commodities as a % of total export earnings
Africa		
99.9	Mauritania	(iron ore 45.0/fish 42.0)
99.7	Zambia	(copper 98.0)
97.9	Rwanda	(coffee 73.0)
97.9	Niger	(uranium 85.0)
95.1	Burundi	(coffee 87.0)
95.0	Uganda	(coffee 95.0)
95.0	Namibia	(diamonds 40.0/uranium 24.0)
94.7	Somalia	(live animals 76.0)
93.4	Malawi	(tobacco 55.0/tea 20.0)
90.0	Ethiopia	(coffee 66.0)
88.9	Burkina Faso	(cotton 48.0)
88.5	Sudan	(cotton 42.0)
84.3	Mali	(live animals 58.0/cotton 29.0)
83.3	Togo*	(phosphates 47.0)
82.0	Guinea Bissau	(cashew nuts 29.0/groundnuts 23.0)
79.3	Tanzania	(coffee 40.0)
76.3	Mozambique	(fish 27.0/prawns 16.0)
72.0	Chad*	(live animals 58.0/cotton 29.0)
71.6	Senegal*	(fish 32.0)
68.7	Zaire	(copper 58.0)
68.5	Ghana*	(cocoa 59.0)
63.2	Sierra Leone	(diamonds 32.0)
61.5	Kenya**	(coffee 30.0)
56.9	Zimbabwe**	(tobacco 20.0)
48.0	Gambia	(groundnuts 45.0)
46.2	Lesotho	(mohair 24.0)
6.5	Angola	(95.8 inc. oil)
–	South Africa	
–	Western Sahara	
Latin America		
91.0	Chile	(copper 46.3)
89.7	Paraguay**	(cotton 30.7/soya 23.6/wood 22.3)
69.3	Colombia*	(coffee 51.0)
61.5	Peru*	
49.4	Brazil*	
46.9	Bolivia	(tin 26.0/natural gas 48.5)
29.2	Ecuador*	(crude petroleum 45.5)
–	Guyana	

Asia

98.0	Myanmar	(cereals 37.3/wood 35.4)
60.7	Sri Lanka*	(tea 34.8)
45.4	Philippines*	
36.7	India	
34.1	Pakistan	(cotton 21.2)
33.5	Bangladesh	(jute 51.6)
33.1	Nepal*	
18.7	Indonesia	(crude petroleum 51.9)
–	Afghanistan	
–	Bhutan	
–	Cambodia	
–	China	
–	Korea	
–	Macao	

Central America and the Caribbean

90.8	Nicaragua	(coffee 36.0/cotton 26.5)
86.9	Honduras	(fruit 34.6/coffee 25.9)
84.8	Jamaica	(aluminium 60.5)
76.6	El Salvador	(coffee 59.5)
75.7	Dominican Rep.*	(sugar 30.9)
75.6	Panama	(fruit 26.5/fish 23.2)
72.7	Guatemala	(coffee 32.4)
69.7	Costa Rica	(fruits 27.1/coffee 26.5)
64.4	Grenada*	(spices 25.7/bananas 13)
37.0	Haiti*	(coffee 23.9)
12.3	Mexico	(crude petroleum 60.0)
–	Belize	
–	Dominica	(bananas 71)
–	Puerto Rico	
–	St Lucia	(bananas 91)
–	St Vincent	(bananas 28)

Middle East

47.9	Jordan*	(phosphates 23.2)
26.0	Egypt**	(87.5 inc. oil)
–	Israel	
–	Lebanon	
–	Yemen Arab Republic	

* Countries with decreased dependency on commodities in total exports as compared to period 1967–1971.

** Countries with increased dependency on commodities in total exports as compared to period 1967–1971.

No star indicates little change in dependency level.

Note: The countries listed are those in which Oxfam made grants in the period 1989 to 1990. Countries without figures are those not included in the UNCTAD source.

(Source: Adapted from UNCTAD Report on Diversification, Annex II, TD/B/C.1AC/7, July 1989. Figures for Windward Island banana dependency taken from B. Borrell and M-C. Yang (1990): *'EC Bananarama 1992'*, World Bank Working Paper on International Trade WPS 523, Table 2.)

So they are very vulnerable to price instability in these commodities. Even small changes in price will produce substantial variations in their export earnings, making it very difficult for them to plan from one year to the next.

With such a high level of dependence on primary commodities, many Third World countries suffered a considerable loss in export earnings due to the low prices of the 1980s. Between 1981 and 1985, this loss has been estimated at US$553 billion, equivalent to 122 per cent of the total value of the commodity exports of developing countries in 1980. The largest part of this loss was due to the fall in the value of fuel exports, which was in turn due to the drop in oil prices, particularly in 1982–1983. However, even excluding oil, the cumulative loss in the commodity export earnings of developing countries was substantial: US$57 billion, as compared with their value in 1980, amounting to 54 per cent of the latter.[7] However, not only did commodity-dependent countries lose export earnings, they also experienced an inexorable deterioration in their terms of trade.

Put simply, 'terms of trade' can be understood as the purchasing power of exports. If the revenue from a given volume of a country's exports purchases a diminished quantity of imports, then a country's terms of trade may be said to have worsened. Many commodity-dependent Third World countries have suffered from this problem, because the prices of manufactured goods, which they have to import, have increased relative to those of primary products, which they export.

This is not a new phenomenon. The terms of trade for primary commodities have been in decline since the 1920s. As Figure 2 shows, there have been irregular price movements since the beginning of the twentieth century, with peaks followed by troughs. However, the overall trend has been for terms of trade to decline.[8] The decline was most marked in the first half of the 1980s, during which the purchasing power of sub-Saharan Africa's exports fell by 50 per cent.[9] While there was some improvement towards the end of the 1980s, by 1989 the purchasing power of primary commodities was still 22 per cent below its 1980 level.[10]

Between 1980 and 1989 terms of trade for those countries in which Oxfam works fell, on average, by 16 per cent, compared with the increase of 12 per cent enjoyed by the industrial countries (see Figure 5). Figure 6 shows percentage changes in terms of trade for the 15 Oxfam countries which were worst affected. Rwanda (which relies on coffee for 73 per cent of its export earnings) experienced the greatest decline, of minus 47 per cent.

For many years some economists[11] have argued that developing countries should reduce their dependence on primary commodities,

Figure 5: Percentage changes in terms of trade for selected groups, 1980–89

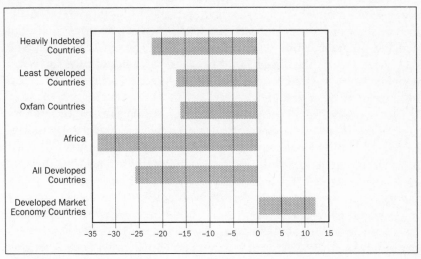

(Source: *Handbook of International Trade and Development Statistics 1989*, New York: United Nations, 1990)

Figure 6: Percentage changes in terms of trade for selected Oxfam countries, 1980–88

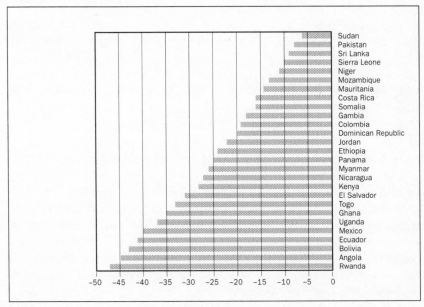

(Source: *Handbook of International Trade and Development Statistics 1989*, New York: United Nations, 1990)

because a number of structural factors make a continuing deterioration in their buying power very likely.

The first factor concerns the nature of the commodities themselves, the low 'income elasticity' of their demand, and the effect of the introduction of substitute products. In developed countries long-term demand for many primary commodities is 'income-inelastic', meaning that rises in income levels will not lead to significantly increased demand. For example, when people's income increases, they are unlikely to drink more coffee.

The second factor concerns the nature of primary-commodity producing countries. Large companies from the rich industrial countries can dominate and structure international markets in a way that is denied to small unorganised Third World commodity producers. Thus they are denied the full gains that they could earn through trade.[12]

One way to overcome the structural problems of declining terms of trade would be to develop a manufacturing base. Many countries have done so. The growth of manufactured goods in world trade averaged 4.9 per cent between 1980 and 1989 (compared with a growth of 1.7 per cent in primary-commodity trade). However, much of this expansion has taken place in the newly industrialising countries of East Asia, such as Taiwan, Korea, and Singapore, and in some other developing countries, such as Mauritius, which have experienced strong economic growth as a result. Other countries are actually producing and exporting fewer manufactured goods than they were in the mid-1970s.

Many of them fall into the United Nations' category of 'least developed' countries, or LDCs. One criterion for categorisation as an LDC is that no more than 10 per cent of a country's Gross Domestic Product comes from manufactured goods. The number of countries with LDC status grew from 24 in 1971 to 42 in 1989.[13] Of the 72 countries in which Oxfam worked in 1989–1990, 25 have LDC status.[14] The manufactures that they do produce are overwhelmingly (around 70 per cent) concentrated in low-technology industries, such as textiles, or are concerned with processing primary commodities produced in the country.[15]

The reasons for the failure of many of these poorer developing countries to develop their manufacturing bases are complex. To do so they need money to invest in the necessary technology and training, and markets to sell to. Declining export earnings and unfavourable terms of trade mean that many developing countries face deteriorating deficits in their balance of payments. These have had to be financed through external borrowing and aid. But the resulting debt-service obligations, aggravated by high interest rates, absorb much of the poor countries' export earnings. This meant that transfers to developing countries went from a positive US$37 billion in 1980 to a negative US$1 billion in 1989.[16]

Price instability in their export markets makes it difficult to plan, while the world's stock of Foreign Direct Investment (FDI) in developing countries has declined. In 1970 30 per cent of the world's FDI was in developing countries. By 1988 this had fallen to 21 per cent. Most of this is concentrated in the richer countries of Latin America, the Caribbean, and Asia. Only 2.5 per cent of foreign direct investment is in Africa.[17]

Those countries that have managed to build up a manufacturing base face difficulties in gaining access to markets. Industrial countries often bias their tariff structures against processed commodities. Sugar, for example, an important export crop for many developing countries, faces an average tariff of more than 20 per cent if it is refined before being exported to industrial countries. Only about one per cent is charged on exports of the raw product.[18] Developing countries' exports of both primary and processed products also face a daunting array of non-tariff barriers which often exclude them from Northern markets and discourage them from developing a manufacturing base.

This is the 'trade trap' in which many of the poorer developing countries are caught. Most of their exports are low-value commodities, so they cannot afford to diversify into more productive economic activities. If they do, they are penalised by the tariff structures of the industrialised countries, which are biased against processed goods.

The debt crisis and the relative decline in commodity prices were major reasons why the 1980s became known as a 'lost decade' for many developing countries. They ended it poorer than they were at the beginning. Economic growth rates are normally measured by per capita Gross Domestic Product (GDP), that is the annual average value of total production within the country concerned, divided per head of population. Caught in the 'trade trap', many countries, particularly in Latin America and sub-Saharan Africa, recorded declines in their average per capita GDP during the 1980s. In stark contrast others, particularly the newly industrialising countries of East Asia, which had, due to their particular historical, economic and political circumstances, managed to expand their manufacturing bases, recorded an average per capita growth rate of more than two and a half times that of industrial countries as a whole.[19] East Asia's four 'little tigers' (South Korea, Taiwan, Hong Kong, and Singapore) have almost quadrupled their share of total world exports in the past twenty years.[20]

THE VULNERABILITY OF POOR PRODUCERS

For the poor producer, who is Oxfam's primary concern, the problems are in no way confined to those of fluctuating or declining prices. Kabula Mboje in Tanzania experiences the 'trade trap' through the difficulties that she faces in obtaining credit to pay for a tractor to plough her land, the pesticides she sprays on her cotton, or the cloth she wraps it up in to stop the wind blowing it away. She also has to contend with lack of storage facilities for her harvested cotton; difficulties in transporting it over the dusty pitted tracks that serve as roads; delays in payment for her harvested crop; and declining levels of soil fertility in the area that she farms.

Ninety per cent of Tanzania's cotton is grown in the Lake Zone, which incorporates the Mwanza and Shinyanga regions. Here it is estimated that between two and three million people are engaged in cotton production. They all face similar problems. For one thing, credit is provided by the Primary Cooperative Societies, which in turn borrow the money from the banks. But sometimes the banks do not have the money to lend, so the supply of credit to the farmers dries up.

Once it is harvested and sorted, the farmers' crop is sold to the village buying centres, where it is stored in the village storage sheds. But here the farmers face another problem: storage facilities are often limited, and much of the cotton ends up in people's houses or piled up outside, where it is easily spoiled by rain. Eventually the cotton is taken from the village stores by truck to the ginneries. But the high costs of fuel and spare parts mean that there are often long delays. These delays are further aggravated by the poor condition of the village roads, or 'cotton tracks'.

When the cotton reaches the ginneries, it is sold by the cooperative unions to the Tanzanian Cotton Marketing Board (TCMB). But many of the ginneries are operating well below capacity, because they are old and poorly maintained. In the 1987/88 harvest only an estimated 19 per cent of the cotton purchased by the TCMB was actually ginned,[21] thus massively reducing the amount available for export and the potential of farmers such as Kabula to earn a decent living from growing cotton.[22]

The problems faced by Tanzania's cotton producers are compounded by environmental degradation. Oxfam's Country Representative described how cotton production itself has degraded the soil in Shinyanga: 'When people first started growing cotton in the area, it was relatively well paid. They were able to buy cattle with the proceeds, but this led to overgrazing. Then they began using tractors to prepare the land for cotton. This meant that larger areas were cleared and trees uprooted. Now there is less rainfall in the area. Farmers can no longer grow maize, so have switched to sorghum. Because there is little left for fuel, they have to use cow dung and cotton stalks which otherwise would be left to fertilise the land. The result is severe soil erosion and declining soil fertility.'[23]

Such problems are not peculiar to cotton, nor to Tanzania. Oxfam's project experience illustrates the extreme vulnerability of small-scale producers in all parts of the developing world. The following examples show what this means to coffee growers in the Dominican Republic and fisherfolk in the Philippines.

Coffee producers in the Dominican Republic

Rufino Herrera owns three and a half hectares of land in the south of the Dominican Republic. He sets aside one hectare of this land to grow food, but the rest is given over to the production of coffee, and in this way he supports himself and his family of five. Rufino is also General Secretary of an organisation of coffee growers which has been supported by Oxfam since the mid-1980s.

Coffee is one of the Dominican Republic's key exports. It ranks fifth in terms of export earnings after sugar, ferronickel, dore (gold and silver), and cocoa.[24] Nearly half of the country's economically active population, of a total population of around six and a half million, are engaged in agricultural production. Of these, some 70,000 families depend on small-scale coffee production.

Prices of coffee on the world market had been guaranteed to producing nations under the terms of the International Coffee Agreement until July 1989, when negotiations for its renewal collapsed. The result was to send the price of coffee on the international markets plummeting as the bigger exporters, such as Brazil (which accounts for some 30 per cent of world production), off-loaded their stocks.

Coffee prices tend to follow a cyclical pattern of boom and bust on the international markets. Short periods of high prices encourage increased production which, in turn, leads to longer periods of low prices. But the slump of July 1989 was the most serious for many years. It is the smaller exporting countries, such as the Dominican Republic, that suffer most, as those countries that dominate the market (such as Brazil, Colombia and Indonesia) battle for commercial advantage. Countries like the Dominican Republic have no influence over international coffee prices.

The collapse in coffee prices came on top of the economic pressures that producers were already facing due to the measures being taken by the government to cope with its international debt. The removal of subsidies on agricultural inputs had resulted in soaring prices for inputs, such as fertilisers. This put them beyond the reach of many farmers, who suffered declining yields as a result. In addition, high taxes had been imposed on coffee exports to increase government revenue. These have to be paid by the farmer before the crop is sold, which forces many of them into debt.[25]

When coffee prices fell, Rufino Herrera and the 10,000 coffee producers affiliated to the federation of coffee producers that he leads could no longer cover their production costs. They were selling their coffee on the international market for around US$85 per quintal, whereas it was costing them between US$105 and US$110 to produce. When asked why the farmers in his federation continue to grow coffee, he pointed out that they wouldn't stand any better chance of survival if they abandoned production. Many have, but most of these have ended up in shanty towns, adding to the country's swelling ranks of unemployed.[26] The only way that they do survive is by selling through alternative traders, as described in Chapter 14.

Fishing in the Philippines

Jun lives in a small fishing community in the southern Philippines island of Mindanao. The *barrio*, Santa Rosa, is perched between a large coral reef and a coconut plantation in the shadow of the Philippines' highest mountain, Mount Apo. Many of its small wooden houses are built on stilts. At high tide the sea washes under them.

Jun grew up in Santa Rosa. His father was a fisherman. He remembers being taken out as a young boy in his father's small boat and helping him to haul in the nets full of fish. There was never any shortage of fish in those rich seas, and the family lived comfortably off the catch, selling what they could not eat at the local market.

But as Jun grew older, it seemed that there were fewer fish in the sea. He and his father were having to spend longer and go farther out to sea to fill their nets. On clear days they could sometimes see large trawlers out to sea. They were rumoured to be from Japan. It was apparent to the Santa Rosa community that the trawlers were sweeping the sea clean of the fish that they relied on for a living.

As Jun's father grew older, he was less able to cope with the long hours at sea. Responsibility for feeding the family fell to Jun, who would set out early each morning to catch fish. Some days he returned empty-handed and disillusioned, and the family went hungry. Then one of his friends invited him to go out fishing with him one night. As they got out to sea, his friend produced a stick of dynamite. He told Jun that if they blasted the coral with it, they would be able to catch the shoals of fish that gather beneath it for feeding and spawning. They used the dynamite that night and returned to shore with their nets full. Jun's father was angry. He warned that if they destroyed the coral, they would also destroy the fish. But Jun took little notice. He knew that this was the only way he could keep the fish coming in and his family fed.

Fortunately, perhaps, his father died before Jun had his accident in the late 1970s, so he was spared the tragedy. One night (they always used the dynamite at night), a stick of it exploded in Jun's hands. He lost both his arms in the explosion. His chest and face were badly burned and he lost his sight in both eyes.

As Jun's father predicted, the coral reef that stretches out to sea in front of the barrio is no longer a rich spawning ground for fish, just an expanse of jagged grey rock. Some people in Santa Rosa still fish, but most have had to find other ways of surviving. For some the answer came when a Japanese logging concession moved on to the other side of the reef. Here truck-loads of logs from the island's dwindling rainforest were dumped daily into the water, awaiting their turn in the sawmill before shipment to Japan. The barrio people strip the bark off the logs, bundle it up, and sell it for a few centavos in town as cooking fuel.

JOHN CLARK/OXFAM

Bataan Province, The Philippines: another area where small-scale fishing is threatened by commercial operators.

There are barrios like Jun's all over the Philippines, an archipelago of 7,100 islands. About eight million people rely on fishing for a livelihood. All of them have experienced problems similar to those of the Santa Rosa community, and most live in conditions of extreme poverty.

Their problems began in 1973 with the signing of the Philippines-Japan Treaty of Amity, Commerce and Navigation. This allowed Japanese merchant and fishing vessels to enter Philippine waters and catch all the fish they wanted. That was followed by Presidential Decree 704, which encourages the export of fisheries products by private businesses, and identifies fishing as a preferred area of investment for foreigners.

These decrees marked the beginning of the plundering of the waters surrounding the Philippines, which used to be among the richest fishing grounds in the world. This process was intensified as the country plunged into debt, and further investment was encouraged to earn desperately needed foreign exchange. Beaten by commercial fishing operators, with their huge nets and advanced fishing gear, fisherfolk such as Jun have been driven to destructive methods of fishing. The setting up of commercial fish farms in many parts of the Philippines has forced fisherfolk into ever-diminishing areas. The result has been rapid environmental degradation. Three quarters of the mangrove forests which line the coasts of the Philippines and serve as important breeding, feeding, and nursery grounds for fish have been destroyed. Only 25 per cent of the Philippines' coral reefs are in good condition, and some 50 per cent of them are in advanced stages of destruction.[27]

Supporting fisherfolk is a priority of Oxfam's programme in the Philippines. At a local level, fisherfolk are organising to improve their conditions, and seeking comprehensive solutions to their problems. At a national level, a coalition of fisherfolk is campaigning for reform of the fisheries laws which have so degraded the environment and contributed to the marginalisation and poverty of their communities.[28]

Governments in the South bear responsibility for many of the problems faced by small-scale producers, including low prices, inefficient marketing structures, lack of credit, inadequate transport or storage facilities, harmful legislation, and development policies that lead to environmental degradation. Yet Third World governments face parallel difficulties. They lack control over international market prices for their exports. Price swings mean that they cannot plan for the upgrading of old industries or attract investment for new ones. Compounding the problems of inadequate resources, tariff structures in Northern markets make it difficult for them to diversify out of primary production.

2

FROM TIN BARONS TO DRUG BARONS:
Commodity dependence in Bolivia

High in the Andean Mountains in a remote corner of Eastern Bolivia, five thousand men go into the heart of a mountain each day to earn their living by mining tin. They have no safety equipment, machinery, plan of the mine, nor strategy of extraction. Each man works for himself, inching his way through the mine's one thousand kilometres of narrow shafts, burrowing deeper and deeper into the seemingly endless depths of the mountain in unbearable heat. Armed only with chisel, hammer, sticks of dynamite, and small bags of coca leaves to numb pain and stave off hunger, they hack their way through the rock seams in a desperate search for the tin-bearing veins.

They live for today. There is little point in planning for the future, or even tomorrow. Many are claimed by the mountain, ending their days buried in its depths under piles of rock. Others slowly cough their way to death from the miners' disease, silicosis. None expects to live more than thirty or thirty five years.

Outside the mine, in the bright Andean sunshine, where the air, at an altitude of 13,000 feet, is so thin that it seems to cut right through you, there are thousands more, women, men, and children, painfully chipping, rolling, washing, grinding and eventually extracting from the mountain's rock tiny piles of smooth grey sand – tin. This is their life blood and only means of survival. Surveying this Kafkaesque scene, a Canadian priest who has lived and worked in the area for more than twenty years remarked, 'It's only a matter of time, maybe months but certainly not years, before this mountain collapses. Then it will be like Armageddon.' His feelings of helplessness and desperation were evident. The Siglo Veinte–Catavi mine, once Bolivia's largest tin complex, has reached the end of its life, reduced to a warren of unsupported tunnels from which the people whose lives depend on it desperately try to scavenge a living.[1]

Their story goes back to 1544, soon after Bolivia had been settled by its Spanish conquerors, when rich deposits of silver were discovered in the mountains around Potosi. The mines were the most prolific the world has ever known, and the silver extracted from them underwrote the Spanish economy for some two centuries. After Bolivia gained independence in 1825, the silver began to run out, and by the end of the nineteenth century once-discarded tin had replaced it as the country's principal export.

The growth of the armaments industry in Europe and North America at the time of the First and Second World Wars, combined with the invention of the tin can, produced a surge in the demand for tin. Output in Bolivia expanded rapidly, and by 1945 its contribution to world supply had reached an all-time high of 48 per cent. Until 1952 control of Bolivia's tin-mining industry was in the hands of a group of wealthy, local capitalists collectively known as the 'tin barons'. Tin mining in Bolivia in the first half of this century was a lucrative business. In many cases tin ores were found in the same geological formation as silver, so the old silver mines and the infrastructure connected to them were used by the tin-mining companies. Tin grades were high, wages low, and investment costs minimal. The 'tin barons' successfully exerted their political influence over successive governments to keep taxes down.

In 1950 tin accounted for three quarters of Bolivia's export earnings. A further 20 per cent of earnings came from the export of other minerals, including copper, wolfram, bismuth, and antimony. But the industry was doing little to develop the economy. Almost all inputs connected with it – clothing, mechanical items, and even some food – were imported. The low wages paid by the industry did little to stimulate other economic activities by way of consumer demand, and infrastructure was tailored solely to the needs of the mining industry.

Working conditions in the mines had changed little in three centuries and wages were pitifully low. The miners' complaints about their situation raised the political consciousness of Bolivian workers and gave birth to the *Movimiento Nacional Revolucionario* (MNR). Under the leadership of Victor Paz Estenssoro, the MNR defeated the ruling military junta in 1952, and the Bolivian tin industry entered the second phase of its history. The new government nationalised many of the mines belonging to the tin barons and created a state mining corporation, COMIBOL.

From that time on, successive governments tried to reduce Bolivia's dependency on tin by promoting other export sectors, notably cash-crop agriculture, crude oil, natural gas and non-tin minerals. As a consequence, tin's contribution to total exports declined as other sectors grew. However, this decline also reflected an underlying decline in tin mining itself.

The central problem was geological. Bolivian ores are found in hard rock and their purity rapidly diminished over time as seams became increasingly thin, and the mines became deeper as the more accessible seams were exhausted. Today it is often more profitable to rework the old slag heaps than to mine at the rock face. But since its very early days the industry also suffered from a lack of investment – in prospecting, the development of new mines, or the re-equipping of existing mines. Then the basic strategies of the governments after the 1952 revolution was to use the earnings of the mining sector to develop other export industries, which ensured a flow of resources away from the traditional mining sector. Attempts to increase productivity in the tin mines focused on reducing manning levels and lowering miners' pay.

Irrespective of these problems, high prices for minerals on the world markets in the 1970s created a climate of optimism. But despite the general drive to increase production, the deep-rooted production problems of the industry meant that production steadily declined over the course of the decade. These difficulties were exacerbated by the debt crisis. As an oil exporter, Bolivia was considered credit-worthy during the 1970s, and borrowed freely as a result. By the beginning of the 1980s, as mineral prices began to fall and its oil surpluses started to dry up, the government had saddled the country with a substantial foreign debt.

The effects of this hit the mining sector hard. Imports were slashed, so there was no money available to buy spare parts or new machinery. COMIBOL was disadvantaged by having to change its foreign earnings into pesos at a highly over-valued exchange rate. There was no investment in the state sector, and the adjustment measures, such as wage freezes and the removal of food subsidies, adopted by successive governments led to a series of general strikes and several lengthy stoppages in the mines. Between 1981 and 1985 production fell by forty per cent.[2]

The troubled tin industry was then plunged into crisis by an unprecedented crash in international tin prices. In October 1985 the price of tin on the international market fell by half – from just over £8,000 to less than £4,000 per tonne. The London-based International Tin Council (the 22-nation body made up of consumers and producers) announced that it was no longer able to perform its function of keeping the price of tin on the world market stable. Quite simply, supply had outstretched demand for too long and, as a result of sudden changes in dollar and sterling exchange rates, the Council had run out of money.[3]

Many countries produce tin, including Britain in its few remaining Cornish tin mines, so the effect of such a drop in prices was widely felt. But nowhere was it felt more acutely than in Bolivia, which, despite declining yields, still relied on tin for nearly 40 per cent of its foreign-exchange earnings. Other major producers were less dependent on it, as they had successfully developed other areas of their economies.

Malaysia, for example, the world's largest producer, derived just 3 per cent of its export earnings from tin, against 19.5 per cent in 1970.[4]

LIFE IN THE MINES

Irrespective of international market prices, productivity levels, or the government's economic policies, life in and around Bolivia's tin mines has always been hard. Oxfam has been supporting projects in the mining areas since the mid-1970s, and the miserable living and working conditions of the miners and their families have been well documented. As one Oxfam field worker wrote in connection with funding for a health project in the area of the Siglo Veinte–Catavi complex in 1979:

... Work conditions in the mines continue to be extremely dangerous and carry the added high risk of infection by TB or silicosis, with the result that tin miners have a scandalously short life expectancy of only 37 years.

... Housing is over-crowded with families of 10–13 crowded into two tiny, badly lit and ventilated rooms, in old barrack housing with a standpipe and one public latrine for each row of 30 houses, and a water system which is frequently cut off. The accommodation is provided free, but is only available as long as the miner continues to work for COMIBOL. If he is dismissed, or reaches retiring age, he is forced to move out.

... Discounts made from the company store, which provides an increasingly limited range of subsidised foods, together with other debts which the miner owes the corporation, can often reduce his take-home wage packet to a small fraction of what he has earned, and many miners live in a state of chronic and perpetual penury.

... Overall, therefore, the living and working conditions of the miners, and of the civilian population of Llallagua–Siglo Veinte, are totally inadequate, and give rise to a host of related health problems. These problems are exacerbated in many cases by the low wages earned, and the inadequate diets available to the bulk of the population. The *campesinos* of the surrounding rural areas suffer the usual problems of inadequate diet, caused by overpopulation and insufficient land, a traditional agricultural system, and the typical set of environmental deficiencies – bad housing, poor water, inadequate clothing, etc., which leaves them prey to malnutrition, gastrointestinal and respiratory problems, and a host of related illnesses, such as TB and bronchial problems.[5]

Conditions in the mining areas deteriorated further following the collapse in tin prices. The government had already announced that it would be re-structuring the country's debt-ridden economy. Its IMF-inspired prescription, a package of measures known as the New Economic Policy, was designed to increase exports and reduce public expenditure. As part of this its nationalised industries, including the troubled state mining sector, were to be subjected to rigorous analysis and cost cutting.

Then came the fall in tin prices. This rendered almost all Bolivia's tin mines irredeemably uneconomic. The government's response was to close down many of the state-owned mines. Twenty thousand miners lost their jobs. Some of the mines were handed over to workers' cooperatives, the Siglo Veinte–Catavi mine among them. Desperate for work, hundreds of people flooded into the area to join the cooperatives. The impact of this influx on the lives of the skilled miners and the surrounding community has been profound, as the following account shows.

Doña Zenobia[6]

Doña Zenobia Reynaga de Chavarria lives in the town of Llallagua which sprawls up the slope of the mountain containing the Siglo Veinte mine. She has a long, indirect association with Oxfam through her membership of the Siglo Veinte–Catavi *Amas des Casas*, or Housewives' Committee, of which she became general secretary in mid-1989. In Bolivia every miners' union has a Housewives' Committee. As their name suggests, they are organisations of miners' wives. The committees have been in existence since 1961, when they formed to demand the release from prison of the miners' political leaders. Over the years they have gained both recognition and respect from the miners' unions and now have a National Committee affiliated to the Miners' Federation. Oxfam has been supporting initiatives taken by the Housewives' Committee to alleviate the problems faced by miners and their families, particularly in the most recent episode of the Bolivian tin miners' history.

By the time we reached the Chavarria household, Doña Zenobia and her family had finished their evening meal and there was the familiar hum of family activity as plates were washed and children settled into their evening activities. She greeted us warmly at the door and led us through the courtyard, which also serves as kitchen, into one of the two rooms that led off it. It was a relief to be out of the biting mountain cold. The atmosphere in the Chavarrias' small sitting room was welcoming but formal, with its wooden upright chairs, lace antimacassars, and pictures of the family on the walls. We were joined by Doña Zenobia's husband, Don Jaime. Tea was bought in by Doña Zenobia's sister, who lives with them and their five children in their two-roomed house. The youngest child, a baby of six months, sat patiently on her mother's knee as she talked.

She told us that news of the government's plans to close down the Siglo Veinte mine complex was greeted with dismay by its 5,000 miners. Not only were their livelihoods at stake, but also those of the 60,000 or so people who lived in the remote mountain area of North Potosi where the mine is situated. The government duly offered the miners redundancy payments and the opportunity to be relocated to other parts of Bolivia if they agreed to leave their jobs. As an added incentive, they systematically withheld pay, food supplies, medicines, and basic services. The immediate effect was one of chronic food shortages. The geographical isolation of the area meant that people were largely dependent on the COMIBOL food stores for their supplies. The removal of food subsidies and the freezing of wages were already causing immense hardship in the area, but with COMIBOL on the brink of bankruptcy and the government's policy of 'relocation', there was virtually no food in the stores. Doña Zenobia described the months following the tin crash when she slept outside the COMIBOL store just to get her monthly ration of bread, the only food available. Apart from bread, she and her family were reduced to a diet of potato peelings boiled into a thick stew.

Under such conditions it was hardly surprising that people began to leave the area. As they accepted the government's offers of redundancy payments and promises of relocation, the exodus began. According to Doña Zenobia, 'Each day twenty to thirty lorries loaded up with people and their possessions were heading out of town. Houses were left empty. The area was simply being abandoned.'

Fighting back
But Doña Zenobia and her family stayed. They were among those who believed that the mine could be made economically viable, and that the real reason that Siglo Veinte had been targeted for closure was to crush the mine's militant trade union. They also believed that the best chance that they had for their own and their children's future was to stay with the mine and fight for their right to work in it. They knew that the alternatives were grim. Many families who did leave the mines were ending up homeless on the streets of La Paz, or drifting into the coca-growing district of Chapare. Here (in the short term) good money was to be found preparing cocaine paste, but the attempts of the US government to clamp down on coca growers and processors made the future look very uncertain.[7]

But those who decided not to leave also knew that no one would be

Bolivia: Doña Graciella, a member of a cooperative of redundant miners, crushing rock to extract tin outside the Siglo Veinte mine.

able to stay without food. Their incomes were much reduced, and there were no supplies in the COMIBOL store. Working through the Housewives' Committee, the PAM (*Programa de Abastecimiento Minero*) set about organising an alternative food-supply system to the area. With assistance from Oxfam and other aid agencies, they set up a programme which provided basic food items at cost price to the miners. To complement this scheme and supplement the diet of the miners, the PAM supported the Housewives' Committee in a scheme that would enable them to grow vegetables. They provided a number of greenhouses, constructed with adobe walls and clear plastic sheeting. In April 1988 Oxfam field staff wrote reporting progress on the project: 'All those involved talk with enthusiasm of the hard work to prepare the ground (sometimes having to blast the rock), finding the adobe for the walls, etc. Men, women and children worked together for long hours and running soup kitchens while construction was going on. It has helped people to get to know each other better, even where they had been working together previously in the same section. People talk of the delight of seeing the fruit of their work, and say it gives them another reason for staying. Men have welcomed women's contribution to the family income.'[8]

Although these schemes made a considerable difference to people, the exodus continued. By 1986 the Siglo Veinte–Catavi workforce had been reduced from 5,000 to 1,000. Determined to keep the mine open, the miners' leaders decided to present a proposal to the government, outlining their plans to make the mine economically viable. In August of that year 900 people from the Siglo Veinte–Catavi mine, and many more from other mines, marched to La Paz, a distance of more than 200 miles, to present their proposal to the government. Doña Zenobia and her three small children, together with other members of the Housewives' Committee, were among them. They were stopped by the army before reaching the city, but the government eventually agreed to make some concessions. Even so, it maintained its efforts to close down the mine. By tripling redundancy payments, the government ensured that the exodus continued until, by the end of 1987, there were only 380 miners on the payroll. With the mine leased to the cooperatives, all the miners were able to do was to keep the processing plant operational while they continued their negotiations with the government to reopen the mine.

Paradoxically, as the local miners poured out of the area, others poured in. Since the government had handed the mining concessions over to cooperative ownership, there was no shortage of unemployed people willing to join the cooperatives. Many are miners who have accepted redundancy from other mines and have no choice other than to return to the mines, but this time without any of the advantages, however inadequate, of employee status, such as safety provisions, union membership, and company housing. And so the story goes back to where it began – with 5,000 men going in and out of the mountain each day under the shadow of almost certain disaster.

FROM TIN TO DRUGS

As a result of the collapse in international tin prices (and at a deeper level because of a complex combination of factors including the legacy of Bolivia's colonial past, its geological structures, and flagrant mismanagement of its tin industry), Bolivia no longer depends on tin for the bulk of its export earnings. In 1990 it accounted for only 12 per cent of export earnings, less than a third of its 1985 level.[9]

Minerals remain the country's chief export. Efforts are being made to attract foreign investment into the mining sector, with production concentrated in zinc, silver and gold. Zinc is now the country's leading mineral export, contributing 17 per cent of export earnings in 1990. Natural gas is the biggest single official export earner, accounting for about 32 per cent of all exports.[10] Non-traditional agricultural exports, such as Brazil nuts, angora wool, flowers, cochineal and essential oils, are also being promoted to boost the decline in income from the mining sector.[11] As a result of these diversification efforts, Bolivia enjoyed a trade surplus in both 1989 and 1990, for the first time since the beginning of the 1980s.[12]

But the official statistics give a very partial picture of Bolivia's economy. Bolivia earns nearly as much from coca, the raw material of cocaine, as it does from all its other exports. In 1990 Bolivia's earnings from coca, the so-called 'informal' economy, were thought to be about US$600 million, while its total legal export earnings amounted to US$860 million.[13] In previous years its earnings from coca had been even greater than its earnings from its legal exports. Bolivia's economic dependency has merely shifted from one internationally tradeable primary commodity to another.

The rise of coca and the fall of tin as the staple of Bolivia's economy are not unconnected. The crash in tin prices in 1985 coincided with a surge in demand for cocaine in the USA, where there are now an estimated 10 million users. Demand was also growing in Europe, particularly Spain and Italy.[14] The indigenous population of the Bolivian highlands have been growing, chewing and using coca ceremonially for centuries. Unlike many other crops, the coca plant grows in poor soil, yields four or five crops a year, and has few pest problems. As people poured out of the tin mines after 1985, the only area of the economy that could absorb them was the rapidly expanding coca industry. It was a choice between simple survival and virtual starvation. Bolivia is now the world's second-largest producer of coca, after Peru. A quarter of the coca it produces is for traditional use. The rest enters the drugs trade.[15] In recent years it has also become the world's second-largest producer of cocaine, after Colombia. From being a simple supplier of leaf to Colombia, Bolivia is now processing an estimated 30 per cent of total output into the final product.[16]

All this provides employment opportunities. Of Bolivia's population of 7.6 million, an estimated 70,000 families, about 300,000 people in all, rely on coca for a livelihood, either through growing it, or through the laboratories where the coca is converted to paste and then to cocaine. Many more benefit indirectly from the millions of dollars generated by the industry that has created an internal market for restaurants, services, construction, vehicle sales, and so on.[17] Without the employment and income generated by coca, Bolivia's economy would not be viable.

That does not mean to say that the vast majority of Bolivian people who depend on the coca industry are doing well from it. Like the tin miners, they are at the exploited end of a vast and lucrative industry. At the going rate of $15 for 50 kilos of coca leaf, peasant producers barely earn enough to support their families.[18] Wages in the illicit processing industries are low, and conditions poor. The whole industry is tightly controlled by drugs cartels in which some individuals, the 'drug barons', like the 'tin barons' of a previous era, are making vast fortunes.

In the same way too that the tin miners were vulnerable to their industry's investment policies, employment practices, and, ultimately, the international price of tin, the coca growers and workers are vulnerable to international drugs policy. For many years the fight against the cocaine trade concentrated on the Colombian drugs mafia. More recently, US drugs policy has focused on its eradication at source. With the backing of US aid money, and in tandem with military action to halt the trade, peasant producers in Bolivia are now being forced to destroy their coca bushes and substitute them with other crops.

Coca is as integral to the Bolivian way of life as tea is to the British, or wine to the French, yet its production is no longer acceptable. 'Imagine how the French would feel if grapes were suddenly found to have narcotic properties that alienated teenagers in New York found a way to abuse and, as a result, French farmers were told to pull up all their vine-yards and plant something else,' was how one community worker described the situation. 'But the real problem,' he added, 'is not in destroying the coca but in finding an alternative way of making a living.'[19]

Coca is most intensely grown in Bolivia's Chapare region, where much of it is destined for the drugs trade. But it is also grown in the area north of La Paz, known as the Yungas, on terraces carved out of the hillsides of the steeply sloping valleys which characterise the region. Traditionally the Yungas coca supplies the domestic market, but even so it is a target for eradication. A UN-backed project, Agro-Yungas, is in the vanguard of coca destruction in the area. According to local sources, it is offering peasant producers in the area sweeteners, in the form of agricultural credits and technical assistance, to help them diversify out of coca, and encouraging them to grow coffee instead. But with the price of coffee so low on the international market in recent years, those farmers who have followed their advice find themselves unable to get a reasonable price for their coffee. As a result they default on their loans, and with no coca to fall back on they fear losing their land.[20] 'And anyway', as one farmer remarked, pointing to his field of stunted coffee bushes, 'even if we could find a market for our coffee, it simply isn't suited to this area. Coca grows like a weed.'[21]

Many farmers in the area have evolved highly efficient structures for the purposes of the production and marketing of their crops, often with union help. For many years they have been trying to diversify production to lessen their dependence on coca, but find themselves facing severe difficulties. One farmer described how he organises his production system so that he has three hectares of land under citrus fruit and coffee, and a further area planted out to vegetable crops, mostly maize, peanuts, and potatoes for family consumption. But he also grows coca. Coca is his insurance policy. Prices for citrus fruits, sold on the domestic market, are very low, and prices for coffee very uncertain. 'Many people round here grow coffee, so when the international price for coffee falls, it's very hard on them. Their income falls and they can no longer afford to feed their families. They become desperate and leave the area to try and find work in La Paz. This has happened a lot in the last few years. We desperately need fair prices and stable markets for our produce. Only then will it be realistic for us to stop growing coca.'[22]

Some farmers' organisations in the area have managed to secure themselves a slot in the export market. One group trades with a Swiss Alternative Trading organisation. Another has a deal with a German company. But the immense need for markets is in no sense being met despite, in this case, there being a clear case of mutual interest between North and South in providing a viable alternative to coca.

3

SWINGS AND ROUNDABOUTS:
Why commodity prices rise and fall

In sealing the fate of Bolivia's tin industry, the crash in international tin prices in 1985 could be said to have altered the course of the Bolivian economy irrevocably. At the very least, it speeded up a change that was already underway. It also showed that the people whose lives depend on tin are extremely vulnerable to international market prices.

The crash in the price of tin was spectacular, but it was by no means the only commodity to suffer from low prices during the 1980s. As we have already seen (in Chapter 1), the prices of many commodities fell during this period. It is difficult to generalise about commodity prices, because they do not all move together. In 1984, for example, when copra and tea prices were high, the price of sugar was very low. Each commodity is influenced by different forces on both supply and demand, which in turn arise as the result of a variety of factors – economic, political, financial. Often it is a complex combination of factors that causes prices to rise and fall.

This chapter looks at some of the factors of supply and demand that influence commodity prices, in an attempt to assess whether current low prices are a temporary problem, or one that is here to stay.

THE DEMAND FOR COMMODITIES

Sixty six per cent of developing countries' exports are destined for developed country markets: the European Community takes 22 per cent, the United States 25 per cent, and Japan 12 per cent. Of the rest, about 26 per cent stays within the developing country group as a whole. In 1970 the developed countries took 72 per cent of developing countries' exports, while the developing countries took only 20 per cent.[1] Although these figures show that the developing world is less reliant on Northern markets now than it was twenty years ago, the industrialised countries' markets, particularly those of the European Community, the USA, and Japan, still absorb the bulk of their exports. It is, therefore, demand levels in these countries that have the most profound influence on the prices of developing-country commodity exports.

The impact of world recession

One of the most important factors affecting the demand for commodities, especially minerals, is the level of economic activity in the Northern industrialised countries.[2] This is because economic growth is closely linked to industrial output, which in turn plays an important role in dictating demand for mineral commodities. In times of recession there is a slow-down in production. Resulting closures of car plants in Britain, for example, will mean that fewer cars are being made, so the demand for the raw materials used to make them falls. Yet the developing countries that supply the raw materials will continue to produce them, first because they have no other source of income, and secondly because of the difficulties involved in slowing down supply. But their raw materials will be competing for sales in a shrinking market-place, and the result will be a slump in prices.

The impact that world recession has on commodity prices is described in a report by the International Monetary Fund: 'When the world experienced a major recession in 1975, responding in part to the oil price shock, commodity prices fell by 16 per cent from the record level of the previous year. As the world economy recovered in the period up to 1980, commodity prices climbed to a new record levels, over 30 per cent higher in nominal terms than the peak of 1974. In 1981, with the world entering another recession, nominal commodity prices declined by 10 per cent, with each major commodity group participating in the fall in prices. The recession continued in 1982 and commodity prices fell by a further 10 per cent.'[3]

In fact, 1981 marked the beginning of a prolonged global recession which continued into the 1990s. Growth in industrial production in the major industrial countries in the first half of the 1980s averaged only 2 per cent a year, compared with 3.4 per cent in the 1970s.[4] Although economic activity picked up slightly after that, there was a further decline in growth at the end of the decade, from 3.25 per cent in 1989 to 2 per cent in 1990.[5] There was a corresponding decline in the growth in imports into industrial countries, from 7.5 per cent in 1989 to 6 per cent in 1990.[6]

The shift away from manufacturing

While economic activity changes from year to year, structural factors will cause problems for commodity exporters long into the future. A number of these have taken place in recent years, the most important of which has been a shift away from industrial products in favour of services. In Britain, for example, services (which include tourism, banking, advertising, communications, and insurance) accounted for 61.8 per cent of GDP in 1987, compared with a figure of 53.8 per cent ten years earlier.[7] The banking, finance, insurance, business services and leasing sector made the most dramatic gains, from 7.8 per cent in 1977 to 18.1 per cent in 1987.[8] The service sector also expanded in the Irish Republic, from 47.1 per cent of GDP in 1970 to 52.7 per cent in 1986.[9] Services use fewer raw materials than industry, so as this part of a country's economy begins to grow, the rest shrinks, at least relatively. As Britain's service sector expanded, manufacturing, as a percentage of GDP, declined from 32.8 per cent in 1970, to 24.2 per cent in 1987.[10]

Even within manufacturing there has been a shift away from industries that use metals towards industries based on electronics. In the more prosperous industrialised countries the demand for some items with high primary-commodity content is nearing saturation, particularly for cars and consumer durables. Furthermore there are no significant new markets for consumer goods with a high primary-product content.

Technological change

No doubt spurred on by high prices for raw materials in the 1970s, a number of technological changes have resulted in a reduction in the amount of traditional raw materials used in the manufacture of goods. This has happened in two ways: one by substitution of one material for another, and the other by materials saving.[11]

The substitution of one material for another is not new, but may have accelerated with the emergence of new materials over the last two decades. The replacement of cotton and other fibres by synthetic polyester fibre in the textile and clothing industry dates back to the 1950s, while the use of optical fibres as a substitute for copper has recently begun in some applications, particularly telecommunications. There are many other examples.[12]

Substitution was one of many factors behind the tin crash. Historically the principal end use for tin was tinplate. In 1963 it accounted for 42 per cent of tin. By 1988 this figure had almost halved, to 26 per cent.[13] Nearly 90 per cent of tin plate is used for packaging, but what was once its competitive advantage in this industry is constantly challenged by a combination of technological developments in other materials, and changes in consumer tastes. For example, the use of aluminium was once restricted to packaging products that are under pressure, such as fizzy drinks, to overcome its poor rigidity. The discovery that by injecting liquid nitrogen into aluminium cans while they are being sealed it is possible to keep the can rigid meant that aluminium could be used as a direct alternative to tinplate for packaging. Similarly, developments in the plastics industry mean that plastic is now the preferred packaging for water-based paints. The plastic containers that have been introduced are made of polyethylene terephthalate, which has the advantage of transparency so that paint buyers can see the colour of the product. Plastic containers can also be made square, instead of cylindrical, which makes them easier to store and handle. Glass has also replaced tin in the packaging of many food products, mainly because it is more attractive and, therefore, preferred by consumers.[14]

Materials saving has been most apparent in the manufacturing sector. Automation based on micro-electronics has cut down on the quantity of raw materials used, by better precision in design and manufacturing, lower rejection rates in production, and marked reductions in the weight and size of products.[15]

Agricultural protectionism

While mineral commodities have been particularly hard hit by these developments, agricultural commodities have been profoundly affected by rising levels of agricultural protectionism.

All the major industrialised countries provide substantial support for their own production of a wide range of commodities, in particular for agricultural commodities. This is not a new phenomenon. The need for such support arose in the first place because of the sharp decline in standards of living in the rural areas of the United States in the Great Depression of the 1930s. Subsequently, apart from the need to rebuild food production capacity after World War II in many industrialised countries, countries in Western Europe faced political pressure to support the incomes of their farmers. Hence the setting up of the European Community's Common Agricultural Policy.[16]

While the aims of these support policies – to boost agricultural production and maintain food supplies – are laudable, dramatic increases across the board in this support since the beginning of the 1970s have resulted in high consumer costs and falling world prices. In 1989 the OECD calculated that the total cost of supporting agriculture in its 24 member countries was ECU 228 billion, of which the European Community, the USA, and Japan spent ECU 88.5 billion, ECU 60.9 billion, and ECU 52.4 billion respectively. The burden on tax payers and consumers is high. In the EC the Common Agricultural Policy has cost a family of four an estimated ECU 21 a week[17] – about £16 – slightly less than the US dairy industry was receiving each week in agricultural support, *per cow*, in 1986![18]

The more farmers are paid, the more they will produce, so the unsurprising result of protectionist policies has been huge increases in production. Industrialised countries that were once major importers of a particular agricultural commodity have become self-sufficient. In some cases they have become major exporters of that commodity. The

CAMILLA GARRETT–JONES/OXFAM

England: shopping for cheaper food in Oxford market as the cost of the Common Agricultural Policy sends European food prices spiralling.

European Community, for example, was a net importer of sugar until the mid-1970s. In 1988 its net exports of sugar amounted to 4.1 million tons.[19] Many of the commodities concerned – grains, meat, dairy products, oilseeds, vegetable oils, and sugar – are also produced by developing countries, and exported to the industrialised countries. But as levels of agricultural protectionism in those countries increased, and there were corresponding rises in production, demand for the developing countries' exports fell, which in turn led to lower world prices. By 1987 the overall prices of these commodities on the international market were half their 1980 level.[20]

THE SUPPLY OF COMMODITIES

Demand is only part of the equation. Supply also plays a major role in determining commodity prices, and there are many factors – political, climatic, and economic – that can affect it. Civil unrest in a major producing country may only threaten disruption of supplies, but even that threat will be enough to make prices soar on the international market. Such events will always be a cause of unpredictable price changes, but there were other factors at work in the 1980s that suggest more structural changes on the supply side.

It would be logical to assume that as prices fell throughout the 1980s, producer countries would have adopted policies that discouraged production, in order to correct the balance between supply and demand. However, the reverse was often true. Production in many commodities increased over the 1980s without corresponding rises in consumption. Coffee, tea, and cocoa, for example, three commodities where demand is relatively stable, all ended the decade with higher stocks than they began with. In most years production had been greater than consumption, which caused a steady build-up in stocks.[21] International market prices for all three have experienced extremely low prices.

The impact of the debt crisis

One explanation for this general increase is that there are strong pressures on developing countries to increase their production of primary commodities as a direct or indirect result of the debt crisis. The problem of debt is often seen as the most critical factor affecting development in the 1980s. It has been a major concern to Oxfam, because debt has affected Third World economies in ways that hurt the poor. Adjustment measures adopted to secure IMF loans tend to be most acutely felt by the most vulnerable sectors of society. The removal of food subsidies, for example, can send the prices of basic foodstuffs soaring, while major reduction in public spending hits basic services such as health care and education. The high social and environmental costs arising as a result of the debt crisis have been well documented by Oxfam.[22] Since the launch of the 'Hungry for Change' campaign in 1984, Oxfam has argued strongly for action to alleviate the debt burden of poorer countries.

The problem of the debt crisis is closely related to that of the Third World's dependence on primary commodities. While instability in the commodity markets is a problem frequently encountered for producer countries in the South, a longer-term problem is the inexorable deterioration in their terms of trade, which in turn is linked to their dependence on primary commodities, and with the debt crisis. On the one hand, declining terms of trade have played a considerable role in the accumulation of Third World debt. On the other hand, the debt crisis has worsened the terms of trade for poor countries.

The rise of indebtedness can, in part, be attributed to the decline in terms of trade in a number of ways. First the debt crisis, at least in part, goes back to the oil price increases of 1973 and 1979. In 1973 the thirteen large oil-exporting nations of OPEC quadrupled the price of oil, and in doing so suddenly found themselves with abundant cash resources. They deposited these so-called 'petrodollars' in the big commercial banks of the United States, Europe, and Japan. Eager for clients to take these deposits (for money at a standstill not only fails to generate profit, but actually loses value through inflation), the banks began to encourage the bigger and apparently more stable developing countries to borrow heavily. They were particularly attracted to Brazil, Mexico, Argentina, Chile, Venezuela, Nigeria, Zambia, South Korea, the Philippines, and Indonesia. Some of these countries were oil importers and so faced much higher import bills. At the same time the temporary boom in non-oil commodity prices, upon which many were dependent, had collapsed. In other words, their terms of trade had declined.

In the oil-exporting countries, such as Mexico and Venezuela, the cause and role of terms of trade in the accumulation of debt was, of course, different. But even there, terms of trade played a vital if indirect role. These nations' terms of trade were favourable. This made them optimistic about investment and growth and accumulating debt. At the same time, they were particularly encouraged to accept loans by the commercial banks, who considered them to be more credit-worthy than non-oil exporters.

It has been estimated that, of the total debt of US$500 billion accumulated by developing countries between 1973 and 1982, about US$260 billion, or just over half, was directly attributable to increased costs of oil.[23]

While falling commodity prices and declining terms of trade were causing countries to accumulate debt, the opposite was also true. The debt crisis was accelerating the collapse in commodity prices, and thus contributing to the developing world's deteriorating terms of trade. Under pressure to pay off their debts, Third World countries needed to achieve an export surplus in order to generate more foreign exchange. Logically this required either a cut back on imports or an increase in exports. In fact, most countries did both. Between 1980 and 1988 the volume of imports for Latin America as a whole fell by 24 per cent – equivalent to a loss of two years of imports.[24] Unfortunately this was not accompanied by effective import substitution, but was done at the expense of growth and development. They also increased exports under the ideology of 'outward orientation' that governed the stabilisation and adjustment programmes of the IMF and World Bank.

The IMF and the World Bank promoted export expansion in a variety of ways, the most important being currency devaluation, a central component of almost every IMF package throughout the 1980s. Devaluation of any nation's currency has the effect of making its imports more expensive, as it takes more local currency to pay for imported goods. At the same time, it encourages export expansion, because the proceeds from export sales increase in terms of local currency. Exports are thus cheaper to produce, and therefore more competitive on world markets.

Critics identify the major weakness of this approach as the blanket way in which it has been applied. Both the IMF and the World Bank claim to design their loan packages around the needs of individual countries. Yet their programmes tend to be very similar to one another, and take little account of the impact that they may have on other developing countries. This is particularly serious when the countries involved are competing exporters of primary commodities. If, for example, Chile devalues its currency and expands its share of the copper market, this is bound to have some impact on other major Third World producers, such as Zambia and Zaire. If they also devalue and increase supply, then the price of copper will fall.[25]

This is, indeed, what happened. Between 1980 and 1985, the quantity of copper ore exports from developing countries rose by 10 per cent, but their earnings from those exports fell by 35 per cent, so the value of their exports fell by 28 per cent.[26] Just to keep their earnings at the 1980 level would have meant a 55 per cent increase in production, which in turn would lead to a further downward pressure on prices.

Evidence of the link between deteriorating terms of trade and the expansion of exports in the service of adjustment programmes is not lacking. World Bank figures show that countries undergoing adjustment programmes increased their export volumes, but that the benefits of doing so were almost entirely wiped out by a deterioration in their terms of trade. Countries that were not undergoing adjustment did not increase their export volumes, and experienced an improvement in their terms of trade.[27]

The effects of biotechnology

Developments in biotechnology also alter the equation between demand and supply, and present both opportunity and threat to developing countries. 'Biotechnology' is a general term used to describe recent advances in the biological sciences that are beginning to make an impact on agriculture, medicine, and industry, with far-reaching social, ethical, and economic implications. As far as agriculture is concerned, three different techniques are being developed with profound implications for farming.

The first is genetic engineering, which enlarges the possibilities of incorporating desirable characteristics, such as disease resistance, into plants. The second is tissue culture, which makes it possible to produce a plant which is identical to the one from which is derived. The third is enzyme technology, which can be used to modify a substance.

The potential benefits of biotechnology are great, provided that the technology is made available to poor producers. However, developments to date suggest that they are more likely to be disadvantaged. The threat that biotechnology poses to developing-country producers can best be illustrated by the impact that it has had on industrialised-country demand for one particular Third World commodity: cane sugar. Through the use of enzyme technology it is possible to extract sweeteners from any starch-containing source. In the 1970s developments in this field in the United States meant that it became technically possible and commercially viable to produce 'sugar' from maize. This substance, known as high-fructose corn syrup, is now widely used by food and drink manufacturers in the USA as a cheap alternative to sugar. But it has effectively shut off the US market to Third World sugar cane exporters, and in doing so contributed to plunging world sugar prices in the 1980s. This in turn caused immense hardship for sugar producers in the worst-affected developing countries.[28]

The problem for developing countries is that much of the research into biotechnology is being conducted in the industrial countries, much of it by private companies, for their own benefit. The stated aim of biotechnology programmes in the European Community, for example, is to improve the international competitiveness of European agriculture. Little account is taken of the impact they may have on the developing world as trade flows change in response to the programmes. One research programme proposes to make soya more suited to the European climate, a move designed to reduce the Community's dependence on imports.[29] The outcome of this could be disastrous for the major exporters of soya, particularly Argentina and Brazil.

But equally, biotechnology could have a positive impact on Third World agriculture in the opportunities that it offers for improvements in quality and yields. For example, current research on coffee, a vital export crop for millions of small farmers in the developing world, may soon make it possible to breed pest-resistant plants with a lower caffeine content. This would reduce the need for applications of costly and environmentally damaging pesticides, suit Northern consumer tastes, and satisfy the recommendations of health advisers.[30]

If small farmers are able to cash in on these developments, they will undoubtedly benefit. They could spend less money on inputs and enjoy new market opportunities. But if the new plants are too expensive for them to buy, they could be further marginalised in world markets, as the benefits would be confined to large-scale producers.

Biotechnological developments are taking place at a rapid pace, and in some cases are already affecting the supply of primary commodities in the developing world. One example is in the palm oil industry. Through the use of tissue culture, Unilever has found a way of speeding up the development of oil palms and increasing yields by around 30 per cent.[31] While this will bring gains for the major producers such as Malaysia, producers of competing oils, such as coconut, groundnut, and oilseed, many of whom are small farmers in poor countries, are already affected by the glut of cheap palm oil on the market. Similar developments are taking place in many other product groups. The challenge of the 1990s will be to ensure that the benefits of these new technologies reach beyond the industrialised countries to the most vulnerable groups of producers in the Third World.

THE CASE OF SUGAR

In 1985 the price of sugar on the world market fell to three US cents a pound. Cane sugar is a vital export crop for many developing countries. They rely on it for foreign-exchange earnings and the industry provides employment for an estimated twelve million people. Yet even the lowest-cost producer could not break even at a price much below twelve US cents a pound. The effect of this price fall was devastating.

First of all, it represented a significant loss of foreign-exchange earnings for a number of countries, such as the Dominican Republic, Guatemala, Fiji, and Malawi. To make up for the shortfall, the governments of these countries would either have had to cut back on imports or resort to borrowing from the international banking community. Either way the indirect effects on people would have been widely felt. Cutting back on imports may typically mean a shortage of certain food items in the shops or of essential agricultural inputs. Borrowing may have entailed the introduction of austerity measures, such as the removal of food subsidies or cuts in public services, to pay the interest on the loans.

But the price fall also had direct, and often tragic, consequences for many of the people involved in the production of sugar. Hardest hit were the sugar workers and their families on the island of Negros, in the Philippines. Negros is one of the larger islands in the Philippines archipelago. While sugar is a relatively important source of foreign exchange to the Philippines, contributing about eight per cent of export earnings a year, it is vital to the economy of Negros. At the time of the price collapse, Negros was producing around seventy per cent of the Philippines' sugar. On the island itself very little else was grown, and the whole economy revolved around its production.

Production was organised on a semi-feudal basis. The plantations, known locally as *haciendas*, were often several hundred hectares in size, and owned by some of the wealthiest families in the Philippines. Most of the *haciendas* employed a small permanent workforce who lived on the plantation. Wages were low and living conditions primitive. During harvest time additional labour was often needed, and this was provided by migrant workers from neighbouring islands. When prices collapsed, many of the *haciendos* saw that it would be uneconomical to harvest

BELINDA COOTE/OXFAM

The Philippines: harvesting sugar cane on the island of Negros.

that year's crop; a quarter of a million sugar workers were thus plunged into unemployment. They had no rights, bargaining power, or social security. More importantly they had no land on which to grow food.

At the time, Oxfam was heavily involved in the relief effort in drought-stricken Ethiopia. When news came through of the desperate plight of the people on Negros, it was hard to believe that there could be a parallel problem of widespread starvation on an agriculturally fertile tropical island. There was an immediate need for food and medicines, to which Oxfam responded, but in the longer term it was widely recognised that if people were to be protected from such devastation, there had to be radical changes in patterns of land ownership and use.

The dramatic fall in sugar prices and the consequent suffering of so many were due to a combination of a number of the factors already described. They were principally caused by the protectionist agricultural policies of the USA and the European Community, and technological changes in the production of sweeteners.

Production and trade in sugar are unique in several ways. Cane sugar is produced in tropical climates, while beet sugar is cultivated largely in Western Europe, the USSR, and North America. But since the beginning of the 1980s sugar has also faced competition from other sweeteners, especially high-fructose corn syrup, produced from maize. Traditionally, sugar trade has taken place between the low-cost tropical producing areas and the developed consuming areas of Western Europe, North America, and Japan.

At the beginning of the 1970s the United States was the single largest sugar importer. It has maintained high domestic prices for sugar by means of guaranteed loans to producers and by controlling the supply of sugar through import quotas. The relatively high price of sugar resulted both in increased production and in increased substitution by the more competitively priced high-fructose corn syrup for use in the food industry. Consequently the USA was able to halve its imports in the first half of the 1980s, most of which came from countries in South and Central America, the Caribbean, and the Philippines. A similar trend was emerging in the European Community. In 1967 the twelve countries which are now members of the European Community were, collectively, net importers of nearly four million tonnes of sugar. Under the Common Agricultural Policy a variety of mechanisms, including guaranteed prices, intervention purchases, and variable import levies, produced massive increases in production. By the mid-1980s the Community was a net *exporter* of nearly four and a half million tonnes of sugar a year.

The impact of these developments on some Third World sugar producers was devastating. Not only did countries such as the Philippines lose their traditional markets; they also faced world market prices that were only a fraction of their production costs of around US12 cents a pound. In December 1984 the price of sugar on the world market fell to 3.51 cents a pound. Meanwhile farmers in the EC and North America were enjoying prices of between 19 and 22 cents a pound.[32]

THE OUTLOOK FOR COMMODITY-DEPENDENT COUNTRIES

Continuing global recession will keep the prices of some commodities low. Agricultural products may benefit from the expected reduction in protectionism (see Chapter 9). Future structural changes in trade patterns in the industrialised countries, and the pace and effects of technological developments, are important but unpredictable factors. There is still much scope for substitution away from traditional materials, and the Northern-based biotechnological revolution is likely to disrupt traditional patterns of world trade.

There is another factor that will have to be taken into account in the 1990s and beyond: the weather. Weather has always had a major impact on supply. An untimely frost in Brazil, for example, may well wipe out the bulk of the country's crop and send prices soaring on the international market. Hurricanes frequently do severe damage to the banana crop of the Windward Islands, with a similar effect. Perfect conditions for cocoa growing in West Africa may produce a bumper crop, but the resulting over-supply may lead to a fall in world prices. .

Until recently the impact of weather on supply would, perhaps, have been considered benignly unpredictable. But with the onset of global warming, weather patterns are becoming increasingly erratic. They could have a major impact on supply. While the inevitability of global warming is now almost universally accepted, the impact of the resulting climate change on agriculture is uncertain. Clearly it will be very disruptive. Third World countries which are heavily dependent on agricultural commodities for food and export will be particularly vulnerable. A substantial rise in temperature could, for example, wipe out the whole of Uganda's coffee crop, and with it its main source of export earnings. The predicted sea-level rise of one metre in Bangladesh by the middle of the next century could ruin what there is of its already very fragile economy by wiping out or displacing two major exports: shrimps and jute.

Experts are particularly concerned about the impact of global warming on semi-arid regions, such as much of sub-Saharan Africa, North East Brazil, and parts of India and Pakistan. In these areas agriculture is closely geared to rainfall and depends not only on rain falling in a concentrated rainy season, but on its timing and distribution within the season. Cropping patterns and agricultural patterns are finely adjusted to the rainfall regime, and even minor changes have major effects on yields.[33]

Predicted climatic change simply underlines the extreme vulnerability of Third World commodity-dependent countries to changes that are largely beyond their control. The next chapter reviews the mechanisms that have been used to try to control commodity prices to shield both producing and consuming countries from unpredictable price movements.

4

'YOU CAN'T PAY THE DOCTOR IN MILLET!':
Controlling international commodity prices

The landlocked central African country, Chad, is rated by the World Bank as the world's third poorest country, after Mozambique and Ethiopia. Its economy is overwhelmingly dependent on agriculture and cattle herding, which together account for almost 50 per cent of its gross domestic product. Cotton, the principal cash crop, is considered to be the backbone of the official economy. Latest estimates are that livestock and cotton contribute 80 per cent of Chad's foreign-exchange earnings.[1]

Cotton cultivation was imposed on Chad by the French in the 1920s to make their Cinderella colony a paying proposition. The southern region of the country where the cotton is grown became known as *le Tchad utile* ('useful Chad') as distinct from the economically unprofitable two thirds of the country to the north. In *le Tchad utile* the French colonial government induced farmers to produce large quantities of cotton for export to Europe, not only in the expectation of supplying the manufacturing industries there, but also in the hope of developing a market for finished cloth in Africa. A common practice was to force farmers to allocate a certain proportion of their land each year to cotton production and sell a quota of their produce to French merchants. Prices were set so low that the farmers could scarcely cover their transportation costs. Inevitably they took a loss on their cotton each year, and had less land available for food crops. The resulting shortfall in food production left large numbers of people very vulnerable to the droughts which periodically hit the country.[2]

Today an estimated 350,000 farmers grow cotton in Chad. Including their families, over two million people, nearly half the population, are dependent on the industry for an income. They are locked into cotton production in the same way that farmers were during the colonial period, only now the imperative is the need for a cash income, rather than compliance with the dictates of the French colonial government.

In Chad cotton production and marketing is controlled by Cotontchad, of which 75 per cent is owned by the Chadian Government, 19 per cent by France, and 3 per cent by local banks. Its activities cover virtually all aspects of the industry, from providing seeds and other inputs to the farmers, purchasing, transporting, ginning, marketing, and manufacturing cottonseed oil and soap. In 1986 Cotontchad came close to bankruptcy following the sharp decline in cotton prices on the international markets during the 1985/6 season (although it was also suffering from years of mismanagement and civil disorder). It was rescued by a loan and restructuring package from a consortium of donors, including the World Bank and the European Community's European Development Fund. However, with international cotton prices remaining weak, Cotontchad continues to face financial difficulties which it tends to deal with, as it always has, by reducing the price it pays farmers for their cotton. In the 1988/89 season they paid CFA 90 (0.18) per kilo, down 10 per cent on the previous year's price.[3]

Bendei Patrice has been growing cotton since 1957. He lives with his two wives and ten children and farms a two and a half hectare plot of land. In most years he divides the land between cash-crop and food-crop production. One hectare of land is devoted to cotton, while the rest is divided between peanuts and millet, with a small area set aside for vegetable production. His job is to tend the cotton crop, while the women devote their time to food production.[4]

The problem for farmers such as Bendei Patrice is that they earn very little from the cotton that they grow, but it is their only source of a cash income. Low cotton prices mean that there is very little cash available, either for individual or more general development needs. People lack very basic requirements such as water. There are no local health services, nor funds for farmers to buy essential agricultural equipment. In recent years Oxfam has been supporting credit and saving schemes set up by village groups.[5] These have helped individual members, and the communities as a whole, but do little to shield farmers from extreme price swings on the international market, such as the fall in cotton prices in 1986. In that year Bendei Patrice's net income from his one hectare of cotton, after he had paid for inputs and the hire of oxen, plough, and local labour, was CFA 84,000 (£167.00).[6] Out of this he was obliged to pay taxes of CFA 3,000 (£6.00), and the same in contributions to his political party. The family had to eke out what was left over the year to cover school fees, clothes, and medical expenses.

Cotton production is highly labour-intensive. With such low returns, it seemed reasonable to ask why he bothered to grow cotton in the first place and didn't concentrate on food-crop production instead. He replied patiently, 'You can't pay the doctor in millet.' But the following year that was all that he had. With such low prices, he had no money left over to buy cotton seeds or inputs. Instead he had to earn what money he could by working on other people's land.[7]

ATTEMPTS TO CONTROL INTERNATIONAL COMMODITY PRICES

Cotton is grown in more than 75 tropical and temperate countries, over fifty of which export it onto the world market. While it is grown in many parts of the Third World, some of the poorest African countries are most dependent on cotton for their export earnings, especially Chad, Mali, Sudan, and Burkina Faso. Its price on the international markets is therefore critical to their development efforts. Like other commodity-dependent countries, these cotton economies have a keen interest in stabilising market prices at levels that adequately reflect their production costs and generate a reasonable income.

The need to control commodity prices has long been recognised, for different reasons, by both producing and consuming countries. The developed countries – the main importers – dislike sharp increases in prices, because they encourage inflation. The developing countries, which depend on exporting commodities for foreign-exchange earnings, find price fluctuations hard to deal with because they make it difficult for them to attract investment or plan for the future.

Attempts to control prices have generally taken two forms: cartels and international commodity agreements (ICAs). They differ in that ICAs are formally negotiated, public agreements made between producers and consumers, while cartels are agreements made between producers alone, and are frequently kept secret.[8]

Chad: Daniel Kada and his wife wait for their cotton to be weighed in the market at Bissi Mafou.

Cartels

The most striking example of a cartel is that of OPEC (Organisation of Petroleum Exporting Countries), whose actions triggered massive rises in oil prices in 1973/4 and 1979. This was a period when some commodity prices, principally sugar and tropical beverages, such as tea, coffee and cocoa, were already quite high. There was also concern over the exhaustion of the world's mineral resource base. This gave rise to a concern in the developed countries that the nations of the South could develop real 'commodity power' and command any price they liked for their commodity exports, particularly minerals, through producer cartels such as OPEC.[9]

As history has shown, these fears were unfounded. Technological developments have continued to reduce the growth of demand for many minerals, and the widespread fears prevalent in the 1970s concerning the exhaustion of resources flowed largely from misunderstandings of the state of the world's mineral reserves, which are much greater than were at one time thought.

The market conditions that promote producer power and therefore indicate the use of cartels have been analysed at length by economists, who have defined five of the most important as follows. First, the commodity should be truly essential for the consumer countries, with few or no close substitutes for its major uses. Demand should be 'price-inelastic', which means that demand does not vary much with price changes. Coffee, for example, is relatively price-inelastic. Its mildly addictive properties ensure that people keep drinking it even if the price does rise, and do not drink any more if it falls. Secondly, supply has to be price-inelastic. In other words, price rises should not trigger increased production. If they do, the strength of the agreement may well be eroded. Many commodity agreements have failed in this way, as countries have unilaterally responded to price rises by increasing production. The third precondition concerns the homogeneity of the product. If the product is truly homogeneous, then producers can compete only on price. If there are many different grades of cotton or types of coffee, for example, then there is plenty of room for producers to compete with one another on non-price grounds. Fourthly, a small number of suppliers should dominate the market. This not only facilitates coordination, but also lessens the risk that non-members will thwart efforts to affect output and prices. Finally, the governments involved should not be heavily reliant on the commodity in question. Dependency seriously curtails their bargaining power, as it would mean that they would be reluctant to cut production.[10]

This is leverage that most Third World commodity producers simply do not possess.

International commodity agreements

Before the First World War, commodity controls generally took the form of cartels. The first attempts to regulate trade in commodities on a multilateral basis did not emerge until 1929, when the world economy plunged into a deep recession, commodity prices plummeted, and protectionist measures proliferated.

In the early 1930s the League of Nations held a conference in London to discuss ways of dealing with the crisis. The conference recognised the importance of increasing the purchasing power of primary-commodity producers by keeping the export prices of raw materials at fair and remunerative levels. They also recognised the damage wrought by protectionist measures, in that they often led to over-production and thus put a downward pressure on prices. As a policy response they suggested the setting up of international commodity agreements (ICAs) which would deal with the problem of over-production through the use of buffer stocks. As a result, ICAs were established in tin, wheat, tea, rubber, and sugar, none of which was successful, as protectionist measures continued to proliferate.

The Second World War caused a major disruption to efforts to regulate world trade. It cut off large parts of the European market, and food shortages led to direct buying by individual governments. It also brought to the fore the views of John Maynard Keynes in his capacity as adviser to the UK government. He was the first true advocate of international and integrated commodity controls. He proposed a comprehensive plan for the introduction of ICAs in a range of goods. He also argued that world trade, development, and monetary policy should be considered in an integrated fashion. The need for this was recognised at the Bretton Woods Conference in 1944, which was designed to reconstruct the world economy. However, the conference, which established the International Monetary Fund (IMF) and the World Bank, failed to establish a comparable institution for trade, although the need for one was recorded.[11] Subsequent negotiations succeeded in producing a constitution for an International Trade Organisation, known as the Havana Charter, in 1948.

While an actual trade organisation was never established, parts of its charter were. Those chapters of the charter which concerned the reduction of tariffs were adopted as a trade accord which became known as the General Agreement on Tariffs and Trade (GATT). Thereafter the GATT became the permanent forum for trade negotiations (see Chapter 9). A further chapter of the charter which related to commodity trading was adopted by the Interim Coordinating Committee for International Commodity Agreements (ICCICA), whose purpose it was to convene discussions for international commodity agreements.

To set up an ICA, producer and consumer countries get together to negotiate its provisions. While each agreement will vary according to the nature of the product and the circumstances of the market, it will operate either through buffer stocks or through export controls, or sometimes a combination of the two. Whichever way the agreement is to operate, the producer and consumer countries must first agree on a price range. This is a band, with a floor and a ceiling, within which it is judged desirable to keep the price of the commodity. The 1977 International Sugar Agreement, for example, established a price range with a floor of US11 cents a pound and a ceiling of US21 cents a pound.[12]

ICAs that use export controls are favoured when the main problem is one of excess supply. They try to achieve a balance between supply and demand by controlling supply through the use of export quotas. Producer countries first have to agree on a 'global quota': the estimated amount that the stronger members of the agreement can sell on the free market at prices within the range. Then the global quota is divided among the exporters. Once each country has been allocated its quota, it has to work out how to keep its supply in line with its export quota. It may do so by reducing production or by stockpiling, or by disposing of its excess production.

The principal aim of buffer stock agreements is to stabilise prices. The buffer stock, which is literally a store of the commodity, is centrally administered and financed by a tax on each tonne of the commodity traded. The International Natural Rubber Agreement is a buffer stock agreement. When there is a glut of rubber on the world market resulting, for example, from increased production in Thailand, the buffer stock manager will intervene by buying sufficient rubber into store, and thus preventing world prices declining below the floor level. When prices once again rise, the rubber can be released from the buffer stock to help keep them stable.

Some agreements also contain measures that relate to consumption of the commodity. Various International Sugar Agreements have, for example, required members to study the effects of sugar substitutes on consumption. The 1972 Cocoa Agreement gave the buffer stock manager authority to divert surplus cocoa to non-traditional uses when the quantity of cocoa held exceeded the maximum storage capacity in the buffer stock.[13]

Some ICAs have clauses that relate to development. The 1990 International Cocoa Agreement, for example, has a clause on fair labour standards: 'Members declare that, in order to raise the levels of living of populations and provide full employment, they will endeavour to maintain fair labour standards and working conditions in the various branches of cocoa production in the countries concerned, consistent with their stage of development, as regards both agricultural and industrial workers employed therein.'[14]

THE CREATION OF UNCTAD

By the 1960s there was considerable discontent in Third World countries at the institutional arrangements governing post-war economic relations. They were particularly disillusioned with the General Agreement on Trade and Tariffs. By now it was apparent to developing countries that the GATT was serving the interests of the industrialised countries, rather than their own. As a result they lobbied for a special conference on trade and development that would be devoted to promoting their own economic interests.

The conference, known as the United Nations Conference on Trade and Development, was held in Geneva in March 1964. At the conference the developing countries called for the creation of a new, comprehensive International Trade Organisation. The new ITO would subsume the GATT and provide an institutional framework for discussions on commodity issues. While they never managed to achieve the setting up of an ITO, the holding of the 1964 conference and the subsequent decision to make UNCTAD a permanent institution was seen as a victory for the Third World, and one that was to have substantial impact on commodity policy. UNCTAD officially came into existence on 12 December 1964, took over all the functions of the ICCICA, and became the centre for global commodity discussions.[15]

UNCTAD has evolved a decision-making process which has been adopted by many other UN bodies. The process involves the development of positions by three well-organised groupings: the Group of 77 (the developing countries), Group B (developed countries), and Group D (the then communist East European states). A fourth 'group' is China. After UNCTAD I, the Group B countries began to coordinate their policies through the Organisation for Economic Cooperation and Development (OECD). The Group of 77 has now grown to a group of 128 countries, which coordinate their activities by continental groupings. Group D has traditionally played a supporting role to G77. Since 1989 they have been speaking as individual countries and only acting as a group on procedural matters.[16]

The philosophy underlying UNCTAD's first decade owed much to Raul Prebisch, the first Secretary General, whose main thesis was that the terms of trade of developing countries were in long-term decline. His policy prescriptions included support for commodity prices, the rescheduling of developing countries' debts, greater market access for exports from developing countries, and compensatory finance for shortfalls in their export earnings.[17]

During the first decade of its operation, market access for commodities formed the basis of UNCTAD's work, through its development of the Generalised System of Preferences (see Chapter 9). From the mid-1970s this was broadened out to ensure a more integrated approach to the range of problems facing developing countries in their pursuit of a New International Economic Order (NEIO).

The New International Economic Order
The idea for a New International Economic Order (NEIO) was formulated by the Group of 77 and debated throughout the 1970s. It came at a time when 'commodity power' seemed to be at its height. The success of OPEC's oil cartel gave rise to optimism in the developing

---

UNITED NATIONS CONFERENCE ON TRADE AND DEVELOPMENT
Dates of Conferences and main decisions taken

1964   UNCTAD I   Dealt with commodities on a case-by-case basis and created a Commission on Commodity Arrangements and Policies.

1968   UNCTAD II   Drew up a draft policy agreement on commodity arrangements and on encouraging the promotion of measures to stabilise international commodity prices.

1972   UNCTAD III   Continued discussions on commodity issues.

1976   UNCTAD IV   Adopted the Integrated Programme for Commodities and reached agreement in principle on the need for a Common Fund.

1979   UNCTAD V   Adopted resolutions authorising the secretariat to carry out studies on the marketing, distribution, and transportation of commodities; the processing of primary products; and compensatory financing.

1983   UNCTAD VI   Deadlock in discussions between G77 and Group B on proposals for emergency action on commodities.

1987   UNCTAD VII   Resumption of dialogue between G77 and Group B. USSR and others signed up for Common Fund. A 'Final Act' was adopted by the conference.

1992   UNCTAD VIII   Theme: 'Strengthening national and international action and multilateral cooperation for a healthy, secure and equitable world economy.'

---

world regarding their potential economic influence. The G77 hoped that the NIEO would 'redress existing injustices' and 'make it possible to eliminate the widening gap between the developed and developing countries'.[18]

The NIEO was to be effected by a seven-pronged Programme of Action which included an Integrated Programme for Commodities, which was designed to stabilise and raise commodity prices, and to increase the export earnings of developing countries.[19] It was decided that the Integrated Programme for Commodities (IPC) should focus on two approaches. The first was to concentrate on negotiations for international commodity agreements for those commodities regarded as being most important for developing countries. Eighteen commodities were identified for coverage under the IPC. Ten of these were designated 'core' commodities, those which are mainly exported by developing countries.[20] The second approach was to establish a Common Fund to finance the buffer stocks of the ten 'core' commodities.

The performance of international commodity agreements

Since the Second World War international commodity agreements have been negotiated to regulate the markets for five commodities: tin, natural rubber, sugar, coffee, and cocoa. Attempts have also been made to establish ICAs in numerous other commodities, including tea, cotton, jute, and copper, but they have all failed to materialise. Of the five that did materialise, only one, the International Natural Rubber Agreement (INRA), a buffer stock agreement, remained in force by the end of 1990. The last International Coffee Agreement (ICFA), which is based on export quotas, was suspended in July 1989. Similarly the International Cocoa Agreement (ICCA), a buffer stock agreement, is to continue until 1992, but without economic provisions.[21] International Sugar Agreements (ISA) have been based on export quotas, but the last agreement expired in 1983. The International Tin Agreement (ITA), a mix of export quotas and buffer stocks, was suspended in October 1985.

Judgements on the performance of these agreements are mixed. Two of them, the sugar and cocoa agreements, are generally judged as having been unsuccessful. Agreements on tin, which span over thirty years, have been more successful, in that they have managed to keep prices mostly within the approved price ranges. The more recent rubber agreement has also met with some success. Successive coffee agreements have often failed to maintain prices within the agreed range, but through use of quotas have prevented prices falling too low or rising too high.[22]

The most important factor contributing to the overall failure of ICAs is a lack of political will to make them succeed. Several factors have contributed to this. One concerns ideology. Many industrialised countries, the main importers of primary commodities, are hostile to intergovernmental market regulations. International commodity agreements are the antithesis of the free-market ideology they are keen to promote in world trade, as demonstrated by the latest GATT negotiations (see Chapter 9.) If ICAs had had the full backing of these powerful consuming countries, they would have had a better chance of succeeding.

Another factor concerns the imbalances that exist between the relative strengths and weaknesses of producers. In any given commodity a handful of countries generally dominates production. For example, Brazil and Colombia have traditionally dominated the world coffee markets, contributing around 40 per cent of global exports, while Malaysia has led production in rubber. If one of these leading exporters fails to support the agreement, it is bound to fail. Critical to their success is the need for producers to reach a consensus so that agreement on market shares or levels of buffer stock financing can be reached. As already shown (in Chapter 3), there were many factors at work, particularly during the 1980s, which created huge imbalances between supply and demand, making consensus between producers very difficult.

Other factors contributing to the failure of ICAs are of a more technical nature. One concerns exchange rates. A major reason for the collapse of the International Tin Agreement was the appreciation of the dollar, which meant that the market was being supported at too high a level. It has been suggested that one way of avoiding this would be by defining support prices in SDRs.[23] Another concerns the drafting of the agreements, which have been criticised for being imprecise.[24] Problems are also created if new suppliers outside the agreement enter the market, or if there are disputes among producers over the allocation of quotas.

The Common Fund
The second part of the Integrated Programme for Commodities, the Common Fund, was advocated strongly by most members of the UNCTAD secretariat, as well as by the G77 developing countries, for a number of reasons. First, they considered that a key reason for the failure of international commodity agreements in the past had been a lack of adequate financing for buffer stocks. The formation of a sizeable fund from which concessional loans could be offered would help to overcome this problem. Secondly, it was felt that money could be saved by creating a joint financing facility, rather than separate ones for each commodity. On the assumption that commodity prices rise and fall at different times, the proceeds from the sale of some stocks could be used

to purchase others. Finally it was argued that having a common fund would spread the risks among governments, as it would cover a number of commodities, rather than just one or two.

The idea of setting up a Common Fund was strongly opposed, from the outset, by the industrial countries. Hence proposals for the Fund were adopted at UNCTAD IV in 1976, but without the support of many of these countries. The debate about the form that the Fund would eventually take was lengthy and acrimonious. Agreement was finally reached in June 1980. It was decided that the Fund would consist of two accounts, referred to as 'windows'. The first account, or window, would be designed to finance buffer stocks and internationally coordinated national stocks in the ten 'core' commodities of the Integrated Programme for Commodities. The second account, or window, would be designed to finance measures other than stocking, such as research and development, productivity improvement, and diversification. The two windows were to be financed separately by direct government contributions of US$400 million to the first and US$350 million to the second.[25]

Once established, the treaty had to be signed and then ratified. Ratification could occur only when the treaty had been signed by at least 90 countries which would collectively account for at least two thirds of the financial subscriptions. The original target for this was March 1982, but it had to be extended several times. Finally, by 1986, 90 countries, including Britain, had ratified the agreement. However, they only accounted for a little under 58 per cent of the subscriptions. Among the non-ratifiers were the USA and the Soviet bloc, which accounted for 15.71 and 10.21 per cent of subscriptions respectively. Finally, at UNCTAD VII in July 1987, the Soviet Union, in a gesture of goodwill towards the Third World, announced that it would ratify the treaty, thus ensuring its entry into force, but without the USA.

In July 1989 the first annual meeting of the Governing Council of the Common Fund took place. By this time 104 countries had ratified the agreement. It was agreed that the Fund's headquarters should be located in Amsterdam.[26] By mid-1991 contributions to the Common Fund had amounted to between $90 million and $100 million. Britain is among the countries which have paid their contributions, but many have not. A further $200 million has been pledged, but not paid.[27]

In the absence of functioning international commodity agreements there is little purpose in the First Window. The efforts of the Fund are, therefore, being concentrated on the Second Window. Several projects have been submitted for funding, but none as yet has started. There is some dispute over whether or not funds should be given as grants, or loans.[28]

COMPENSATORY FINANCING

Most negotiations on commodities since the Second World War have been about regulating market prices, primarily by the use of international commodity agreements. But there have also been negotiations to use compensation payments to deal with the problem of loss of export earnings resulting from declines in commodity prices. These have taken place in the IMF and, to a lesser extent, in UNCTAD. In addition, the European Community has developed a related scheme as part of its Lomé agreements with the African, Caribbean, and Pacific (ACP) countries.

Developing countries have directed most of their attention to international commodity agreements, arguing that the issue of compensation diverts attention away from the need to tackle the root causes of unstable commodity prices. The industrialised countries, on the other hand, have tended to view compensatory financing as a more attractive way of dealing with the Third World's commodity problems than schemes that directly deal with prices and supplies.[29]

The IMF's compensatory financing facility

As early as 1953 a United Nations group of experts suggested that the IMF should offer assistance not only for temporary balance of payments deficits, which was its original function, but also specifically for shortfalls in earnings from commodity exports. This was not taken up seriously by the IMF until the early 1960s. At this time, falling commodity prices prompted developing countries, suffering from resulting balance of payments difficulties, to urge the IMF to consider ways of expanding opportunities for borrowing.

In response, the IMF created a new account in 1963 which granted members slightly greater borrowing rights. This Compensatory Financing Facility (CFF) gave members the right to borrow the equivalent of 25 per cent of their quotas in the face of a decline in their merchandise export earnings. For an IMF member country to borrow from the CFF, three conditions have to be met. First, there has to be a balance of payments problem. Secondly. the shortfall in earnings must be temporary and beyond the country's control. Finally, the beneficiary government has to agree to cooperate with the IMF in finding appropriate solutions to its short-term balance of payments problems.[30]

The Group of 77 have criticised the CFF on the grounds that it is too restrictive and does not go far enough. They have argued that compensatory financing should take the form of grants, not loans, and should not carry any conditions. Several amendments were made to the Facility, the main ones being increases in the percentage that members can draw. In 1988 the CFF was abandoned and replaced by the

Compensatory and Contingency Financing Facility. This new facility provides members with overall access to Fund financing of up to 122 per cent of their quota, but still requires them to cooperate with the IMF over stabilisation programmes designed to deal with balance of payments difficulties.[31]

The Lomé Convention's STABEX scheme
The discussion of compensatory financing during the 1970s and early 1980s was influenced by an agreement reached between the European Community and a large group of African, Caribbean, and Pacific (ACP) countries in 1975. Known as STABEX (the Stabilisation Fund for Export Earnings), this agreement was a major component of the first Lomé Convention, signed in 1975. (For more on Lomé and a list of ACP countries, see Chapter 10.)

Under STABEX the European Community agrees to compensate ACP countries included in the Lomé Convention for shortfalls in their earnings from commodity exports to the Community with the stated aim of

> ... remedying the harmful effects of the instability of export earnings and to help the ACP States overcome one of the main obstacles to the stability, profitability and sustained growth of their economies, to support their development efforts and to enable them in this way to ensure economic and social progress for their peoples by helping to safeguard their purchasing power ...'[32]

STABEX is essentially an aid scheme, with transfers being made to the ACP countries for 'the benefit of economic operators adversely affected by this loss [of export earnings], or, where appropriate, to diversification, either for use in other appropriate productive sectors in principle agricultural, or for the processing of agricultural products'.[33] When the scheme was first set up, it covered only twelve products. The list has since been extended to 49, covering a wide range of natural resource and agricultural products. Sugar is covered under a separate scheme, known as the Sugar Protocol. Minerals are dealt with under SYSMIN, 'Mining Products: Special Financing Facility', which is separate, but similar to STABEX.

When STABEX was established in 1975, it was agreed that the least developed ACP countries, 43 of the 69, should be exonerated from repayment, but that the others would be obliged to pay if the market recovered, although no interest would be charged.[34] This system changed under Lomé IV, which began in 1990 for a ten-year period. All transfers are now given as grants. This was prompted by the low levels of loan repayment under previous Lomé agreements: 0.9 per cent under

Lomé I, 7.5 per cent under Lomé II, and 11.6 per cent under Lomé III.

Under Lomé IV there have also been changes in the rules about the way in which STABEX transfers are used. They must be used either in the specific sector which recorded the loss of export earnings, or in other agricultural sectors. Under Lomé III, funds could be used in 'other appropriate sectors'. Lomé IV also attempts to link STABEX to adjustment reforms. Where there is already an adjustment operation designed to restructure production and exports or to achieve diversification, STABEX funds must be used to support it. Changes have also been made to the dependency thresholds. STABEX is now applicable to products representing five per cent of a country's total export earnings, or one per cent for least developed, landlocked, or island countries. Under Lomé III, the thresholds were 6 per cent and 1.5 per cent respectively.

Unstable commodity prices during the 1980s placed immense strain on the STABEX budget. Between 1975 and 1988, applications amounted to ECU 3.271 million, double the ECU 1.723 million provision.[35] In 1988 alone legitimate claims for shortfalls arising in 1987 were 35 per cent in excess of the fund.[36] This led to requests from the ACP countries for the Fund to be topped up. Accordingly the EC put a further ECU 245 million into the Fund for 1987 to 1988. This was considered by the Community as a political gesture in exceptional circumstances, but has subsequently been quoted by the ACP as a precedent for further top-ups.[37]

STABEX accounts for 14 per cent of the current European Development Fund aid budget for the ACP states. But only a small number of countries benefit. Its distribution is distorted, so that in 1989 63 per cent of transfers went to only two countries: Côte d'Ivoire and Cameroon. Five more countries accounted for a further 28 per cent, which means that 91 per cent of the transfers went to only seven countries. Only twenty countries received any STABEX money. The commodity distribution is even more distorted. Coffee accounted for 70 per cent of transfers, cocoa and cocoa products for 20 per cent, and wood for 6 per cent. Applications were made in respect of only thirteen products in all.[38]

While STABEX is sometimes referred to as the jewel in the crown of the Lomé Agreement, and on balance has been greeted by the ACP countries as a substantial innovation and a novel approach to the problems of the commodity sector, it is also criticised for its limitations, particularly in terms of its selective commodity coverage, which does not extend to processed products. In the view of the British government STABEX has failed to make any significant positive impact on the economic development of the recipient countries: 'While one of the intended uses of STABEX is for diversification, it can reduce the effect of market forces and discourage adaptability to them ... STABEX to date has provided foreign exchange without any link to economic reform.'[39]

It has also been criticised for being selective by country, since only ACP states are eligible. However, a small scheme called COMPEX (Compensation For Loss of Export Earnings for non-ACP countries) is now in operation for the least developed non-ACP countries. COMPEX was set up in 1987 for a five-year period. It signalled the EC's commitment to the United Nations Programme for Action for the Least Developed Countries, formulated at a conference held in 1985. It is a provision of ECU 50 million to help to stabilise export earnings mainly in the agricultural sector. Transfers, which are in the form of grants, may also be used to support diversification programmes. Disbursements have been made, among other countries, to Bangladesh, for its jute and tea industries, and to Nepal for its hides, skins, and lentils industries. Its continuation beyond the end of 1991 has yet to be discussed.[40]

BACK TO BENDEI PATRICE

None of this has added up to much for small-scale producers such as Bendei Patrice, who remain as vulnerable as ever to unstable commodity prices. Neither international commodity agreements nor commodity cartels have been much help to him in his efforts to make a living out of cotton.

Cotton meets none of the market conditions necessary for the forming of cartels. It is a heterogeneous commodity, with many different grades being produced. There are several substitutes for cotton. Synthetics, especially polyester blended with cotton, have slowed the growth of cotton consumption over the last few decades. It is grown in both tropical and temperate climates, and produced by more than 75 countries worldwide. Major producers include powerful countries such as the USA, the Soviet Union, and China. Attempts have been made to establish an international commodity agreement for cotton, but without success. Between the 1950s and the 1970s cotton prices on the international market were relatively stable, mainly due to US policy to hold large cotton reserves and pay a generous support price to its farmers. In effect it was holding a world buffer stock. In 1965 the USA abandoned its stocking policy and reduced its price-support programme.

This is when serious discussions on setting up an ICA for cotton began. But agreement was never reached, because of the conflicting positions of producer countries. Some believed that an agreement would be unworkable because of competition with synthetics, others because of the heterogeneous nature of the product. Many did not want to regulate the market, because it would restrict their opportunities to increase their market share.

Cotton prices rose substantially in the mid-1970s in the wake of the oil price shocks which substantially raised the price of synthetic petroleum-based fibres, cotton's main competitor. At this time there was little incentive for an agreement. The USA and Soviet Union were particularly opposed to market intervention. As major producers they would have had to pay considerable sums towards the financing of a buffer stock. The poorer developing country producers, such as Chad, who may have benefited from a more regulated market, lacked any power in the negotiations, due to their marginal position in the world market.

The slump in prices during the mid-1980s was wholly due to increases in production in the major producing countries.[41] While Chad was unable to benefit from a more regulated market, it did receive some compensatory payments through STABEX following this fall in cotton prices. In 1987 disbursements to Chad amounted to 5.4 per cent of the total STABEX budget, and in 1988 they accounted for 2.2 per cent.[42]

The next chapter looks at another method of dealing with price instability: earnings insurance protection. This is the way in which big companies deal with the problem. They protect themselves against price fluctuations by trading on the futures markets.

5

HEDGING YOUR BETS:
Price stabilisation and the futures markets

PATTY AND GEORGE GO BUST

Back in the mid-nineteenth century, Patty and George made their living from farming 50 acres of land in Wisconsin, USA. It was good land, which made them a modest but decent living: enough to feed, clothe, and school their three children and keep a roof over their heads.

Their main crop was corn, which they sold each year to the local grain merchant. One year, with the corn safely harvested, they set off for town to sell it, in festive mood. The hard work of harvesting was over for another year, and it had been a good year. The rains had come at the right time and in the right quantity. The corn had grown tall and strong and ripened to gold in the summer sunshine, which had continued to shine throughout the harvest. When they reached the grain merchant, they were delighted to find that their efforts would be rewarded by exceptionally high corn prices. With the deal done, they returned home and began planning how to use their windfall gain. They decided to build an extension to their small farmhouse that winter, and invest in some new farm machinery and tools. The profits from their corn harvest would not quite cover the amount of money they needed, so they decided to take out a loan from the bank. They were confident that they would be able to repay it in a couple of years.

Winter came and went. With the extension completed, farm machinery purchased and the corn planted, they waited for harvest. It was another good growing season and the corn yield was high, but this time when they reached the grain merchant, bad news awaited them. The price of corn had plummeted. Two consecutive years had produced bumper harvests, and stocks from the previous year were still high. Quite simply supply had outstripped demand. The price being offered by their merchant was only a fraction of that paid the previous year. Patty and George returned home crestfallen. That evening they sat on their porch looking out across their harvested fields, and worked out what it would cost them to transport the grain to town, and how much they would make on the sale. It didn't take them long to discover that they would actually make a loss on the transaction. It would be cheaper to dump the grain in the Mississippi.

And that is what they did. The fruits of their harvest ended up on the river bed. The bank foreclosed on their loan, and Patty and George went bust.

TRADING ON FORWARD CONTRACTS

One of the farmer's greatest enemies, whether a North American grain farmer or a small-scale Latin American coffee producer, is price uncertainty. Price uncertainty means that you do not know, from one year to the next, what your income is going to be. It means that you cannot plan for the future, or even guarantee yourself reasonable financial security in the present.

The Chicago Board of Trade says that it was to protect grain farmers such as George and Patty against violent price swings that it began trading on forward contracts in the mid-nineteenth century. In fact, the precedent had already been set by the Osaka Rice Exchange, which had been using forward contracts for rice since 1730.[1] There are even claims that forward contracts were used as early as the thirteenth century in England by Fountains Abbey to sell wool.[2] Had the option been available when George and Patty took out their loan, they could have fixed the price of next year's harvest. The actual corn may not even have been planted. Or, if it was, then when it was harvested and ready for sale the following year, part of it would have already been sold, at a fixed price, thus guaranteeing them a proportion of their income. So if prices had dropped in the meantime, only a part of their crop would have had to be sold at the lower price.

Table 2 shows how this could work for a coffee producer. In the table, two prices are used. The *spot price* is the daily price for a particular commodity, given by the current balance between supply and demand.

Table 2: Buying on a Forward Contract

Date	Coffee prices per tonne Spot	Futures	Farmer's transaction	Farmer's bank balance Payment	Receipt	Balance
Sept'91	£480	£500	Sells 100 tonnes of coffee at £500 per tonne	—	£50,000	£50,000
June'92	£380	£400	Buys 100 tonnes of coffee at £400 per tonne	£40,000	—	£10,000
			Sells 100 tonnes of coffee at £380 per tonne	—	£38,000	£48,000

The *futures price* is the price that people can buy or sell at now, although the physical commodity is not delivered until, say, three months' time. Roughly speaking, the futures price is the spot price that is expected in three months' time.

At the end of the 1991 harvest, the farmer decides that she wants to guarantee herself the current spot price, of £480 per tonne of coffee, for at least part of her harvest the following year. She reckons that she will harvest around 200 tonnes of coffee in 1992. She does not want to sell it all on a forward contract, in case her harvest fails for some reason, so she decides to sell half of it on a forward contract. Accordingly she sells 100 tonnes of her next year's coffee at the current futures prices of £500 per tonne. Although no financial flows take place at this time, she technically has £50,000 in the bank.[3]

The 1992 harvest comes around and she harvests 200 tonnes of coffee, as predicted. But by now the price of coffee has fallen. The spot price at the time she wants to sell is only £380 per tonne. She stands to make £20,000 less in 1992 than she made in 1991. But she has already sold half her coffee at the 1991 futures price. She is able to buy back her forward contract at the new price of £400 per tonne. Then she can sell all of her coffee at the current spot price of £380 per tonne. Hence she cuts her losses by half. She sells her coffee for £38,000, but receives an extra £10,000 on her forward transactions. By selling on forward contracts, she has successfully managed to insure part of her crop against a price fall, and thus guarantee herself a proportion of her following year's income. Had the spot price in 1992 been higher than in 1991, she would then have gained on the spot market, but lost on her forward contract.

This simple model illustrates the two main functions of forward markets. The first is known as *price discovery*. The farmer was able to discover the price she would be able to receive for part of her crop the following year, even though she had no idea what the spot price would be at that time. Thus, the farmer can use the price as a basis for planning how much crop to plant, what equipment to purchase, and how much fertiliser and other inputs to buy. The second function is known as *hedging*, the dictionary definition of which is to 'reduce one's risk of loss on (bet, speculation) by similar transaction on the other side'.[4] This is just what it does. It reduces the uncertainty of income for the farmer, and hence plays an important role in guaranteeing the price she can expect to receive for her crop.

TRADING IN FUTURES

Since the days of George and Patty, and the founding of the Chicago Board of Trade, trading on forward contracts has become increasingly sophisticated. Basically, the days of simple forward buying, as illustrated above, are over, although the principle remains the same. Nowadays people and companies trade in *futures*. The main difference is that money has to be put up front, in what is known as a 'margin account'.

To return to the coffee farmer. She would have sold her coffee on a futures contract in the same way as already described. But she would have had to pay a deposit, known as an 'initial margin', which would have been lodged in a margin account. Then as the price of coffee moved, normally on a daily basis, there would be corresponding adjustments made to her deposit, known as a 'variation margin'. If the price went up, she would have to pay the extra. If it went down, she would have received the balance. Thus the amount required in her margin account would be constantly changing. What this basically means is that she would have to be very credit-worthy to put up the sometimes extremely large sums of money involved.

The Chicago Board of Trade's idea of protecting producers by trading in grain futures trading quickly caught on. Futures trading now takes place in capital cities in many part of the world, including Tokyo, Hong Kong, Jakarta, and Buenos Aires, although the main trading centres are Chicago, Paris, New York, and London. A huge range of commodities is traded in these centres, including oil, metals, agricultural commodities, and money. There are even plans for a futures market in electricity in Britain.

To allow futures trading in a commodity, the commodity must have certain characteristics. Most importantly, there must be an agreed standard that can be traded. In futures trading it must be possible to trade like with like. For this reason some goods are rarely traded on the futures market. Tea, for example, is still sold mainly through auction, as described in the following chapter. This is because there are so many different varieties and grades that it is impossible to set a single price.

In London, futures trading evolved out of the public auctioning of imported goods. In the eighteenth century, commodity traders used to meet in coffee houses in the narrow streets around Mark and Mincing Lanes just behind the City's most famous landmark, the Tower of London. Here they would buy and sell goods by public auction. Samples of the goods – the tea, coffee, cocoa, and spices – would be openly displayed, filling the streets with their rich aroma. The rest, which had arrived by ship, was stored in warehouses which lined the river.

However, the mere buying and selling of these goods did not provide the shippers, in particular, with insurance for their cargoes. Their ships had to undergo long and hazardous voyages to get the goods from Asia or Latin America to the City of London. They needed some guarantee that they would be able to cover their costs and pay their crews, and so the practice of buying and selling in the future began. To do this, merchants in the City of London had to take views on what the forward price of a shipment of, for example, copper, would be in three months' time – its expected date of arrival from Santiago. They would do this by assessing the likelihood of its arrival, on time or at all, and the projected demand for it. The merchants trading in this particular commodity would gather in a coffee house in Mark Lane, stand around a ring drawn in the sawdust on the floor, and shout out their projections – a practice known as dealing by 'open outcry' – until the hammer fell and the price was fixed.[5]

Today there is no aroma of spices in the City of London: only the pervasive smell of exhaust fumes from the cars, buses, and taxis that fill the streets. Many of the elegant old buildings have been replaced by modern office blocks. Trading no longer takes place in coffee houses, nor in the pubs and wine bars that have replaced them, but in smart modern office buildings. However, the system by which the prices of commodities are fixed, and its principles, remain much the same. It has, of course, evolved over the years, and continues to do so as communications become more sophisticated and increasing use is made of computers.

There are three main commodity houses where commodity trading takes place. One, the London Futures and Options Exchange (FOX), deals in 'soft' commodities, such as coffee, cocoa, and sugar. The International Petroleum Exchange (IPE) deals in oil. Only a few commodities are still traded by 'open outcry'. The others are all done by computer from the confines of individual offices in the City. The other commodity house, the London Metal Exchange (LME), deals in 'hard' commodities – copper, lead, nickel, zinc, tin and aluminium. Here all trading is done by 'open outcry'. Similar arrangements exist for some of these and other commodities in the New York and Chicago markets.

For the uninitiated, the world of commodity futures trading is at best bewildering and at worst incomprehensible, as the following account of a visit to the London Metal Exchange reveals:

> You will find the exchange inside Plantation House in Fenchurch Street. Speak there to Mr Sampson and you will be allowed into the viewing gallery. Speak to him nicely and he will take you on to the floor of the exchange. It will, for he will have thoughtfully so arranged it, be 12.29 p.m.

> At 12.30 a bell will ring, and Mr Sampson will explain that high-grade copper dealing has begun and will last five minutes. There will be about 300 people – most of them men, all of them white – in the hexagonal room. Around 25 of them will be sitting in a ring in the middle, the rest crowding round the circle. Some will be

leaning over the back of the ring, others leaning out of foam-padded booths, attached to three or four telephones.

The men in the middle will wave, roar, shout, signal, scribble, bellow, gesture, gesticulate, scream, flail and turn pink. This is during the early stages of the five-minute session. Thereafter things will begin to get a little bit heated. What are they gesticulating? A little book provided by kind Mr Sampson is of some help. A limp wrist with three fingers displayed signifies 'Three offered'. Two fingers mean in this context something quite different from the way in which they are used by London taxi drivers. They mean 'Two bid'. Two fingers bent double, as if by arthritis, denote 'two and a half trading'. I have to be frank and admit I cannot help much with the meaning of these.

What are they shouting? Again it is difficult to be quite sure. The dialogue runs: 'Nine offered ... Six seven ... One nine eleven ... Seven five six ...' These were snatches from here, there and everywhere. But every half-minute or so everyone in the room will unite in an apparently spontaneous chant of, say, 'Nineteen offered'.

Meanwhile further gnomic, staccato conversations will be carried out between the characters outside the ring. Such as: 'Mel, can you cover the price?' or 'Stoo, tell Tel he's done total 13 warrants.' Or: 'Dougie, what's fixing?'

The last thirty seconds of the five minutes will be like the last 30 seconds of a Frank Bruno fight. One plumpish dealer may well turn even more seriously pink than his colleagues and scream several times to the world at large: 'Ninety-five to sell, 95 to sell', and then just as a bell sounds: 'Ninety I'll give.' And so it is that the price three months ahead for 65 per cent of the world's copper is fixed.[6]

The frantic activity described was being carried out by commodity brokers and their clerks. Brokers act as the sales agent between the producer and the consumer. In order to trade on the floor of either the London Metal Exchange or London Fox, the broking firms have to become members, which involves buying their way in. Once in they are allocated a phone booth in the trading ring, marked with a silver plaque bearing the company's name. Some companies even equip their brokers with special outfits. Part of their job is to hedge on behalf of their clients, in other words to buy and sell commodities in the future, as already described. Each commodity is traded in standardised lots, the size of

LONDON METAL EXCHANGE

Trading in action on the London Metal Exchange.

which depends on the value of the commodity concerned. Copper, for example, is traded in lots of a tonne, tin in five-tonne lots. They are assisted by clerks who, while trading is in progress, spend their time on the telephone to their offices, which are simultaneously taking orders from companies that want to buy or sell the commodity in question. As these orders come through, the balance between supply and demand becomes apparent and thus the price, both current (spot) and future, is set for the day.

However, hedging is not the only activity on futures markets. There is also *speculation*. Commodity speculators do not have any direct interest in the goods being traded. They do not, for example, want to receive the actual coffee or copper. Nor do they produce it. They simply buy and sell, in the hope that they have guessed future price movements correctly. In doing so they keep the price moving, ensuring liquidity in the markets. Speculators are welcomed in some futures markets, particularly in the USA, where the extra liquidity in the markets is viewed as essential to their smooth running. In others they are viewed suspiciously as profiteers, and either discouraged or tolerated. This difference in views stems from the difference of opinions on the effects that they have on the markets. Some maintain that speculation dampens excessive price swings. Others maintain that speculation has a destabilising effect on prices.

FUTURES MARKETS AND DEVELOPING COUNTRIES

Had Patty and George been farming in the USA in the twentieth century, they could be selling their grain on futures or direct to a local grain merchant, who would probably sell the grain on to a big trader such as Cargill. In turn, Cargill would be trading its grain on the futures market, thus insuring itself against adverse price movements. There would then be some measure of guarantee on the price for Patty and George, who would also be assisted by government farm subsidies.

In many commodities the world of futures trading is very much the world of transnational corporations and large state companies. The reason for this is simple. To trade in futures requires capital. To hold a margin account you have to be credit-worthy, and the sums of money involved are great. As a result, it is these large companies who benefit from the transactions and control the marketplace. Most futures contracts are designed to suit their requirements in terms of grades, maturities, and so on.

Futures trading can be a simple and effective way of stabilising producer prices. Yet the prohibitive sums of money involved exclude the involvement of the people who most need stable prices. Few developing countries trade in futures. The contracts may be too short for them. They may require twelve-month contracts, but most are for three months; or twelve-month contracts are 'illiquid', meaning that there is insufficient trading on twelve-month contracts to keep the price moving. Moreover, developing countries lack the necessary credit. In short, they are disadvantaged in a market that is controlled largely by Northern-based, credit-worthy corporations.

One solution that has been suggested is that an international body such as the World Bank could underwrite margin payments, so that developing countries could make better use of futures markets.[7] No progress has been made towards this, however. Alternatively, developing countries could find other ways to hedge. For instance, banks could offer loans, with repayments levels linked to commodity prices.

It is not the principles of the market that are at fault. If those same principles could be applied on a small scale, millions of producers in developing countries could, in theory, benefit. If a Bengali jute farmer, for example, were able to sell some of next year's crop in a forward contract, it could make the difference between being able to feed his family one or two meals a day. It would help to reduce the unpredictability of his income, by insuring him against price fluctuations.

State marketing boards in some countries give a fixed price to growers for their commodity. Often this is calculated as a moving average of the world market price over a given period of time. In this way, producers have been able to take advantage of more stable domestic prices. Although there are examples of successful marketing boards, other have been discredited on grounds of corruption and inefficiency. Some have collapsed due to mismanagement, and others have been dismantled, leaving producers vulnerable to fluctuations in market prices.

Domestic futures markets are sometimes suggested as an alternative to state marketing boards. Hungary has developed a small domestic grain futures market, in which trading takes place in the local currency. In Argentina a futures market for grain has developed, where trading is in dollars. Through these, farmers are offered a price for their goods in advance of sale, and thus price uncertainty is reduced. Domestic futures markets could serve a useful purpose in managing domestic price risk. The need to do so has become all the more pressing with the failure of traditional price stabilisation mechanisms such as international commodity agreements.

6

THE PRICE OF A CUP OF TEA

While the slump in primary commodity prices has had a profound impact on Third World producers, it has hardly been felt by consumers in the Northern industrialised countries. When, for example, the International Coffee Agreement collapsed in 1989 and coffee prices fell to half their 1980 level, there was no immediate change in the price paid for coffee by consumers. In fact, international commodity prices are only a fraction of the amount ultimately paid for the product by the consumer. This is because the real value in commodity trading is not in the primary production of sugar, coffee, or tin, but in the subsequent activities, such as the processing, packaging, transporting, and retailing, that occur in the product's journey to the consumer.

This chapter traces one commodity, tea, in its journey from the tea picker to the tea drinker. There is no particular significance in the choice of tea. Like all commodities the marketing patterns of tea are, to a great extent, dictated by its physical characteristics. So while each commodity has its own peculiarities, they all tell much the same story. Oxfam's experience of the tea industry comes from working with tea workers in a number of countries. In common with many other primary-commodity producer groups, such as the Bolivian tin miners, tea workers tend to work long hours for very little money. They lack access to basic services, suffer health problems, and are poorly educated. They are, in every sense, at the end of a long and complex chain that links them to the consumer.

THE CONSUMER

By the end of the 1980s the world's population was steadily drinking its way through around 2.2 million tons of tea a year.[1] Each year the global increase in tea drinking outpaces that of population.[2] In short, tea is a growth industry. The historian Henry Hobhouse puts its popularity down to its theine content. Theine, like caffeine, is a mildly stimulating drug, harmless if taken in sensible doses. Tea is also cheap and practical in those parts of the world where there are dangers in drinking unboiled water.[3] Barring the Gulf State Qatarians, the Irish and British drink more tea than anyone anywhere in the world. In Qatar the average amount of tea drunk per person is five and a half cups a day. In Britain and Ireland the average is about four cups per person per day, still considerably more than in the rest of Europe, where the figure is less than one cup a day.[4]

Since the beginning of the 1960s the pattern of world tea consumption has changed significantly. People in the industrialised countries are drinking less tea than they were twenty years ago. Substantial as it may seem, the British four-cups-a-day habit is only half of what it was at the beginning of the 1960s.[5] This is partly due to the increasing popularity of coffee, and the growing market for soft drinks. But it is also due to the introduction of the tea bag. Tea bags have a convenience value over loose tea, with the result that tea bag sales now far outstrip sales of packaged tea, providing some blenders/packagers with as much as 75 per cent of their revenue.[6] This partly accounts for the decline in consumption because the tea bag, while more expensive, uses far less tea per cup than loose-leaf tea. However, this decline has been more than compensated for by a rapid growth in consumption in the Middle East, North Africa, South Asia, and the USSR. In many countries in these regions rapid growth in population and incomes has led to a steady increase in tea drinking, a trend that looks set to continue well into the 1990s.[7]

THE PRODUCER

Tea comes from an evergreen bush that thrives in the wet regions of the tropics and subtropics. As Tables 3 and 4 show, Asia dominates the world tea industry, with India and China alone producing more than half the world's tea, and accounting for nearly 40 per cent of world tea exports. But tea is also important as an export crop for a number of much smaller developing countries. In 1989 Sri Lanka, for example, accounted for nearly a fifth of world tea exports, yet tea provided more than one third of the island's foreign-exchange earnings between 1982 and 1986. Tea is also an important export for Kenya and Malawi, and significant to the economies of a small number of other very poor countries such as Rwanda and Tanzania, as Table 4 shows. Kenyan tea is the main supplier to both the British and Irish markets, providing 49 per cent and 34 per cent respectively of their tea supplies. India has cornered 33 per cent of the Irish market and 18 per cent of the UK market. Other suppliers include Sri Lanka, Indonesia, Rwanda, and Malawi.[8]

There are three ways in which the physical properties of tea have dictated its marketing patterns. The first is that tea needs to be processed immediately after harvesting. This means that processing has to take

Table 3: Major tea producers, 1989

Country	Thousand metric tons	% of world production
Asia		
India	684.1	27.8
China	558.9	22.7
Sri Lanka	207.0	8.4
Indonesia	156.0	6.4
Bangladesh	39.1	1.6
Africa		
Kenya	180.6	7.4
Malawi	39.5	1.6
Zimbabwe	17.9	0.7
Tanzania	16.1	0.7
Rwanda	13.0	0.5
Latin America		
Argentina	40.0	1.6
Brazil	14.8	0.6
Other countries	493.1	20.0
Total	2460.1	100.0

(Source: Food and Agriculture Organisation of the United Nations: *Tea*, New York: FAO, 1990)

place close to where it has been grown. Secondly, tea has a limited storage life and needs to be sold quickly. This is one reason why it is generally sold through auction. Finally, in terms of processing there is virtually no scope for adding value to tea. Once the leaf has been dried and cured, all that there is left to do is blend and package it, or granulate it to make 'instant' tea, the most recent innovation in the tea market.[9]

It is the first characteristic that has had most influence on the way in which the production of tea is organised. On-the-spot processing requires large-scale production to justify the use of expensive processing machinery. Tea, therefore, is generally grown on a plantation, or estate, with a factory attached. In most countries at least some of the production is carried out by smallholders – farmers living near a tea factory. Their harvest will generally supplement that of the main estate, although occasionally they are the only suppliers. The income they earn from it is likely to be their only source of cash to supplement their otherwise subsistence economy.

In some countries, such as Indonesia and Sri Lanka, the estates and factories are state-owned. In India, plantation ownership is

Table 4: Major tea exporters, 1989

Country	Thousand metric tons	% of world exports	% of export earnings*
Asia			
India	220.7	20.0	5.7
China	211.9	19.2	–
Sri Lanka	204.2	18.5	34.8
Indonesia	114.7	10.4	
Bangladesh	23.4	2.1	6.1
Africa			
Kenya	163.2	14.8	17.1
Malawi	39.0	3.6	20.0
Zimbabwe	14.0	1.3	–
Tanzania	13.0	1.2	5.0
Rwanda	10.8	1.0	8.0
Latin America			
Argentina	43.3	3.9	–
Brazil	9.4	0.9	–
Other Countries	34.3	3.1	–
Total	1101.9	100.0	

* UNCTAD Report by the Secretariat on Diversification. REF: TD/B/C/.1/AC/7, July 1989.
(Source: as for Table 3.)

predominantly private, while in Kenya there are a large number of smallholders (although the processing is done by a parastatal organisation, the Kenya Tea Development Agency (KTDA)). One legacy of British colonial history is extensive British corporate involvement in the tea industry at all stages of production. Until the Sri Lankan tea estates were nationalised, many of them were owned by British companies. They still dominate the African tea industry. Booker McConnel, Finlays, and Brooke Bond all own or manage large estates in Malawi and Kenya, while the Commonwealth Development Corporation has shares in the KTDA and in tea estates in both countries.[10]

In tea production it is the owner of the tea factory who bears all the costs of production up to the point of sale to the blender/packers; payment of estate labourers or smallholders, processing, transport to the port, shipping, insurance, warehousing and brokerage fees. The tea factory may be owned by a parastatal, private company, or foreign transnational. Whichever, the living and working conditions of the estate labourers, or the standard of living enjoyed by smallholders, depend on how much they are paid by the tea company owner. Being at the end of the production chain, they are the most vulnerable to internal state or company policy, or external market forces.

Tea workers

Sevanthamma has picked tea all her life. She lives with her two children and her husband on one of the 'labour lines' on the estate in Sri Lanka where she works. These are rows of huts, provided free to workers by the estate owner. Each family occupies one small room. Sevanthamma's room has neither water nor electricity. She has partitioned off one corner to serve as the cooking area.

Her day starts at 4 a.m., when she gets up, fetches water, and prepares breakfast. She has to report for work by 7 a.m., having dropped her two younger children off at the estate's primary school. On some days she has a long walk to the area of the estate where she will be working that day. If she is late, she could lose a full day's work, or have money deducted from her wages. She spends the rest of her day picking tea. She normally works until 4 p.m., with a break for lunch. If the crop is particularly heavy, she may have to spend longer picking and often does not get home until 6 p.m. Then her domestic routine begins once again: washing, cooking, cleaning, and caring for her children.

Her wages are paid every month, calculated at a daily rate of about £0.50 a day. In some weeks she will be given only three or four days' work, depending on how much tea is ready to be picked. So her wages tend to be much lower than in most other sectors of the economy.[11]

Like nearly all Sri Lanka's tea workers, Sevanthamma is of Tamil origin. Her grandmother was bought to Sri Lanka, aged 13, in 1913, to pick tea. The island was under British colonial rule at the time, and as the Sinhalese refused to work on the estates, they recruited labour from South India. These so-called 'Estate Tamils' have remained culturally and physically isolated on the island, where they are regarded by the Sinhalese majority as second-class citizens. Health and education facilities are inferior compared to those available to other sectors of the population, and their wages are lower.

For these reasons tea workers have, since the mid-1970s, been a priority target of Oxfam's programme in Sri Lanka. Project funding has mostly aimed at improving their working and living conditions. The Oxfam-supported organisation Satyodaya works with Tamil estate labourers and Sinhalese farmers in the villages that surround the tea estates in the Kandy district of the central highlands of the island. Through community organisation, it works to increase the educational and health status of these groups and to manage income-generation and welfare projects. It also aims to promote better understanding between Tamils and Sinhalese.[12]

Sri Lanka: 'Labour lines' on a large government tea estate near Kandy.

Conditions on tea estates in Bangladesh have, for many years, also been of concern to Oxfam. Back in the 1970s and early 1980s Oxfam supported a campaign designed to improve conditions on estates owned by the Scottish company, James Finlay, the biggest single producer of tea in Bangladesh. At that time conditions on those estates were described as follows:

> To describe the tea workers as slave labour would not be accurate, since they receive wages; but the similarities between their situation and that of a slave labour force are considerable, in that the attitudes and policies of their employers completely dominate every aspect of their lives. They live inside the gardens in 'labour lines' (housing) provided by the company. They are issued by the company with cheap rations of food stuffs they cannot otherwise afford. They depend on the company for any elementary education or medical care that may come their way, and even for their water supply. They are required if necessary to work as personal servants to estate managers; and they are generally unable, because of cultural isolation and high unemployment, to leave the gardens and find alternative work.[13]

A more recent study shows that overall conditions in the Bangladesh tea industry remain extremely poor.[14] It focused on women workers on a tea estate in the Sylhet region. As in Sri Lanka, the tea workers live on 'labour lines', rows of huts scattered all over the estate. Since 1977 tea companies in Bangladesh have had a legal responsibility to replace 10 per cent of the mud, bamboo, and thatch huts with cement houses that have tin roofs. But as the study shows, only a very small proportion have done so. The vast majority of workers still live in the old style housing:

> These one-room huts, measuring about 8 ft by 8 ft, have no doors. The old thatch roofs ... are leaking badly and rotting away. The floors are made of earth, there are no windows, and no separate kitchen. These homes are meant to house a maximum of four people, but up to six adults and four to six children often live, sleep, cook and eat their meals in them ... The physical environment of the labour lines is extremely poor. In the garden, attack by the mosquitoes is tremendous, and the labourers do not have any mosquito nets to protect themselves. Many are also attacked by cold, 'flu and diarrhoea. There are many labourers who suffer from malnutrition due to lack of food, and as a result their power to resist diseases becomes very weak.

As far as education was concerned, the study showed that fewer than three per cent of women on the tea estate were literate. Although a primary school had been recently established, few people could afford to send their children there, as it would deprive the family of the vital income that the child could earn on the estate.

Wages on the plantation were extremely low in comparison to those paid in other industries, and the workers on the estate were described as 'unhealthy and skinny'. To increase their basic daily wage many work over-time, for which they are paid piece rates, but even so, the 'majority of the plantation workers, especially the women workers on the Tea Estate, cannot eat two meals a day, let alone buy the bare necessities.'[15]

Responding to this the company, James Finlay, says, 'Overall the picture is not one of which we are particularly proud.' However, they add that 'All our children attend primary schools, where there are also free crèches which supply food and milk to the children ... wages are negotiated on a nationwide basis. Standards of housing and so on are subject to the Labour Act.'[16]

The company stresses the difficulties that tea companies face due to low prices for tea on the world markets: 'We have made very small profits in the last few years and there have been no dividends paid in the last decade to our shareholders.' They go on to say, 'What is needed in Bangladesh is to bring the yields and productivity of the estates up to a level comparable to the rest of the world. We are working on that and have a very major uprooting and rehabilitation programme. As the success of the rehabilitation is realised, we will have more money to add to our already considerable expenditure over labour health, welfare, education, housing and so on.'

Tea production is also of concern to Oxfam in Malawi. But here the focus of concern is on the impact that the industry has had on the local economy, rather than on the plight of workers. The industry is concentrated in the Mulanje District, in southern Malawi. Mulanje is one of the most densely populated regions in the country. But the problem is exacerbated by two factors. First, much of the area is unsuitable for cultivation, either because it is very hilly, or marshland. Secondly, much of the area is not available for cultivation, because 10,000 hectares of it is used for growing tea. The result is that there is enormous pressure on land, with not enough available for smallholder cultivation. Hence the size of landholdings in the area tends to be very small: the majority are less than half a hectare, and often fragmented, so families are cultivating tiny plots of land scattered over a large area. As these small plots have to be heavily cultivated, the soil has gradually become less productive.

All this makes it difficult for families to grow enough food to support themselves all year round. Ninety per cent of households run out of food before the next harvest is due. The main source of income to supplement subsistence farming in the area is from the tea estates. But wages in the industry are low. Malawian tea workers are among the lowest paid in the world. The daily rate is equivalent to about £0.25 – 18 per cent of the rate paid to Zimbabwean tea workers, and half the rate paid in Sri Lanka.[17] This means that there is a general lack of purchasing power, which in turn contributes to extreme poverty in the region.[18]

Oxfam is currently funding a community development programme in Mulanje District aimed at assisting the region's most vulnerable farmers and communities.[19] Tea production is just one of a complex combination of factors that has contributed to poverty in this region. But it illustrates how this type of large-scale production for export can contribute to rural poverty, through low wages and by limiting the land available for smallholder cultivation.

PROCESSING

Tea is classified according to the processing procedure used, which results in three classes of tea: black tea (fermented after plucking), green tea (unfermented), and oolong (semi-fermented). Over 90 per cent of exports consist of black tea. Most green tea exports come from China.

The processing of tea is relatively straightforward, and starts immediately the leaves have been picked. The harvested leaves first go through a 'withering' process to dry off excess moisture. Then they are put through rollers, so that the juice left in them is spread evenly over the leaf particles. After this, they are left to ferment, a process of oxidation during which the leaves change colour. Once their smell and colour are judged correct, the leaves are fired to stop fermentation, and then sorted into grades.

The best grades are large, long-leafed, and well twisted. They are known as Orange Pekoe. Then come the broken grades with names like Golden Broken Orange Pekoe. Then come the 'dusts', which are not the tail end of the tea trade, as their name suggests. They can be used in tea bags and can often fetch high prices on the open market. These are known as 'orthodox' teas, named after the machine used in their manufacture. There is also CTC (Cut, Tear and Curl) tea, which is processed through the more capital-intensive CTC machine. The smaller fragments of leaf produced by this process are ideal for tea bags, as they infuse more quickly.

After processing, the tea is packed in plywood tea-chests, or – more commonly nowadays – into five-ply foil-lined sacks ready for sale to the manufacturers, known as blender/packers in the tea industry. Some blender/packers buy direct from the tea estate. A few buy on forward contracts, but the vast majority purchase tea from public auctions.

THE AUCTION

There are tea auction centres in all the major producer countries: India, Bangladesh, Sri Lanka, Kenya, Cameroon, Singapore, and Indonesia. These account for about 90 per cent of all auction sales of tea.[20] Tea sold in Britain and the EC is generally sold through the London Tea Auction, which was established in 1834 and was, for many years, the world's leading auction. Its importance diminished in the 1970s as British tea consumption fell and the volume auctioned in producer countries increased. All the auctions follow similar sales procedures. Up to the point of sale, all costs are born by the producer. If the tea is being sold at the London auction, the producer's post-production costs will include transport to the port, shipping to London, insurance, and any warehousing involved. The producer will also pay a commission to the broker in London for selling the tea.

Auctions, as buying and selling institutions, are operated by brokers. Each producer will have a broker to whom the tea will be delivered for tasting and assessment of market value. For the London Landed Auction, that is the sale of tea warehoused in the UK, the brokerage fee was 1.75 per cent of gross sale proceeds in January 1988. For the selling of tea at the Offshore Auction, which deals with tea still aboard ship and en route to its final destination, the brokerage fee is 2 per cent. The broker may also act as agent for the seller, dealing with documentation, warehousing, and collection and remittance of proceeds. For this service an additional fee of 1 per cent of gross sale proceeds is charged. A further £8.50 per lot is levied as a sale charge for London Auction teas.[21]

Only four tea brokers now operate at the London Auction.[22] The brokers draw samples from the tea warehoused for auction, taste it themselves as an aid to pricing in the catalogue, and send out samples to any buyers for whom they may also be acting.[23] The London Auction is held weekly at Sir John Lyon House. Each broker selling that day has a catalogue of lots, and auctions it from the podium in the small auction room. The buyers sit in the body of the room, though it soon becomes apparent that only three or four are doing much bidding. These are the representatives of the so-called 'Big Four' companies who dominate the tea industry in Britain and elsewhere. They are Brooke Bond, Premier Brands, Allied-Lyons, and the Cooperative Wholesale Society.

The auctioneer states a lot, for instance Pekoe Dust, 60 chests, starting at 95. This means that the broker's minimum valuation on this lot is £0.95 per kilo. The bidders may bid up from this figure, or may come in at a lower figure. If a lot does not come in at his calculated minimum, the auctioneer withdraws it, and it goes on to the 'outlist', for sale later by private treaty, or else to be 're-printed' into the catalogue of a later auction.[24]

The bidding progresses by a penny per kilo at a time, never straying very far from the brokers' own valuation, except when a scarce item, such as an early Darjeeling, comes in. The movement from lot to lot is swift, and the whole auction, with four brokers presenting landed and offshore catalogues, can be over in three or four hours. While representatives from the 'Big Four' companies dominate the bidding for most lots, other buyers in the room occasionally ask for parts of lots. They do this by shouting out to the main bidder, for instance, 'I'd like twenty, please'. This means that they want to take twenty chests out of the lot, which may contain sixty chests, at the price currently on the table. This practice is widespread at all tea auctions. It enables smaller buyers to procure tea from lots which would otherwise be too large for them. Yet, frequently, the voice requesting a part-lot comes from another major bidder. This has led to speculation that on occasions the major companies collude to keep prices low, splitting lots rather than bidding against each other.[25]

The broker extracts a further 0.5 per cent of the auction price from the buyer, for a grand total of 2.25 per cent commission on gross sales – 2.5 per cent from offshore sales. In 1987 the average price of tea sold at the London Auction was £1.051 per kilo. The total amount of tea sold in the same year was 52,968,000 kg, giving a total sale price of £53,238,136. The brokers' 2.25 per cent cut of this comes to £1,197,857.[26]

Tea prices

The amount that tea sells for at auction is determined by a number of factors. The sharp rise in tea prices in 1984, for example (see Figure 7), was mainly due to India's ban on all exports of CTC tea in the first five months of that year in order to protect its domestic market. Drought, which adversely affected production in Kenya, Sri Lanka and India, also put pressure on international supplies.[27] Poor harvests caused by drought in India were again a factor in the price rise at the end of the decade, at a time when political unrest in Sri Lanka was having serious consequences for its tea industry. A tea workers' strike in 1989 to demand a rise in the minimum wage was estimated to have cost Sri Lanka 20 per cent of its crop.[28] Meanwhile in the USSR, fall-out from the nuclear disaster at Chernobyl has affected tea production and forced the government to buy from external markets.[29]

Attempts to regulate the price of tea through international agreements have proved largely unsuccessful, mainly because producers have been unable to agree on market shares.

THE BLENDER/PACKAGER

Eighty per cent of tea drunk in the UK, of a total market valued at £600 million a year,[30] will have been blended and packed by one of the 'Big Four' companies. The largest of these is Brooke Bond Foods Ltd, which

Figure 7: London tea auction prices, 1978 to 1989

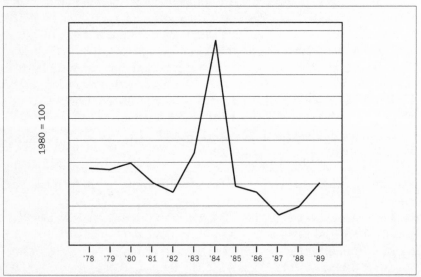

(Source: UNCTAD: *Handbook of International Trade and Development Statistics, 1989,* New York: United Nations, 1990)

includes the two tea companies, Brooke Bond and Liptons. Both are subsidiaries of Unilever PLC, making it the world's biggest tea company. Unilever made its first foray into the tea market in 1872, when it acquired Liptons, a Glasgow firm which, by that time, dominated the tea trade in the USA. In 1984 Unilever expanded its tea operations by its take-over of Brooke Bond. Brooke Bond was even more established than Liptons, and had been selling, blending, and growing tea since 1861.[31] With the popular Brooke Bond brands (PG Tips, Choicest and D), Unilever now controls an estimated 30 per cent of the UK market.[32]

The second largest blender/packer in the UK is Premier Brands Ltd – makers of Typhoo, Ridgeways, Melroses, and Glengettie – which has cornered 21 per cent of the market.[33] Premier Brands used to be the food arm of Cadbury Schweppes until a management buy-out in May 1986. Three years later it was acquired by Hillsdown Holdings PLC. It has subsidiaries in the USA, France, Ireland, and Italy. Third on the list is Lyons/Tetley Ltd, a subsidiary of Allied Lyons PLC, with 18 per cent of the market[34] and brand names such as Tetleys and Quick Brew. Allied Lyons has extensive marketing interests outside the UK: it is the market leader in Ireland, and has a share of the US and Canadian market; in Australia it holds second place after Unilever. Fourth comes the Co-operative Wholesale Society, the Co-op, with 12 per cent of the market.[35]

It is mainly the 'Big Four' who supply the major retailers with their 'own-brand' teas, although which company supplies which retailer, and with how much tea, is never publicly disclosed. Retailers' 'own brands' account for about 30 per cent of the total tea market.[36] The remainder of the market is taken up with the 'speciality teas', such as Ridgeways (a subsidiary of Premier Brands) and Jacksons of Piccadilly, which account for about 10 per cent of the market, and a miscellaneous grouping which includes instant teas, such as James Finlay's brand 'LIFT', and the various regional brands, such as Taylors of Harrogate for the remaining 10 per cent.

After purchase, the original teas are blended. All popular brands are a combination of teas which may come from as many as thirty different sources. Skilled blenders will mix together the various available teas so that the taste, if not the origin, remains consistent, and satisfies the blender's requirements of strength, flavour, and colour. In general, North Indian teas (particularly from Assam) are used to give strength; Sri Lankan, South Indian and Indonesian teas give flavour, and African teas give colour.[37]

After blending, the tea will be packaged. The ever-increasing popularity of tea bags means that around 85 per cent of all UK tea is bagged.[38] The growing popularity of tea bags over loose tea is good news for the consumer, if cost takes priority over quality, and for the manufacturers, who get more money for less tea. A 125 g pack of loose tea makes on average 55 cups of tea. A 250 g pack of tea bags contains 80 tea bags and makes between 100 and 150 cups of tea.[39] The retail price of ordinary tea bags works out at some £1.08 per 250 g, as opposed to £0.93 per 250 g for the same tea in packaged form.[40] The consumer saves around 15 per cent on each cup of tea drunk, but the producer sells less tea overall.

Once the tea has been blended and designated loose or bagged, all that remains to do is package it. It is in the design of the packaging that the companies compete most intensely for a share of the retail market. However, the scope for change is limited. In 1989 Premier Brands decided to boost its tea sales by a relaunch of its most popular brand, Typhoo. In looking at ways of doing this, they decided that as the blend was already near-perfect, all that was left was to redesign the packaging. The resulting new-look Typhoo tea bags were sealed in foil pouches, in tear-strip packs. The machinery required to do this cost the company £8 million. It then hired advertising agency Leo Burnett to market the product. They added a support line 'OO that's NOO' to the old advertising slogan 'You only get an OO with Typhoo'. The bill for the relaunch was £6 million.[41]

Blender/packagers enjoy a price mark-up of around 50 per cent, which makes it a lucrative business even for small, independent companies. They can often beat the 'Big Four' on price for a given tea at auction, because they know the exact size of their market, and their overheads are lower. What they are unable to do is expand their market. The four major companies maintain their grip on the market in two major ways. First through massive advertising campaigns, such as Premier Brand's re-launch of Typhoo, and secondly by offering discounts on bulk sales to retailers for 'own-brand' labels.[42] Neither tactic would be within the means of more modest operations.[43]

Of the four companies, Unilever is by far the largest. Apart from its dominance of the UK tea market, Unilever has also captured 62 per cent of the Australian tea market, via Bushells and Lipton, 30 per cent of tea sales in Canada, 49 per cent in the US market, and 95 per cent of packaged tea sales in India and Pakistan.[44] Unilever's subsidiary, Lipton Far East, has been blending and packing tea in Singapore since 1978, from where it supplies most of the South East Asian region with black tea. It has also started marketing green (unprocessed) tea, which is still the preferred drink in many parts of the region. Unilever is well aware that South East Asia is a dynamic growth area, and is concentrating its efforts there with the aim of considerably expanding its market. It has also made significant inroads into the fast-growing Turkish market, where its operations are fully integrated.

Tea-time in Turkey

Unilever's Turkish operation is probably indicative of the way in which the company would like to see its tea operations going in producer countries. Up until 1984, tea production in Turkey was controlled by the government parastatal Caykur. However, in 1984 the market was opened to private companies. Unilever was already well-placed to take advantage of the change of policy via its subsidiary, Dosan, which produced canned foods and tomato paste.[45]

Dosan sited a new factory in an area of high unemployment on the Black Sea. The aim is to provide 4,000 tonnes of Turkey's annual consumption of 120,000. The Unilever operation buys its tea direct from the 61 buying centres which it has established in the hill villages where the tea is grown. The advantages of this to the 3,000 registered tea growers who supply the Dosan factory is that they do not have to bear the costs of transport, insurance and documentation for their tea. They are also spared the costs of processing.[46] By using another Dosan plant at the industrialised end of the country for blending and packing, Unilever maintains a verticality of integration that few Turkish companies could afford to match. Packing machinery was shipped in from a Brooke Bond factory in Manchester.

Unilever is aiming for a modest 3.5 per cent of the Turkish market. But tea consumption in Turkey is growing fast. With a population that is increasing at a rate of around a million a year, consumption rose from about 1.44 kg a head to 2.65 kg a head between 1980 and 1986, putting it only slightly behind the UK as one of the world's major tea consumers. Between 1980 and 1987 the area of Turkey's land under tea cultivation and production increased by a third. At the same time, exports dropped from 5,243 tonnes to only 177 tonnes.[47]

Through strategic positioning Unilever has been able to enter the tea industry in a country with huge potential for an increasing market. As the growing industrial population of Turkey turns increasingly to convenience foods, inevitably the packaged tea sector of the market will increase its share. Unilever will be in a strong position to dominate the sector, and eventually the market.

WHOLESALERS/RETAILERS

In most countries the major intermediary between the manufacturer and the retailer is the wholesaler, who makes bulk purchases from producers for resale to retailers. But in the last thirty years, as retail power in industrialised countries has become increasingly concentrated in the hands of a relatively small number of supermarkets or chain stores, these mega-retailers have tended to buy direct from the manufacturers.

The retailer buying tea direct from the manufacturer can expect to make a mark-up of about 20 per cent. Jackson's Ceylon Tea Bags, for example, were being bought at the trade price of £11.78 for 12 boxes of 50 bags in 1989. Their retail price was £1.19, a mark-up of 21.4 per cent.[48]

However, the smaller retailer cannot hope to compete with the supermarket at the cheaper end of the range. In April 1989, for example, PG Tips was listed at a trade price equivalent of about £0.55 a packet, yet Tesco was selling it for £0.48, complete with a voucher offering 5 pence off the next packet purchased.[49]

The price of a cup of tea

Oxfam's main concern in the tea chain is with the ways in which the industry contributes to rural poverty in the producing countries. The need for improved pay and conditions on many tea estates is apparent. But to achieve this, two factors have to be taken into account. The first is the price of tea on the international market. Put simply, this means that the estate owners have to earn enough from their tea sales to be able to pay decent wages. The second factor relates to how those earnings are distributed. The benefits of good prices then have to reach the workers and their families. Clearly, in many cases they do not.[50]

Developing countries also need to be able to maximise their returns on their exports. In October 1991 medium-quality tea was selling in the London Tea Auction for £1.10 a kilo. The retail price was nearly four times that amount, even though the tea only has to be blended and packaged between the auction rooms and the retailer.[51] If producing countries were able to blend and package the tea before it was exported, they could substantially increase their share of the profits from the industry. Likewise they could export more if Northern consumers could be persuaded to revert to loose, rather than bagged, tea.

However, the obstacles to achieving either of these objectives are formidable. In the words of the company chairman of James Finlay: 'This is simply something which Brooke Bond, Premier and so on would not accept, but even if they did, the very high costs of transporting materials out to these countries and bringing the tea back in a packeted form would more than offset the advantage. The packeting companies like Brooke Bond and Premier would still want to advertise their products. Prices on the shelf would be much the same or even more. The producer would not be better off.' In his view, 'It is a myth that more tea would be drunk if it were in a packet rather than tea bag form.'[52] In short, it would mean changing Northern consumer habits and breaking the grip that the large tea corporations have on the market.

7

THE CASE OF COCONUTS:
Market power and the vulnerability of small producers

Tea can only be drunk. The coconut, by contrast, can be used in many different ways. In Britain the large nut with its brown 'hessian' coating frequently turns up in fairgrounds, but is only occasionally found whole, in food stores. However, its hard white flesh is used in a variety of ways, both edible and non-edible. In its desiccated form it can be found in cakes, biscuits, and confectionery. As an oil it is used in artificial milk products and ice cream, and as a glossy coating for biscuits. As an oil in non-edible products it can be found in a range of products that include soaps, washing-up liquids and powders, toothpaste, cosmetics, adhesives, pharmaceuticals, industrial oils, and fire-fighting equipment. Copra cake, a by-product of coconut oil, is used extensively by European countries as a cattle feed.[1]

COMPETITION FOR COCONUTS

But there are disadvantages in being so versatile. Coconut oil is just one of many sources of vegetable oil that compete in a highly complex market (see Table 5). Unilever, one of the world's largest processors of vegetable oils, divides them roughly into three groups. The first consists of those which are used predominantly in foods: soya, ground nut, cotton seed, sunflower, rape seed, sesame, and olive. The second group contains those with both edible and non-edible uses: palm, palm kernel, and coconut. The third group consists of those used mainly for industrial purposes: linseed, castor, and tung.[2]

Copra's main competitors are oil palm and soyabean, which together account for more than 30 per cent of world exports of vegetable oils. Its nearest substitute is palm kernel oil. Palm kernel oil and palm oil come from the same plant, the oil palm. The fruit appears in the form of bunches of nuts. Beneath the outer skin of each nut is a layer of fibrous pulp, known as the pericarp. Ordinary palm oil is processed from this. Inside the pericarp is the seed, from the inner kernel of which comes palm kernel oil. Palm oil is used locally in areas of production as a cooking oil. Its major use as an export commodity is as an ingredient in edible fats. Palm kernel oil is 'harder', and closer to coconut oil. It has good lathering qualities that make it suitable for use in soaps and detergents. It is also used in margarines, cooking oils, and confectionery, in much the same way as coconut oil, and for much the same reason.

Africa used to dominate the oil palm business, with Nigeria, Zaire, and Benin producing some 70 per cent of the total by volume. At the end of the 1950s Côte d'Ivoire started growing oil palm, and ten years later as synthetic rubber began to displace natural rubber, Malaysia switched its attention to oil palm.[3] Malaysia now dominates the palm oil market, accounting for nearly 70 per cent of exports (see Table 5). Oil palm is principally a plantation crop, unlike coconut, which is grown by small farmers. The oil palm has a higher production potential per acre than any other oilseed crop, and production has been increasing steadily over the years. It is undoubtedly seen as the oil plant of the future, in terms of current investment and research. In the field of biotechnology it has proved particularly amenable to tissue-culture techniques. Unilever has used tissue culture to speed up new variety development, and has succeeded in increasing yields from the new trees by 30 per cent. The

Table 5: Vegetable oil exports (in metric tons) in 1988

I	II	III	IV	V
1	Palm oil	2,590,153	96%	Malaysia 69%, Indonesia 13%
2	Soya oil	1,840,689	44%	USA 26%, Argentina 23%
3	Sunflower	1,080,377	36%	Argentina 35%
4	Olive oil	995,471	14%	W. Europe 86%
5	Rape & mustard seed	864,919	4%	
6	Coconut	721,914	91%	Philippines 57%, Indonesia 15%
7	Palm kernel oil	390,025	91%	Malaysia 67%
8	Maize	254,002	17%	W. Europe 40%
9	Groundnut	211,472	74%	Africa 47%, Argentina 13%
10	Cottonseed	174,622	43%	USA 51%, Brazil 25%
11	Castor	128,027	3%	Brazil 43%, India 21%, China 18%
12	Linseed	87,317	60%	Argentina 56%
	TOTAL	9,338,995		

Key
I   Oil's rank in terms of volume exported
II Oil type
III Metric tons exported in 1988
IV Percentage of exports coming from Third World countries
V   Major exporters and their percentage of column III

(Source: FAO: *Trade Yearbook, 1988*, Volume 42, Rome Tables 118 to 129 inclusive, New York: United Nations, 1990)

company expects that before long oil-palm yields will be two to six times greater than those of the older varieties, a development seen by other experts as 'threatening the position of traditional cultivators and the producers of rival vegetable oil crops, such as ground nuts and coconuts'.[4]

Copra competes with soya in cooking oils and fats, solids such as margarine and spreads, and the large and lucrative animal-feed business. In this soya has the edge over copra, because of the high protein content of the residue left after crushing and milling to produce oil. Soya is less of a 'Third World' crop than either coconut or palm oil. Over half comes from North America and Europe. Major Third World producers are Brazil and Argentina. Because of soya's particular strength as a base for valuable animal feeds, and palm oil's strength as a suitable candidate for advanced plantation techniques using tissue culture, the coconut is the most vulnerable of these three oil sources. Of the three it is also the most important as a small-scale farm crop, providing a livelihood for a large number of people in rural areas, particularly in the Philippines.

BELINDA COOTE/OXFAM

The Philippines: Coconut farmers and their families, forced off their land to make way for a commercial palm-oil plantation, take refuge in shanty villages on the island of Mindanao.

THE TREE OF LIFE: COCONUTS IN THE PHILIPPINES

The tall, graceful coconut palm thrives in tropical climates, particularly in sandy loams and deep alluvial soils close to sea level. It can be found in most parts of the tropical world, but grows most profusely in South and South East Asia and the Pacific.

The coconut is exported on to the world market in five different forms. It may be exported whole or desiccated. It may be exported as copra (the dried white flesh), as coconut oil (which is derived from the copra), or as copra cake, a by-product of coconut oil. By far the most important of these is coconut oil, which, in value, accounts for around 65 per cent of all coconut product exports. (See Table 6.)

The Philippines is the world's major supplier of coconut products. In 1988 it accounted for 57 per cent of world coconut oil exports and about half of the copra cake and desiccated coconut market. Indonesia, the next largest exporter, accounted for 15 per cent of the coconut oil market and nearly 40 per cent of the copra cake market. Other exporters include Malaysia, Sri Lanka, Côte d'Ivoire, Papua New Guinea and Vanuatu.[5]

While Northern consumers are largely unaware of the extraordinary versatility of the coconut and the wide range of products in which it can be found, people in the countries in which coconuts grow are only too aware of their versatility and value. In the Philippines, the coconut palm is called 'the tree of life'. It supplies the Filipino people with wood for their houses and furniture, thatch from its leaves for their roofs, an alcoholic drink from its flower, food, drink and soap from its nut, and cooking fuel from the nut's shell.

Apart from its domestic significance, the coconut is the country's single most important export crop, providing the country with about six per cent of its total export earnings. It also, directly or indirectly, provides a livelihood for a third of the population, nearly twenty million people.[6] While there are some large coconut plantations, production is predominantly on a small scale, with about three quarters of all holdings devoted to coconut averaging less than five hectares.[7]

Table 6: Value, in US dollars, of world coconut-product exports in 1988

	US$	
Coconut oil	721,914,000	64.9%
Desiccated coconut	145,552,000	13.0%
Copra cake	128,633,000	11.6%
Unprocessed copra	91,171,000	8.3%
Whole coconuts	24,824,000	2.2%
Total	1,112,094,000	100%

(Source: FAO: *Trade Yearbook, 1988*, Volume 42, New York: United Nations, 1990)

The producers

Situated among the handicraft displays in the Oxfam shops, it is usually possible to find a selection of small, brightly coloured wooden parrots. Sometimes they are sold on sticks as potted-plant supports, and sometimes as mobiles. They come from the Philippines, and they could be said to symbolise the fortunes of the archipelago's coconut industry. The men and women who so painstakingly carve and paint them do so because they are unable to make ends meet from their only other form of income generation – coconut production.

Rural poverty and the coconut industry in the Philippines are virtually synonymous. There are two main reasons for this. This first concerns the way in which land ownership is organised in the Philippines, and the second concerns the increasing marginalisation of coconut products in international trade.

Domingo and Christita Belleza Sendini hold one of the Philippines' half million coconut tenancies – a hectare of land with one hundred trees on it. They live, together with their seven children, in a small *barrio* a few miles inland on the island of Marinduque. The setting looks like a tropical paradise: low, steep, wooded hills, covered with elegant 70-foot coconut palms, the sun dappling thatched-roof houses on stilts. In the valley bottoms are occasional fields of rice, and under the trees are patches of lawn-smooth grass where water buffalo graze.

The Sendinis harvest their trees every 40 to 45 days. They either do this from the ground with a knife attached to a 70-foot pole, or scale the trees to reach them from above. The main danger is injury from falling coconuts, for they hit the ground with immense impact. Coconut farmers in the Philippines always try to harvest before there is any chance of the coconut falling out of the tree and hitting a passer-by. Once the nuts are harvested, the Sendinis strip off the thick green outer skin to reveal the brown nut. They crack open the nut and scoop out the firm, white copra flesh from inside. This is dried on a rack over a fire, fuelled with the discarded husks.

The Sendinis' harvest makes P300 (£8.89) every forty days, but they get only one third of that, P100 (£2.96).[8] The rest goes to the landlord, as is common in the Philippines. So their annual income from coconuts amounts to about P800 (£23.73), a little less than an agricultural worker, paid the minimum wage, would earn in one month.[9] They supplement their income by weaving baskets and gathering firewood, and through occasional work on a neighbour's rice fields. They can also make the coconut shells into charcoal, but the returns are low. From the two thousand nuts they gather each harvest, they can make about twenty pesos, or P160 (£4.74) a year.

Their landlord does not allow vegetables to be grown on his land, even though coconut trees grow better if they are intercropped. This is because he fears that if they do, they may be able to claim ownership of the land should a comprehensive land reform programme be implemented. But the Sendinis do have a small vegetable patch next to their house. They are allowed to grow bananas, and they plant cassava on the unused land in the hills. Their diet mainly consists of cassava, and rice when they can afford it. They supplement this with a few vegetables, pork, and fish. When the copra price falls, they cut back on the pork and fish.

If the Sendinis owned the land that they cultivate, they could triple their income from coconuts, and substantially increase the amount of food they are able to grow by inter-cropping. The Department of Agrarian Reform estimates that about 20 per cent of the agricultural workforce are sharecropping or leaseholding tenants, like the Sendinis.[10] But arguably it is worse still to be without land, reliant on agricultural labouring jobs – the lot of at least half the agricultural workforce in the Philippines.[11]

Not far away from the Sendinis, in a valley with steeper hills and no rice fields, just past a fork in the dirt road there is a small house on the right up a little rise. In it live Salvador and Nelda Seco and their baby daughter. They have no land. Salvador earns a living harvesting coconuts. Coconut harvesters get paid for every one hundred nuts they cut. The amount they earn varies according to the international price, but usually ranges between P3 and P7 per one hundred. The number of nuts Salvador can cut also varies, depending on the season, on competition from other cutters, and on demand from the mills. On an exceptionally good day he may cut as many as a thousand nuts, for which he would earn between P30 (£0.88) and P70 (£2.07).

The Secos pay a rent of P20 (£0.59) a year for their house. As they have no land, they have no opportunity to supplement their income by growing food. Instead they carve parrots.[12] The parrots, which are carved out of a fast-growing island soft wood called 'lanete', or 'deta', start off as an unmarked block of wood, about three inches high and one inch in diameter. It takes Salvador four minutes to carve it into the shape of a parrot, which Nelda then sands. They sell the parrots to a workshop on the sea shore. Here they are painted. There are about twenty painters, most of whom are women.

Levels of pay are determined by the number of orders from marketing outlets. The fewer orders there are, the less work there is available. In mid-1991 there was enough work for only about one third of Marinduque's parrot carvers. The work that is available is distributed between them, so that each carver currently earns around P15,000 (£333.33) a year. Painters can earn up to P100 (£2.22) for an eight-hour day.[13] But because the orders are insufficient to keep them in full-time work, their annual average earnings are about the same as a carver's.[14] Wages for parrot production compare unfavourably with other sectors of the economy. The minimum daily wage for factory work in Manila is P127.84 (£2.84).[15] Yet despite this, the parrots are a lifeline to those people of Marinduque, who otherwise must rely on coconuts for an income. Provided that retail outlets, such as Oxfam, keep buying the parrots, the people are, to some extent, protected from the vagaries of the international market place and adverse weather conditions which can so dramatically affect their income from coconuts. One typhoon can wipe out their earnings from coconuts for six months, or longer.

Processing copra

After harvesting, the nuts are de-husked and the flesh dried to make copra. This first stage of processing is almost always done by the farmer. The copra then begins its long journey to its final in-country destination: the oil mill or copra exporter. First the farmer sells it to the *barrio* buyer. The *barrio* buyer sells it to the town buyer. The town buyer sells it to the intermediary dealers, and they sell it on to the oil mill or copra exporter. This whole process, according to the Philippine Coconut Authority, takes about two months.[16]

Such a long marketing chain means that the farmer's share of the final price is low. One study estimates that landowners receive around two thirds of the Manila price, while the tenant's share is a third of that.[17] Because the farmers receive so little for their copra, many are forced to sell in advance to the *barrio* buyers. Sickness in the family, for example, may mean that they need cash between the forty-day harvests. When this happens, they are tied to the particular *barrio* buyer who has advanced the loan, and cannot sell them elsewhere, which weakens their bargaining power considerably.

The mills

There are 43 copra mills in the Philippines. A number of them are owned by multinational corporations, among which are Unilever, Proctor and Gamble, and Colgate Palmolive. The biggest mills can crush up to 1,000 tonnes of copra a day. The Philippine-owned San Miguel Corporation's Lucena City Oil Mill Refinery has a capacity of 400 tonnes, which puts it in the middle-sized range of mills. Its heart is a 70-foot high production hall, crammed with 18 massive crushing mills. The US-built machines have a nineteenth-century look about them, as cranks and chains clatter noisily round to drive the presses.

The plant absorbs 34 truckloads and 20 jeeploads of raw copra each day. As the copra awaits processing in piles outside the production hall, it is completely covered with black copra beetles, many of which get taken into the press with the copra. Once inside, it is pressed to squeeze out the coconut oil, which runs in channels under gratings in the floor. Twenty-four tankers a day take the oil to Batangas, a port about 100 kilometres away, and then to Rotterdam. From another part of the machine the copra cake is expelled. It takes ten 16-tonne trucks to take one day's output to Batangas.[18]

The export market

The Philippines exports nearly 85 per cent of its coconut products, mostly in a semi-processed form such as crudely refined oil. More than 60 per cent of them go to the European Community. A further 25 per cent go to the USA.[19] Nearly 80 per cent of the world's coconut oil is imported by the EC and the USA, each taking roughly half that amount.[20] Exports of copra cake nearly all go to Europe, while 70 per cent of desiccated coconut exports go to Europe and the USA. However, once these products have left the Philippines, they quickly get lost in the processing chain.

Much of the coconut oil is used in margarine, where it can be interchanged with a number of other oils, such as palm oil, soya, or sunflower. In Europe, Unilever dominates the margarine market, where it accounts for an estimated 60 per cent of all purchases of fats and oils.[21] The amount of coconut oil used in its products depend on the oil's price and availability. In much the same way as in the tea industry, Unilever is involved in all stages of coconut production. It owns plantations, one of the largest mills in the Philippines, and the refining operations – Unimills BV in the Netherlands. It also manufactures all its own end-products in which coconut oils are used. Its operations are broken down into four areas: food products, detergents, personal products, and speciality chemicals – all of which use coconut products.[22]

COMPANIES AND COMMODITIES

The coconut is a particularly vulnerable commodity. In nearly all its commercial uses another source of vegetable oil could be substituted for it. If this should this happen, the Philippines stands to lose its annual coconut revenue of around US$600 million, and a third of the population would lose their main source of livelihood.[23] Its survival as an export crop relies on the commercial decisions taken by the handful of transnational companies which control the vegetable oil industry. The central role played by these and other companies in international trade is illustrated by the cases of tea and coconut. In the United States it has been estimated that the transnational companies (TNCs) generate as much as 90 per cent of all trade. In Britain over 80 per cent of all exports are accounted for by local and foreign-owned TNCs, and the situation is similar in other countries. They are a major force in the development of new technologies, and they control a major proportion of all direct foreign investment.[24]

Oxfam's research into tea and coconut production has inevitably led to a focus on one transnational corporation, Unilever – inevitably, because this vast UK/Dutch-owned corporation is the largest food company in Europe, ranking sixth over all. It also dominates the tea and vegetable oils markets. Had cocoa or coffee been chosen for study, the focus would have been on the Swiss conglomerate, Nestlé – the second-largest food company in Europe, ranking eighth overall.[25] Whatever commodity had been chosen, there would have been one or more transnational corporation playing a leading role in all stages of its production and trade.

Unilever is listed as a food-processing company, although it also runs salmon farms and plant-breeding institutes. It makes shampoos, cosmetics, washing powders, and toilet cleaners. It sells chemicals, manufactures pregnancy-testing kits, and owns textile factories and restaurants. It has principal group companies in 19 industrialised countries and 37 developing countries, and employs more than 300,000 people world-wide.[26] Through its extraordinary range of products and activities it has penetrated nearly every area of our lives. The sheer size of its operations dwarfs the economies of most developing countries. In 1987 Unilever's turnover of £16.5bn was larger than the total Gross Domestic Product for the Philippines, of £15.7bn. In the same year its pre-tax profits of £1.3bn were greater than Tanzania's total GDP of £1.2bn, while its profits (after tax) of £0.7bn were greater than Chad's GDP of £0.6bn.[27]

The growth of companies such as Unilever has been achieved mainly by company take-overs. In the last decade these have been happening at a breathtaking pace, which has led to predictions that by the end of the century the global food industry will be dominated by no more than ten corporations.[28] Hillsdown Holdings plc, for example, has achieved its leading position in the UK tea market through buying up smaller tea companies. In the mid-1980s it acquired the food arm of Cadbury Schweppes and renamed it Premier Brands. Premier Brands proceeded to absorb Melroses, Ridgeways (formerly of Tate and Lyle), Typhoo (formerly of Cadbury Schweppes), and Glengettie Tea (formerly of Lloyd Piggot Co.). Hillsdown Holdings ranks 191 in the European Top 500 Companies, but is Europe's seventh-largest food group and one of the 'Big Four' tea companies.

The result of these company take-overs is fewer but larger companies. The consumer may face the same array of competing brand names, but

Table 7: UK market concentration

Product	Parent companies	% of UK market	Major brand names
Tea*	Unilever	33	Brooke Bond, PG Tips
	Allied Lyons	22	Tetley, Quick Brew, Red Label
	Cooperative Wholesale Society	10	"99", Rich Leaf, Indian Prince
	Hillsdown Holdings	13	Typhoo, Melroses, Ridgeways
	Own-label	16	e.g. Sainsbury's, Tesco's
	Others	6	
Soluble coffee	Nestlé	54	Nescafé, Gold Blend
	Philip Morris	22	Kenco, Maxwell House, Café HAG
	Unilever	7	Red Mountain, Choice
	Own-label	15	e.g. Sainsbury's, Tesco's
	Others	2	
Chocolate confectionery (cocoa)	Mars	30	Mars Bar
	Hillsdown Holdings	26	Cadbury's Milk Chocolate
	Nestlé	28	Rowntrees, Dairy Box
	United Biscuits (Holdings) Ltd.	3	Terry's
	Philip Morris	2	Jacob Suchard
	Others	11	

*A different source was used for these figures from that used in Chapter 6, in order to separate out the 'own label' category from the others.

(Source: Adapted from Mandy Jetter: 'Fair Trade Mark – Preliminary Report', November 1990)

they will be owned by only a handful of companies. In the UK well over half the tea and coffee that we drink and the chocolate confectionery that we eat is produced by only three companies: Hillsdown Holdings, Unilever, and Nestlé (see Table 7). Competition between these companies to increase their market shares is intense. Some of these large corporations have been criticised by Third World interest groups, including Oxfam, on specific issues. To name but a few, Nestlé has faced criticism over its promotion of infant formula in Third World countries; James Finlay for conditions on its tea plantations in Bangladesh; Tate and Lyle for employment conditions on Jamaican sugar estates; and pharmaceutical companies for their Third World marketing policies. Yet without them, the international trading system, as we know it today, would collapse. While these campaigns can be seen as vital checks and balances on specific aspects of company policy, the real challenge of the 1990s and beyond is to ensure that the transnational companies' immense power and influence is used in a way that genuinely enhances the overall development of Third World countries.

8

1492 AND ALL THAT:
Third World goods and First World markets

On 3 August 1492 Christopher Columbus set sail from Spain and, heading due south-west, was to 'discover' the palm-fringed islands of the Caribbean three months later. On his voyage home he wrote to his patrons, Ferdinand and Isabella, the King and Queen of Spain, describing the Caribbean as a region that 'fairly throbs with great promises of all kinds of wealth', 'great trade and profit,' 'great mines of gold', and 'a thousand other things of value', lands 'rich for planting and sowing and for livestock of every sort', 'all ... more richly supplied than I know or could tell.'[1] Two voyages and six years later, he also laid claim to that huge land mass that we now know as Latin America. Columbus' discovery of 'The New World' marked the beginning of a relationship between Europe and the Americas that was based on extraction. It began with gold and silver, but extended to include a range of goods, of which sugar and tobacco from the Caribbean were to prove the most durable.

One of his first landings was on the island that he named 'Española' – the island now divided between Haiti and the Dominican Republic. It was, according to the Republic's Minister of Tourism, the island he loved best. To attract tourists in 1992 to coincide with the quincentenary of its 'discovery', the government of the Dominican Republic embarked on a cosmetic clean-up of its capital city. The dusty sprawl of Santo Domingo was to be beautified, and a mighty lighthouse, in honour of Christopher Columbus, erected in its midst, all to promote tourism.[2]

Oxfam has been supporting community projects in Santo Domingo's urban slum areas for many years. These poor communities are facing additional problems because of the government's beautification programme. Street trading, by which many poor people in Santo Domingo make a living, has been banned. Slum areas have been cleared to make way for avenues, parks, and monuments, and entire communities have been re-located away from the city to areas where basic amenities such as water, electricity, sewerage or waste disposal do not exist. As a result, a recent outbreak of typhoid in one of these haphazardly erected, re-located shanty towns claimed many lives.[3]

Many of the people who live in Santo Domingo slums are there because they have been forced off their land by rich land-owners wanting to turn it over to large-scale production for export. Others have been driven to the city in search of work because they could no longer make a living from agricultural production, especially coffee, due to low prices on the world market. The irony is that these slum dwellers whose homes are being bulldozed have become double victims of a trading pattern that was first established in 1492, and has consigned some countries to the category of 'Third World'.[4] This early extraction of goods from the Caribbean islands determined their future role in the world economy: that of providers of raw materials to Northern markets. The unequal exchange on which this arrangement was based has contributed to the region's impoverishment and to the wealth of the importing nations of the 'First World'.

For the last five hundred years Third World commodity producers, such as those in the Caribbean, have relied principally on the industrialised countries to provide them with markets for their goods. This remains true today. As already seen, 66 per cent of developing country exports are destined for developed country markets, predominantly in the USA, EC, and Japan. These industrial superpowers are willing recipients of exports from developing countries, when the market conditions are right. Trade is essentially about meeting demand in the importing country. But this demand is determined not only by the consumer, but by the companies who help to shape it through advertising campaigns. Imports from developing countries are, therefore, essentially tailored around the requirements of the importing companies, such as Nestlé and Unilever. This has both advantages and disadvantages for the exporters in the South. On the one hand, it provides them with markets for their produce and the foreign exchange that they need to import goods. On the other hand, the commercial interests of those companies do not always concur with the interests of the developing world.

One area where there is conflict is in the processing of primary commodities. As we have already seen (in Chapters 6 and 7), the real value added in commodity trading lies in the processing of commodities. Developing countries would gain far more from their exports if they were able to process them before exporting them. It would help them to develop a manufacturing base. It would encourage investment, create employment, and increase their foreign-exchange earnings. But Northern-based companies and importing countries would stand to lose from developing countries making more of the value added from their primary commodities. One of the ways in which their interests are protected is through the use of escalating tariffs.

RICHARD ENGLISH/OXFAM

Dominican Republic: For many small farmers forced off their land by low coffee prices and rich landowners, a slum area of the capital, Santo Domingo, offers the only chance of a home.

TARIFF BARRIERS

Tariffs that escalate are tariffs that increase with each stage of processing. For example, as Table 8 shows, cocoa beans entering the European Community carry a 3 per cent tariff. If they come into the Community in the more highly processed form of cocoa powder, they carry a 16 per cent tariff. Likewise processed coffee is penalised by high tariffs. The EC

Table 8: Tariffs[a] on tropical products by degree of processing in major world markets (per cent or value-based equivalent)

Product group	EC	Japan	USA
Coffee			
Raw	9.0	0.0	0.0
Roasted, ground	16.5	20.0	0.0
Extracts, preparations	18.0	20.5	0.0
Tea			
In bulk	0.0	12.5	0.0
For retail sale	5.0	20.0	0.0
Extracts, essences	12.0	17.3	..
Cocoa			
Beans	3.0	0.0	0.0
Paste	15.0	15.0	0.0
Butter	12.0	2.5	0.0
Powder	16.0	21.5	0.4
Chocolate	..	26.7	1.9
Spices			
Unground, unprocessed	7.5	1.2	0.7
Ground, processed	11.8	6.6	4.5
Essential oils			
Essential oils	4.5	2.4	0.9
Mixtures	5.3	7.5	4.4
Preparations	6.6	..	5.3
Vegetable plaiting materials			
Raw	0.5	5.0	2.2
Plaits	3.4	5.7	5.2
Basketwork, wickerwork	6.2	9.4	6.6
Oilseeds, vegetable oils			
Oilseeds	0.0	1.0	1.8
Vegetable oils	7.2	6.1	3.5
Fatty acids, fatty alcohols	8.8	5.0	4.3
Margarine	25.0	35.0	12.5
Soaps	6.9	6.5	4.0
Tobacco			
Unmanufactured	30.0[b]	0.0	15.9
Manufactured	81.0	68.9	16.8
Rice			
Unmilled	12.0[b]	0.0	4.3
Milled, processed	23.0[b]	16.7	2.7

tariff on unprocessed coffee beans is 9 per cent, while soluble, or instant, coffee carries a tariff of double that amount.[5]

While this protects the commercial interests of companies such as Nestlé and Philip Morris who dominate the UK coffee market, it does little to help the Third World develop a manufacturing base around its own primary products. Tariff escalation applies to nearly all tropical

Manioc, roots, tubers			
Fresh, dried	6.0	11.3	13.5
Flour	6.0	12.5	0.0
Meals, starches	30.0	25.0	0.0
Bananas			
Fresh, dried	20.0	18.0	0.4
Flour, prepared	17.0	25.0[c]	3.5
Tropical nuts			
Unshelled, crude	2.2	10.5	5.6
Shelled, prepared	15.0	20.5	6.3
Tropical fruit			
Fresh, dried	8.0	8.8	10.7[d]
Preserved	11.3	21.1	10.7[d]
Prepared, fruit juices	23.6	28.2	35.3[e]
Tropical wood			
In the rough	1.2	0.4	3.4
Simply worked	3.0	2.6	1.5
Veneers, plywood	4.0	8.9	4.4
Wood articles	4.9	..	6.3
Rubber			
Natural rubber	0.0	0.0	0.0
Simple manufactures	3.7	3.6	4.7
Tyres, tubes	3.6	4.7	3.1
Other articles	4.8	4.6	5.2
Jute			
Raw	0.0	0.0	0.0
Processed	..	..	0.0
Yarns	5.3	8.0	4.1
Woven fabric	8.7	16.0	1.8
Made-up articles	7.7	9.3	3.8
Sisal, henequen			
Raw	0.0	0.0	0.0
Processed	..	..	8.0
Twine, cordage	12.0	6.5	4.1

[a] Simple averages of post-Tokyo or applied (1984) MFN duty rates, whichever are the lower.
[b] Estimated.
[c] Banana flour, not for feeding purposes.
[d] Tropical fruit, fresh, dried, preserved and prepared.
[e] Fruit juices only.

(Source: UNCTAD: *Uruguay Round - Papers on Selected Issues*, New York: United Nations, 1989, Table 4, pp. 349-50)

products, such as tea, coffee, spices, wood, rubber, and jute, entering the three main Northern industrialised markets. Having to pay such high duties on processed goods actively discourages Third World exporters from developing their own processing industries. So they remain locked in the role of primary-product exporters.

The use of escalating tariffs on processed primary commodities is just one way in which the developed countries protect their own industries and inhibit the growth of a manufacturing base in many developing countries. There are many other ways. One of these concerns controls on textile imports.

NON-TARIFF BARRIERS

Textiles and clothing are a crucially important export sector for many Third World countries, comprising between 20 and 25 per cent of their total manufactured exports. For some of the poorest countries this is the one area into which they have successfully diversified away from primary commodities. Production processes are relatively simple and labour-intensive, making it an ideal first step into industrialisation. During the 1980s cotton fabrics became the most important processed product exported by LDCs (Least Developed Countries), especially Malawi, Botswana, and Tanzania. In Bangladesh, clothing has emerged as the most important export item, overtaking jute in 1987/88, with 36 per cent of exports.[6] However, development in this sector has, in many instances, been severely impeded by the Multi-Fibre Arrangement.

The Multi-Fibre Arrangement

The Multi-Fibre Arrangement (MFA) is what is known as a non-tariff barrier. In other words, the importing country has resorted to a method other than use of the conventional tariff to limit, or exclude, unwanted goods. It was first introduced in 1974, though it grew out of earlier controls on cotton textiles dating back to 1962. It was supposed to be a temporary arrangement. Declining textile and clothing industries in the North argued for protection against the growing pressure from cheap imports from the Third World so that they could restructure and maintain profitability.

Under the MFA, member-countries are either 'importers' or 'exporters'. The importing countries, which include Britain, are allowed to limit imports by setting quotas on imports from the exporting countries which include Bangladesh, the Philippines, India, Hong Kong, and Singapore. While these quotas were in place, countries like Britain were supposed to 'structurally adjust' their own clothing and textile industries to make them competitive under free-market conditions. If that were not possible, they would be encouraged to diversify.

Failure on the part of the importing countries to make the necessary adjustments to their industries has meant that the original four-year agreement has now been renewed five times, thus stretching the definition of 'temporary'. However, pressure from the exporting countries to abolish it has resulted in a commitment from the EC and USA to phase it out gradually. Hence its most recent extension, in July 1991, was only for a period of seventeen months, so that the parties can await the outcome of the Uruguay Round (see Chapter 9) before deciding what arrangements will replace it.

Voluntary export restraint

Non-tariff barriers, such as the Multi-Fibre Arrangement, take many forms, and are frequently used by industrialised countries to keep competing goods out of their own markets. One device which has been increasingly used against developing-country manufactured products is the 'voluntary' export restraint (VER).

If one government is worried about the harm a specific import is doing to its own producers, it requires another government, on pain of retaliation, to restrict its exports of the goods in question. The use of these voluntary export restraints has spread in the last decade from textiles and clothing to cover steel, cars, shoes, machinery, consumer electronics, and more.

The VER can be effective only if the government imposing the restraint is as powerful, or more powerful, than the one accepting it. Hence it is a device which is used mainly by the USA and the EC and, more recently, by Japan and South Korea. Currently there are about 300 VERs in existence. Many of these are directed at exporters from industrial countries, but some are aimed at developing countries. Among the developing countries which have 'volunteered' to restrict their exports are Brazil, Mexico, and Bangladesh.[7]

Countries will often 'volunteer' to restrict their exports when they are threatened with what are known as anti-dumping measures, which are designed to stop countries 'dumping' their exports on other countries at below-market prices. Under the regulations of the GATT (see Chapter 9), the importing countries are allowed to raise a tariff equivalent to the dumping subsidy used by the exporter. However, the problem is that the rules on anti-dumping are so vague that they are widely open to abuse. If Brazil, for example, wants to sell its footwear in the USA, the threat of US anti-dumping action may well be enough to persuade Brazil to restrict its exports voluntarily. Thus while anti-dumping measures are sanctioned by GATT regulations, they are frequently used as a protectionist measure, particularly by the European Community and the USA.

SUPPORT FOR NORTHERN AGRICULTURE

Manufactured goods are not the only area in which there is a clear conflict of interests between industrialised countries and Third World exporters. The other main problem area is agricultural products that compete with commodities produced in the North. Included in this category are cereals, meat, dairy products, oilseeds/vegetable oils, and sugar.[8] The policies used by the industrialised countries to protect these sectors vary between countries. The shape they take in the European Community is dictated by its Common Agricultural Policy (CAP), which supports farm production through three main mechanisms: guaranteed minimum prices; protection against imports (including levies and other import controls such as duties, tariffs and quotas); and export subsidies to boost sales of surpluses on the world market.[9] In the United States of America the major forms of government assistance to agriculture are direct payments to producers, import restrictions, input subsidies, and export subsidies. Japan uses a variety of measures which include import quotas, import tariffs, input subsidies, and price-support mechanisms.[10] They are all designed to encourage levels of domestic production and protect farmers and agro-industries from cheap imports.

However, their effects are different. The measures used by Japan are used to underpin rice self-sufficiency. By imposing import barriers, they reduce market outlets for rice exporters, but they do not produce surpluses. The measures used by the USA and the EC, on the other hand, support output substantially in excess of domestic demand, so they do produce surpluses.

As we have already seen (in Chapter 3), these surpluses have put a downward pressure on world market prices for agricultural products, as well as closing off markets to Third World exporters. Chapter 3 showed that their negative impact on developing countries has been most visible in the sugar industry. However, any developing country which relies on Northern markets for its agricultural exports is vulnerable to measures taken to protect or promote the interests of their influential farming lobbies or industries. One example is the Philippines' coconut industry which, in recent years, has been threatened in both its main export markets.

Soya's revenge

> In Washington one finds today 'No coconut oil' stickers on food products such as bread. US airlines, particularly United Airlines, serve peanuts with 'No Coconut Oil, No Cholesterol!' labels.[11]

The American consumer has been led to believe that coconut oil is a health hazard. This is not as a result of medical evidence, but due to a campaign waged by American soyabean growers in the mid-1980s. At that time they perceived tropical oils to be a threat to their own market. This led to attempts to discredit tropical oils on health grounds.

The row started in 1984. At an annual conference of oilseed producers, the Malaysian delegation extolled the virtues of palm oil at the expense of soyabean oil, and followed this with a month-long palm oil sales blitz in the USA. This antagonised US soyabean growers, whose producer organisation, the American Soybean Association (ASA), decided to fight back. The Association mounted an attack first on palm oil and then on other tropical oils, namely palm kernel oil and coconut oil. They claimed that they were unhealthy because they contain saturated fats. Health-conscious Americans had only recently been made aware of the link between saturated fats and the build-up of cholesterol, which in turn is associated with coronary heart disease.

The Philippines coconut industry was caught in the cross-fire. Nearly half its coconut oil exports go the USA. Of this around 40 per cent goes to the food industry. A major part of its export earnings from the industry were suddenly under threat, and the country stood to lose $100 million in foreign-exchange earnings.[12] The government coconut authority, UCAP (the United Coconut Association of the Philippines), launched a campaign to save the position of one of the country's major exports in its most important single market.

They set out to challenge the ASA's health allegations by showing them to be based on incorrect scientific information. What they were able to prove was that although coconut oil is a saturated fat, its chemical structure seems to contribute to *low* levels of cholesterol in the blood, rather than the opposite. Soyabean oil, on the other hand, acquires properties similar to saturated fats when hydrogenated. As 70 per cent of soyabean oil used in the United States is reported to be partly hydrogenated, they argued that the claim that soyabean oil contributes to the lowering of blood cholesterol levels is not valid.[13] They were also at pains to point out that coconut oil is not significantly in competition with soyabean oil in the USA home market. In the food industry it is mostly used as a spray oil for crackers, or a frying oil for snack foods, in which it was not in competition with soyabean oil as much as with fully hydrogenated oils of a higher price range.[14] Thus, they argued, the soyabean producers' fears of being displaced by coconut oil were unsubstantiated.

But the Philippines coconut authority still had a trade war on its hands. Through mounting a massive anti-tropical oils campaign, the ASA had backed draft legislation which, if passed by the US Congress, would exclude tropical oils from American food products on health grounds. The UCAP set out to prove that the proposed legislation was nothing more than an unjust trade barrier against imported oils, disguised as a measure to protect consumers' health. The battle was bitter and costly, but eventually the proposed legislation was thrown out of Congress on the grounds that it was unfair and discriminatory. Subsequently new legislation was introduced, requiring products to be labelled as containing saturated fats if they contained tropical oils. While this was considered to be much less harmful than the previous legislation, it still meant that the coconut industry has had to continue to fight its corner for the American market. It has done so through a massive media and information campaign which 'enjoins Americans to believe the experts and not the laymen regarding coconut oil health claims'.[15]

Aflatoxin strikes back

While the embattled Philippines coconut industry was under threat on one side of the Atlantic, it was also facing difficulties on the other. This time the problem was a poisonous mould, belonging to the family Aspergillus Flavus, called aflatoxin. Aflatoxin is commonly found in the tropics, in the same way that other moulds such as penicillin are found in temperate climates. The concern about aflatoxin is that it has been found to be highly carcinogenic in animals. At very low levels it can reduce resistance to diseases. At higher levels it can induce mycotoxicosis, leading to cancer. The problem is that the mould is extremely difficult to destroy, as it can survive heating up to 650 degrees fahrenheit.

The mould spores are present in copra as well as other commodities such as ground nut, cassava, brazil nuts, barley, and palm kernel. In their dormant state they are not dangerous, but the very slightest change in temperature can cause them to grow very quickly. The poison is not found in edible coconut oil, because it is destroyed in the refining process. But it is a problem when the copra is converted to animal feed, because the mould thrives when it has a food source containing amino acids, minerals, and vitamins. The best chance of preventing the mould from developing is to dry the copra thoroughly after the coconuts are harvested. But there is a problem with this. In the Philippines, copra comes from 900,000 small farms which on average are only a few hectares in size. The methods used by the farmers to dry their copra are primitive. Either they scoop out the flesh and place it over a fire, in the way that the Sendinis do, or they simply cut the nut in half and leave it to dry in the sun, as most farmers do on the island of Mindanao. They have no way of testing the moisture content of the copra before selling it, and as a result aflatoxin levels in Philippines copra are high.

The issue of aflatoxin in copra first came to the fore in 1970, when the

US Food and Drug Adminstration served a writ on a copra meal trader in California. It was claimed that the company's warehoused products contained excessive quantities of aflatoxin. Although the shipments were later allowed to proceed when it was shown that all traces of the poison were removed by refining crude oil into edible oil, the issue had been raised. It was subsequently recommended that there should be no more than 20 parts per billion of aflatoxin in copra meal, the same as the limit established for the US peanut industry ten years earlier.[16]

The USA no longer imports copra, but the European Community does. In fact, it is now the sole buyer of copra cake for animal feed.[17] But from the end of 1988 the Community set a maximum aflatoxin contamination level of 200 parts per billion in all raw materials used in animal feeds, comfortably above the 175 parts per billion met by most Philippine copra. However, compliance to this rule is left to the individual country, provided that the ceiling is not exceeded. What has alarmed the Philippine coconut authorities is that Germany and the Netherlands, the major importers from the Philippines, have indicated much stricter requirements of 50 and 30 parts per billion respectively, which would automatically exclude Philippines copra from the market.[18] Most feed for cows contains between 20 and 25 per cent copra meal. Its inclusion in cattle feed is said to produce better-quality milk and higher yields, but even so it would be relatively easy for the industry to turn to other sources, such as soymeal or sunflower seed meal, both of which are produced in large quantities within the Community. This has led to speculation in the Philippines that the EC's ruling on aflatoxin levels is really a trade measure designed to protect the Community's own oils and fats market.[19]

The answer may never be known, but the problem is being taken seriously by the Philippines Coconut Authority. The World Bank has recently pledged a loan of US$121 million to the industry, to be spent over a five-year period. Part of the money will be spent on drying equipment to reduce the risk of contamination by aflatoxin; the industry says that the equipment will be made widely available to small farmers.[20] Whether or not this will make it possible to reduce aflatoxin to levels low enough to satisfy Dutch and German importers has yet to be seen.

The American soyabean lobby attempted to raise a non-tariff barrier against coconut oil, by claiming it to be a health hazard, because it perceived it to be a threat to its own share of the US vegetable oils market. Likewise the EC's ruling on aflatoxin levels acts as a non-tariff barrier on copra imports. While this is in part due to a justifiable health concern, it could also be seen as a way of excluding copra from the Community's market in the interests of promoting its own sunflower and soya industries.

PROTECTIONISM: ON THE RISE

While both tariffs and non-tariff barriers serve much the same purpose, the advantage of exclusion by a tariff barrier, rather than by a non-tariff barrier, is that it is visible, fixed, and calculable. The exporting country knows where it stands. The non-tariff barrier, on the other hand, takes many forms and is sometimes harder to identify. As already shown, they range from the more visible, tangible type (such as the use of quotas on imports) to the more obscure (such as health-labelling requirements).

In recent years the use of non-tariff barriers has increased considerably, while the use of tariff barriers has decreased. In 1981 and 1982 the General Agreement on Tariffs and Trade (GATT) recorded 600 different types of non-tariff barrier. A decade later, people had stopped counting. As one European Parliamentary Committee pointed out: 'It is impossible to draw up a comprehensive list of non-tariff barriers, as human ingenuity in this area is boundless.'[21]

The problem is that the figures alone show that non-tariff barriers raised by industrial countries more often discriminate against exports from developing countries than they do against goods from other industrial countries. The overall share of developing-country exports that face non-tariff barriers is roughly 20 per cent, twice the share of exports from industrial countries. Worst affected are Third World agricultural exports. About 26 per cent of these face non-tariff barriers, while around 18 per cent of manufactured goods are affected.[22]

A curse or a blessing?

This chapter has focused on the negative impact of certain protectionist policies, used by the industrialised countries, on Third World country exporters. There is little doubt that these policies are being used to protect business interests in the North in a way that is damaging producers in the South. However, there would undoubtedly be social costs involved in the removal of some of these protectionist measures, especially the Multi-Fibre Arrangement.

While there is a clear case for arguing for the abolition of the MFA, on the grounds that it is severely damaging Third World industries, there are genuine fears in some countries that its abolition will have grave economic and social consequences. Portugal, for example, relies on textiles for a third of its exports. The industry also provides employment for 30 per cent of the country's workforce.[23] In cases such as this, the government would need to provide the investment and retraining required to reduce the social costs of adjustment.

The issue of protectionism is complex, and cannot be addressed in general terms. It is true that selective protectionist measures can be used positively. They can help to promote food security in developing countries. By erecting barriers to control the import of cheap subsidised foodstuffs from other countries, particularly from the North, and by subsidising their own food production, developing countries can take real steps towards achieving self-sufficiency in food. Selective protectionist measures have a role in supporting infant industries which could become competitive in open markets in the fullness of time. They can also be used to protect consumers from harmful products, and can play a vital role in protecting the environment. This makes it difficult to define what constitutes a harmful trade barrier and what constitutes a beneficial trade barrier, for whom and for what purpose. These tensions are at the heart of the discussions taking place on the General Agreement on Tariffs and Trade.

9

REGULATING WORLD TRADE:
The General Agreement on Tariffs and Trade

The proposition that free trade will produce higher incomes for national economies and improve the world economy is central to conventional economics. Competition, so the argument runs, will lead to specialisation, higher output, and greater efficiency. This is true for all producers, be they individual company or country, since it will force them to concentrate resources in areas where they enjoy the greatest cost advantage over their competitors, specialising within an international division of labour. In a nutshell, this is the theory of 'comparative advantage', developed by the Scottish economist, David Ricardo, in the early nineteenth century.

A hypothetical example: Bangladesh can produce textiles at much lower cost than, say, the UK. However, the UK can produce machine tools more cheaply than Bangladesh. In theory, the UK could try to become self-sufficient in textiles. But most trade economists would argue that it should concentrate on producing machine tools to export to Bangladesh. With the foreign exchange thus generated, it could then import more textiles than could be produced by diverting the labour and capital from machine tools into textile production. Conversely, by producing textiles and exporting them to the UK, Bangladesh would be able to import more of the machine tools it needs to develop its manufacturing sector than it could produce by similarly diverting resources. British consumers get cheaper cloth than domestic producers could supply, and Bangladeshi manufacturers get access to cheaper machine tools, maximising the efficiency of their investment. The world economy gains, because both are maximising their potential revenues.[1]

But free trade has never existed in the real world. Today's developed countries industrialised behind high tariff barriers and other trade restrictions, many of which remain in place. Similarly, many efficient and competitive industries, North and South, would never have survived without a period of initial protection. Without heavy state intervention in the 1950s and 1960s, South Korea – one of the world's most efficient electronics producers – would still be dependent on exporting stuffed teddy bears assembled in foreign-owned plants. Stated differently: a static approach to comparative advantage ignores the potential which might be released by a period of protection.

Quite apart from these considerations, there are other forces which undermine genuinely free trade. For instance, the 'free market' in which African cocoa exporters operate is composed of two or three powerful Northern transnational corporations (TNCs), whose turnover may exceed the exporting countries' entire GDP. This massive discrepancy in economic power has important implications, since it means that TNCs are able to use markets to their advantage. Also, the technologies needed for production are often the private property of the TNCs, and made available to developing countries only on the TNCs' terms.

For all this, free trade has remained an ideal to which almost all governments proclaim their commitment, even while transgressing its principles. And it is on the principles of free trade and comparative advantage that the General Agreement on Tariffs and Trade is premised.

THE GENERAL AGREEMENT ON TARIFFS AND TRADE

The dismantling of trade barriers, in a trading system that is underpinned by rules of conduct, openness, and a mechanism for arbitration, is the purpose of the General Agreement on Tariffs and Trade, or GATT. The GATT is the main forum for debating and negotiating the rules and standards of international trade. As we have seen in Chapter 4, the GATT was born out of efforts after World War II to reconstruct the world economy. The proliferation of protectionist measures during the depression of the 1930s was seen by many as an important factor contributing to the outbreak of war. Free trade was, therefore, to be one of the pillars of the new world order. [2]

The Bretton Woods Conference which established the International Monetary Fund (IMF) and the World Bank in 1944 failed to create an organisation of equivalent status for trade. Instead world trade was to be organised and monitored by 'agreement'. Those countries which sign up for the GATT are known as 'contracting parties'. The agreement they contract is serviced by a permanent secretariat based in Geneva. Despite its somewhat inferior status in comparison to the IMF and World Bank, the GATT has exercised considerable influence on the world economy in the last 45 years. The contracting parties are a large group of countries who believe that their best economic interests are served through a multilateral trading system based on open markets. As such they agree to respect certain basic principles governing world trade.

There are four key principles. The first is that any protectionist measure should take the form of *tariffs* rather than import quotas or other non-tariff barriers. The second is that if one contracting party lowers its tariffs against another's exports, there should be matching reductions by the other member. This is known as the principle of *reciprocity*. For example, if Japan agrees to import manufactured goods from France duty-free, then the French must do the same for Japan. Thirdly, no contracting party should grant preferential treatment to another country or group of countries. This is the principle of *non-discrimination*. It means that contracting parties have to extend to each other the most favourable terms negotiated with any trading partner. This is known as the Most Favoured Nation (MFN) treatment, and exceptions are permitted only where there are regional trade agreements, such as those negotiated between the ACP countries and the EC under the Lomé convention. Finally, members agree to commit themselves to periodic multilateral negotiations on tariff reductions.[3]

Hence the Agreement is based on these different rounds of multilateral negotiations. So far, seven rounds have been completed, as summarised in Table 9. The eighth round, the Uruguay Round, was launched in 1986. During the thirty years up to the mid-1970s, the GATT made significant progress towards reducing tariffs, the main inter-war barrier to trade. The average tariff level on manufactured goods fell from 40 per cent to 10 per cent. Agreements reached in the 1973–1979 Tokyo Round brought a further reduction to 5 per cent. However, the Tokyo Round took place against a backdrop of a fast-deteriorating trade environment. Growth in the world economy had slowed dramatically since the 1960s and was further destabilised by the oil price rises of the 1970s. Chronic balance of payments problems in the USA, the world's largest trading nation and the driving force behind GATT liberalisation, gave rise to protectionist pressures. In Europe, too, rising unemployment and 'stagflation' – high inflation and low growth – led to inward-looking policies which conflicted with liberal GATT principles.

Concern in both the USA and the EC focused on the older more labour-intensive industries which were particularly vulnerable to foreign competition. Unfortunately, these industries – textiles, footwear,

Table 9: GATT negotiating rounds

Round		Dates	Number of countries	Value of trade covered
1	Geneva	1947	23	$10 billion
2	Annecy	1949	33	(unavailable)
3	Torquay	1950	34	(unavailable)
4	Geneva	1956	22	$2.5 billion
5	Dillon	1960–61	45	$4.9 billion
6	Kennedy	1962–67	48	$40 billion
7	Tokyo	1973–79	99	$155 billion

steel, and electronics – were precisely those in which developing countries were establishing a comparative advantage. GATT commitments prevented the developed countries from resorting to tariff protection. However, they did not prevent them from introducing a new genre of protectionist measures: the non-tariff barriers discussed in Chapter 8.

DEVELOPING COUNTRIES AND THE GATT

From the outset, developing countries were unhappy with the GATT. They felt marginalised in the negotiations, which concentrated on industrial products – an area which is not of great interest to the vast majority of Third World countries. They also argued that 'equal treatment of unequals is unfair', thus rejecting two of the GATT's fundamental principles: non-discrimination and reciprocal trade liberalisation.[4] It soon became apparent to them that the GATT was not designed to address their problems.

Their dissatisfaction with the GATT led to the creation of UNCTAD (the United Nations Conference on Trade and Development) in 1964. This was set up as an organisation which would be responsible for creating 'an international trading environment that would facilitate the growth of developing countries and not thwart it'.[5] A year later an additional chapter was added to the GATT which gave developing countries what is known as *special and differential treatment* (S&D). It marked the GATT's acceptance of the principle that Third World countries needed discrimination in their favour. In practice it meant that developing countries would not have to make trade concessions which are incompatible with their development needs.

These new principles were given concrete expression during the second session of UNCTAD in 1969, when agreement was reached on the principle of a *generalised system of preferences* (GSP), based on exceptions to the GATT rules concerning the principles of reciprocity and non-discrimination. The stated aims of the GSP were to increase the export earnings of Third World countries, promote their industrialisation, and accelerate their rates of growth. The scheme assists developing countries by helping them to export their manufactured and semi-manufactured goods to industrialised countries through the granting of tariff preferences – that is, a partial or total reduction of customs duties. The industrialised countries had to draw up a list of goods and countries to which they would give preference.

It took some time for this to happen. It was 1971 before the first GSP scheme, that of the European Community, was drawn up. Japan followed soon after, then the other industrialised countries. The USA was the last to have its scheme ready, in 1976. In all cases the scheme was for a period of ten years, but was extended unconditionally in the international trade negotiations of the GATT's Tokyo Round in 1979. By the end of the 1980s, 200 countries were GSP beneficiaries, while only three schemes, those of the USA, the EC, and Japan, accounted for 90 per cent of GSP imports.[6]

In theory, the GSP schemes should cover almost all Third World exports. In reality, as we have seen in Chapter 8, many goods are excluded by a variety of complex measures including quotas and other non-tariff measures. The EC, for example, does not grant preferences on metals or most agricultural products, and severely restricts them on textile imports. It thus excludes the three categories of exports most important to most countries in the Third World.[7] As a result, in 1983 only 11 per cent of EC imports from countries that are beneficiaries of the GSP scheme received preferential treatment – a mere 2.7 per cent of its total imports. The USA was much the same, with 12 and 4 per cent respectively, while Japan was only marginally better with 18 and 4 per cent.[8] One study estimated that preferential imports to the major industrialised countries have a market share of between 7 and 22 per cent. Although these are proportionally small, the author argues that in absolute terms they are significant, amounting to between US$2.4 and US$7.6 billion in terms of 1984 prices.[9] However, the scheme is generally judged to have had a very marginal impact on the Third World exporters that it was originally designed to benefit. Because of its emphasis on manufactured goods, those countries with a more highly evolved industrial base (those that need it least) have done best out of it. The three largest beneficiaries of the scheme are Hong Kong, South Korea, and Taiwan, which alone account for 44.2 per cent of the increase in exports under the GSP.[10]

In January 1990 the European Community announced plans to overhaul and upgrade its GSP system in recognition of its very severe limitations. It hopes to make the system more attractive by extending the range of products that it covers, increasing the number of countries covered to include some of the poorer ones in Eastern Europe, and making the system clearer and simpler to use. These changes will be introduced in 1992, and it is the EC's hope that they will be adopted by other countries.[11]

THE URUGUAY ROUND

Very few people in Sub-Saharan Africa have heard of the Uruguay Round, yet it will sound the death knell for Africa. It is good to go along to see how you are being prepared for sacrifice.[12]

(Thomas Ogada, Kenyan Representative to the United Nations at Geneva)

When the Tokyo Round of GATT negotiations was completed in 1979, the industrialised countries argued that a new round would be needed in the near future. They felt that the world's trading environment was becoming increasingly complex and that GATT rules were no longer able to provide the measure of discipline that was needed to prevent tensions between countries, and the widespread use of non-tariff barriers. They also wanted whole new areas of trading activities to be brought into the Agreement.[13] Most developing countries did not want a new Round. They argued that the GATT should first deliver on past promises, such as the removal of tariffs on tropical products, and that the inclusion of new issues on the agenda was unacceptable.

However, a new round was launched in September 1986 at Punta del Este in Uruguay, with 105 countries participating. The original organisation of the Round is summarised in the box below. Fourteen negotiating groups were established to work on goods, and a separate structure was

---

Organisation of the Uruguay Round

The **Trade Negotiations Committee** supervises three Committees which are set up in negotiation groups:

A The Committee of Negotiations on Trade in Goods (CNG), which is subdivided into 14 groups of negotiations:

1   Tariffs.
2   Non-tariff measures.
3   Products based on natural resources.
4   Textiles and clothing.
5   Agriculture.
6   Tropical products.
7   GATT Articles.
8   Examination of agreements and arrangements stemming from multilateral trade negotiations (Tokyo Round).
9   Safeguard measures.
10 Subsidies and countervailing measures.
11 Trade-related aspects of intellectual property rights (including trade in counterfeit goods) (TRIPs).
12 Trade-related investment measures (TRIMs).
13 Settlement of trade disputes.
14 Functioning of GATT (FOGs).

B The Committee of Negotiations on Trade in Services (CNS)

C The Monitoring Committee: it is understood that, with regard to trade in goods, the Ministers are committed to taking no new measures that are incompatible with the General Agreement ('standstill commitment'), and to gradually eliminating existing measures which are incompatible with this agreement ('rollback commitment').

(Source: *GATT Briefing No 1*, June 1990, published by RONGEAD, France.)

---

set up to deal with services. Unlike previous rounds of multilateral trade negotiations which primarily focused on trade barriers for goods, the Uruguay Round negotiations included trade in services, the protection of intellectual property (TRIPs), and international investment flows (TRIMs). Also, for the first time, agriculture was included in the liberalisation process. Textiles and Clothing, an area of trade governed for nearly three decades by a regime of its own, the Multi-Fibre Arrangement, as a derogation of GATT rules and principles, was also included.

THE NEW ISSUES

In the last few decades there have been tremendous advances in technology. As we have seen in Chapter 3, technological progress has revolutionised industrial techniques, while biotechnology, for example, has created new opportunities in agriculture. But there have been advances in other areas as well, perhaps most crucially in information and communication systems which have transformed service industries, such as banking, insurance, and aviation. With improvements in computers and telecommunications technology, production and markets have become globalised, and suppliers, consumers, goods, and data have all become internationally mobile.

Nearly all these advances have taken place in the industrialised countries, through the research and development programmes of the transnational corporations. What this means is that the world is becoming increasingly divided between those countries that have developed advanced technologies, and are, therefore, 'technology-rich', and those countries that have not and are, therefore, 'technology-poor'. The technology-poor countries include the developing countries and the newly emerging democracies of Eastern Europe.

The inclusion of the new issues – services, TRIPs and TRIMs – in the Uruguay Round was at the behest of the technology-rich countries, led by the United States. They see the issues as inter-related and complementary to one another in achieving their objectives of optimising the use of their new and emerging technologies, and maintaining their comparative advantage in this area of international economic activity. Hence they want to be able to extend their service industries, increase their investment opportunities, and protect their technologies from adaptation or imitation.

Services

World trade in services has grown much faster than trade in goods, to US$560 billion annually by 1988.[14] The technology-rich countries argued for their inclusion in the GATT on the grounds that this is a growing area of economic activity and trade, and should be brought under GATT rules and disciplines in order to expand world trade and make the GATT more relevant to a changing world economy.

The immediate problem was one of definition. The service sector includes economic activities as varied as telecommunications, transport, electricity, data processing, banking and insurance, and educational and health services. The intangible nature of these activities, and the unique issues that each service raises, make them difficult to regulate through a multilateral agreement that treats them as a single sector. They may cross from one country into another as a flow of information (data processing, design, entertainment), or as a consumer or supplier of services (tourism, education, professional services). They may cross as a flow of money and financial services, or as a cross-border shipment of goods (repair services). Hence, transborder trade in services is often difficult to detect, and equally difficult to regulate.[15] Governments generally regulate their flow not by border barriers, as in trade in goods, but through foreign-investment policies or domestic regulatory policies. The technology-rich countries, the main exporters of services, want to see these barriers detected and made more transparent, so that they can be eliminated, or at least made more consistent.

The position of the technology-poor countries is somewhat different. Although services constitute an important component of their economic activities, most of their industries focus on traditional services such as education and transport, which lack dynamism and have low productivity. None (or very few) of their services operates trans-nationally. Their priority is to expand and develop their service sectors, and make them more dynamic components of their economic development. They argue that the policies and legislation they use to regulate the transborder flow of services are not motivated by protectionist considerations, but by strategic needs related to public order or consumer protection. The development of certain sectors crucial to the efficiency and growth of the rest of the economy is also an important consideration. They feel that they have little to gain from liberalisation of trade in services, because they are generally the main importers. They also fear that the adoption of international undertakings will undermine the development of their own infant service industries.[16]

Trade-related Investment Measures (TRIMs)

The world's stock of foreign direct investment (FDI), which in 1988 totalled US$861 billion, is becoming increasingly important in international trade.[17] But the nations that invest, primarily the industrialised countries through transnational corporations, are frustrated by the measures used by host-country governments to regulate their investments.

Trade-related Investment Measures, adopted by host-country govern-ments to attract and regulate foreign investment, are mainly of two kinds. The first consists of investment incentives such as loans, tax rebates, or the provision of services on preferential terms. The second relates to requirements that investors must fulfil. A typical TRIM of this nature would require the investing corporation, for example, to restrict imports of certain components in order to encourage local production.

The developed countries want to see an international investment regime which establishes rights for foreign investors, and reduces constraints on TNCs. The view of developing countries is that while they need foreign investment, certain investment measures or performance requirements are necessary to channel foreign investment according to their own national policy objectives. The also argue that if their own TRIMs are to be liberalised, then the restrictive business practices of TNCs should be brought under international control.

With more than a third of world trade now conducted within companies, through their subsidiaries, TNCs are in a strong position to exploit discrepancies between national regulations, repatriate increased profits through transfer pricing, limit technology transfer, prohibit exports, and tie purchasing to their chosen suppliers. These mono-polistic practices are not regarded by investing countries as part of the TRIMs agreement, but many developing countries regard the TRIMs liberalisation agenda as one-sided if such practices are not dealt with.[18]

Trade-related Intellectual Property Rights (TRIPs)

Negotiations about TRIPs are concerned with achieving more, not less, protection. The developed countries want to ensure a minimum worldwide standard of protection of intellectual property, in order to protect the technology developed by their firms, and so maintain their competitive position in world markets. They also want the system to extend to living matter. Northern companies trading in pharmaceuticals, biotechnology, communications, electronics and computer software, among others, would benefit as a result. They argue that inventors and investors have a moral right to the returns from their inventions. They also maintain that the economic welfare of developing countries will increase if they adopt patent and copyright systems, because it would encourage inventions designed for the particular conditions of developing countries.[19]

The developing countries, on the other hand, argue that intellectual property protection has nothing to do with trade, and should be dealt with by the World Intellectual Property Organisation, a United Nations body. Their fear is that patent protection, particularly in areas such as food, pharmaceuticals, and chemicals, will inhibit their development efforts to meet basic needs. In pharmaceuticals, for example, they need to build up local capacity to manufacture cheaper, generic versions of essential drugs to meet national health needs. Increased patent protection would prevent them from doing this. It would allow the transnational pharmaceutical companies to dominate local markets with their more expensive brand-name products. Developing countries therefore maintain that, in cases such as this, the larger public interest must take precedence over commercial interests.[20]

The patenting of living matter would also have profound implications for Third World agriculture. Developments in the biotechnology field are highly dependent on freely available genetic resources of the South. But the products of these developments would be patented and exported to the South at high prices.[21] It could become illegal for farmers and herders to renew their stock biologically without permission or payment of royalties. Prices for patented genetically engineered 'miracle' seeds and breeds would be far higher. In addition, the developing world would increasingly lose access to scientific information and technology transfer.

In all three areas (services, TRIPs and TRIMs) there has been a sharp divide between North and South. Debate throughout the Uruguay Round negotiations has been acrimonious. Developing countries have taken a defensive position against what they regard as the largely unwelcome prising open of their markets by Northern-based transnational corporations and an erosion of their national sovereignty.

If the outcome of the negotiations is unsatisfactory from the point of view of developed countries, the USA, in particular, will continue to pursue its overall objectives in these three areas through its domestic legislation. The framework for it to do so is already embodied in US trade law, most recently in the 1988 US Trade and Competitiveness Act. Clauses in this act, known as 'Special 301' and 'Super 301', enable the US Trade Representative to threaten, and use, retaliation when countries impede its commercial activities through unreasonable restrictions. Their definition of unreasonable restriction covers any policies or practices that deny (a) 'fair and equitable' opportunities for the establishment of an enterprise, (b) adequate and effective protection of intellectual property rights, and (c) market opportunities for US goods. The USA has already used this legislation as leverage to change patent laws in a number of countries, including South Korea and Brazil.[22]

Textiles and clothing

The Multi-Fibre Arrangement (already described in Chapter 8) has a quasi-official status as a special derogation from GATT rules. It was established at the behest of the industrialised countries, the main importers of textiles, to protect their industries from cheap imports from the developing world. It is a non-tariff barrier sanctioned and administered by the GATT, and provides clear evidence that the GATT is not, as is sometimes claimed, a 'free trade' organisation, unless in the interests of its more powerful members.

However, the industrialised countries are committed to phasing out the MFA and re-integrating textiles into the GATT. Discussions during the Uruguay Round have mainly concerned the terms on which it should be re-integrated. European manufacturers believe that textiles should not be returned to GATT disciplines until the rules on dumping, subsidies, and TRIMs have been strengthened, while developing country exporters are simply anxious to see the end of it.[23]

Agriculture[24]

Before the Uruguay Round, agriculture escaped GATT disciplines. Various waivers were introduced in the 1950s which reduced the applicability of GATT's provisions to agricultural products. Although agriculture figured in the Kennedy and Tokyo rounds, it was dealt with on the understanding that GATT disciplines could not be applied.

Agriculture was included on the Uruguay Round agenda because farm spending in the Northern industrialised countries, particularly the USA and EC, had reached record levels, with high costs to consumers and tax-payers. The need to bring it under control and reduce surpluses had become a pressing policy issue on both sides of the Atlantic – so pressing that the USA made it clear from the outset of the round that it would walk out of the GATT, jeopardising the future of world trade, rather than accept a failure to reach agreement on this issue.

The inclusion of agriculture on the agenda made the Uruguay Round of critical importance to the developing world. Agriculture is of far greater significance to Third World countries than it is to the industrialised world. It accounts for an average of 20 per cent of their GDP (compared to only 3 per cent in the North), for two-thirds of employment and, in many countries, the bulk of their foreign-exchange earnings.[25] As we have seen in Chapters 3 and 8, Northern agricultural protectionist policies have resulted in low prices and loss of markets for agricultural exports from developing countries.

The agriculture negotiations have proved the most difficult area to resolve in the Uruguay Round. Failure to reach an agreement in this area caused a break-down in the talks at the end of 1990. It was eventually agreed to extend the talks for a further two years, with the latest date for completion being mid-1993. This time the problem is not one of a North-South divide, but of a split between the European Community, supported by Japan and the Nordic countries, and the United States, supported by the Cairns Group, a coalition of fourteen developed and developing countries.[26] The disagreement between the two groups is not on the need to deal with the problem, but on how to deal with it.

The arguments, which are complex and technical in nature, boil down to what constitutes a subsidy. The USA has been demanding the withdrawal of all *direct* export subsidies within five years. This constitutes a frontal assault on the EC's Common Agricultural Policy, which could not survive in its present form without them. But it also leaves untouched the US system of Deficiency Payments, which is the main source of US export subsidies. These, at least in the US view, are 'general income support' measures, rather than a direct export subsidy.

It is likely that the USA and EC will eventually find some way of accommodating their differences, and an agreement that liberalises agricultural trade will be reached. But while welcoming a reduction in agricultural support policies in the North, developing countries fear the implications that this may have for their own food-security policies.

GATT AND FOOD SECURITY

As the spectre of famine haunts sub-Saharan Africa, Oxfam's main concern is that any GATT agreement should foster, and not inhibit, efforts by developing countries to become food-secure. To be food-secure, there must be enough food available in a country to feed everyone. In addition, it must be possible to distribute the food to the people who need it, and for them to have enough income to purchase that food. In ensuring that there is sufficient food available, countries have a choice: they can either buy in their food supplies with money earned from their exports, or they can try to become self-sufficient in food. If neither of these is possible, the outcome is either hunger, or dependence on food aid, or both.

For most developing countries, reliance on food imports is risky. As we have seen, many developing countries export only a few products, which are at the mercy of low or unstable commodity prices. In many cases these countries are also under pressure to pay off debts, so food imports become an added burden on their balance of payments. A further problem is that owing to unbalanced income distribution and high transport prices, imported food often does not reach people in the more remote areas.[27]

The alternative to relying on world markets is food self-sufficiency. One of the most effective ways of increasing domestic food production is to pay food producers realistic prices. The government of Zimbabwe, for example, increased the farm-gate price of maize by 80 per cent between 1979 and 1981, and production tripled over the following five years.[28] Of course, realistic prices are not a sufficient condition for raising output and increasing food security. Farmers also need access to land, credit, and other resources. Infrastructural invest-ment in the transport and storage equipment needed to facilitate the smooth marketing of foodstuffs is also important. However, most economists would agree that remunerative prices are a necessary condition for releasing the productive potential of small peasant producers.

In recent years world cereal prices have slumped. This is because both the USA and the EC have been producing huge surpluses, which are being dumped on world markets at below-production costs. These cheap cereals are then purchased by food-deficit developing countries at knock-down prices. However, this depresses prices for local staple foods (such as millet, beans, and sorghum), lowers household incomes, and reduces the incentive to invest in agriculture. In Europe and North America, farmers have been protected against the effects of this type of food dumping by the trade restrictions outlined earlier. Oxfam is concerned that it should also be possible to protect peasant farmers in food-deficit developing countries from this type of food dumping. To do this, it is vital that a distinction is made between the type of subsidies (such as those used to protect farm production in the USA and the EC) which distort world markets, and subsidies which help countries to reduce their dependence on world markets. If this distinction is not taken into account in a Uruguay Round settlement, Third World food security could be threatened.

The agricultural negotiations illustrate a wider problem faced by developing countries in the Uruguay Round: the erosion of the principle of Special and Differential (S&D) treatment. Granted under a mid-1960s amendment to the GATT treaty, S&D waives the obligation on Third World countries to reciprocate liberalisation measures where this would be 'inconsistent with their development, financial and trade needs'. But the status of S&D treatment has become very unclear in the course of the Uruguay Round, with different interpretations being given to it by North and South. The USA and EC have both indicated that concessions given should be phased out over time. The developing countries argue that a time frame is not acceptable, and that concessions should be available to them for as long as they are needed. What this means is that developing countries may no longer be able to rely on S&D treatment to avoid having to take damaging liberalisation measures.

The issue of food security is central to Oxfam's concerns. For Oxfam, therefore, a 'successful' outcome to the GATT's agricultural negotiations will be one that fully supports the efforts of developing countries to achieve food security, both by enabling them to support their own agricultural production, and by ending the dumping of subsidised exports on world markets. Anything less could, indeed, 'sound the death knell for Africa', as Ambassador Ogada predicted.

Burkina Faso: Selling locally-grown millet in the market at Gorom-Gorom. Millet is a staple food in this area of West Africa.

GATT AND THE ENVIRONMENT

> There are extensive and significant linkages between international
> trade and the environment. Trade relationships and trade
> agreements substantially influence, and can undermine, national
> and international efforts to address ecological problems.
> Unfortunately, trade-environment linkages are rarely recognised
> and poorly understood.[29]

Oxfam project partners in all corners of the Third World understand,
only too well, the links between environmental degradation and trade.
In Chile, Peru, and the Philippines they witness daily the effects of over-
fishing, by national and foreign-owned fleets of trawlers, on the lives of
the small fishing communities that are scattered along their coastlines.

In many parts of the developing world people are forced off good
land into more marginal environments to make way for cash-cropping
geared to the export market. In an effort to survive, they find they must
over-exploit these marginal lands, thus leading to further impoverishment. In Brazil, for example, landlessness and land disputes are major
causes of the destruction of Amazonia. But the reason for the land
problems is the concentration of land in some parts of the country into
large holdings, producing trading surpluses. Mining, timber, and large-
scale agriculture also cause significant destruction of the forest.[30]

Yet, until recently, GATT negotiators have viewed the environment as
a strictly non-economic factor which has little to do with the
negotiations in the Uruguay Round. They did not see it as their job to
take into consideration environmental factors in the trade liberalisation
process. Yet liberalisation measures can threaten efforts being made by
national governments to protect their environments. For example, in
1985 Indonesia banned the export of raw logs, to encourage value-added
manufacturing and thus generate more foreign exchange for less raw
material, and take the pressure off the Indonesian rainforest. A number
of other countries followed suit. If GATT introduces a ban on export
controls that does not take into account the need for countries to protect
their fragile environments, it will mean that these countries will be faced
by potentially ecologically devastating free trade in raw timber, or
comprehensive GATT-backed sanctions.[31]

The attitude of GATT negotiators to the environment gradually
thawed during the Uruguay Round, thanks largely to the vigorous
lobbying efforts of concerned groups. The Nordic countries and others
have called for the activation of the GATT Environment Committee,
which was convened in 1971 but which has never met. Many developing
countries are reluctant to see any extension of GATT powers into other
areas, and are not so enthusiastic about this move. They would rather

see trade and environment discussed in a more open forum, such as UNCTAD or in the UN Conference on Environment and Development (UNCED) process. Those calling for the convening of the GATT Environment Committee are hoping that it would comprehensively examine the Agreement's effects on the environment.

Environment had been officially 'recognised' by the GATT by the end of 1990 to the extent that it is now possible to recognise environmental protection as a mitigating factor in the dismantling of trade restrictions.[32] Articles of GATT grant exemptions to allow trade measures to 'conserve exhaustible natural resources'. But they can be applied only inside the country applying the measures, and a recent GATT ruling reinforced the limitations of these exemptions.

In August 1991 a GATT dispute committee ruled that a US law banning imports of yellow-fish tuna from Mexico was contrary to international trade rules. The ban had been imposed as a punitive measure to prevent the death of dolphins who swim above the tuna and get caught in the Mexican industry's drift nets. This was the first test of whether environmental considerations, extending beyond a country's jurisdiction, can be a factor in restricting imports. The GATT's answer was 'no'.[33] This ruling could mean that any attempt to conserve habitats or resources in other countries, or in the global commons (the sea, for example), cannot rely on trade sanctions. It puts into jeopardy existing agreements such as the International Convention on Trade in Endangered Species (CITES), the Montreal Protocol on ozone protection, and others painstakingly developed since the beginning of the 1980s which rely on trade sanctions. It raises questions over the development of future agreements, such as conventions on biodiversity and climate change due to be signed at the UNCED or 'Earth Summit' in June 1992.

But the dispute panel ruled, in addition, that countries may not raise barriers against goods which are produced in environmentally unfriendly ways. The point here is that the cost of timber, for example, produced in sustainable ways will be greater than that produced in unsustainable ways, because the costs of replanting or regeneration will be included or 'internalised'. Unsustainably produced timber would obviously have more ready market access because it is cheaper than sustainably produced timber – unless barriers are erected against it. Hence, for example, Dutch efforts due to come into effect in 1995, aimed at supporting the sustainable logging of tropical forests by the use of trade measures, could be challenged in the GATT. When environmental costs, of whatever kind, involved in production are not 'internalised', because they are supposedly 'free', goods are artificially cheap and are, in effect, subsidised. But GATT does not even recognise this type of 'subsidy', let alone try to remove it, and thus in practice encourages the continued exclusion or 'externalisation' of environmental costs of production. And artificially cheap, environmentally 'subsidised' goods will clearly dominate the market unless the 'subsidies' are removed or trade measures are erected against them.

All this seems a far cry from the people with whom Oxfam works, such as the dispossessed peoples of sub-Saharan Africa, or the destitute fishing communities of poor Third World countries, yet their plight underlines the complexities of the issues. The overturning of the US ban represents a blow to the global environment yet, for Mexico, it represents a boost to its economy. As noted above in relation to the convening of the GATT Environment Committee, developing countries are ambivalent about the inclusion of environmental concerns in the GATT. On the one hand it offers opportunity, as in the Indonesian timber case. On the other hand, for many people in the South, the power of the Northern environmentalist lobby represents a new form of imperialism and a threat to their development efforts. People in the South stress that any concern for the global environment necessitates tackling poverty and North/South inequality. If debt burdens were eased and commodity prices improved, then pressure to over-exploit natural resource systems would be reduced. A significant reduction in poverty in the South would benefit both the global environment and world trade.

THE IMPORTANCE OF THE GATT

The GATT is often accused of being a club that regulates world trade to suit the interests of its most powerful members, particularly those of the USA and the EC. Hence it is criticised for its lack of democracy and also for its lack of transparency, in that negotiations take place behind closed doors. The evidence to support these criticisms is overwhelming.

In recent years a number of proposals have been put forward to create a new trade organisation. The model favoured by the South is a new International Trade Organisation (ITO), with broad economic objectives, to replace the GATT and UNCTAD. A proposal by the European Community for a new Multilateral Trade Organisation (MTO) is more limited in scope. The MTO would be a kind of 'Super-GATT', which would incorporate the new areas discussed in the Uruguay Round, such as services and intellectual property, but would not deal with the broader economic objectives envisaged by the South in its proposals.[34]

Yet while there are powerful arguments to support the need to reform the GATT, to take account of the interests of its weaker members, it is equally important to preserve its key underlying principle: that of a multilateral world trading system. The next chapter looks at some of the consequences for developing countries of unilateral trade arrangements, and the emergence of new trade blocs.

10

GOING BANANAS:
The impact of trade blocs on developing countries

Every year between June and October, farmers in the Caribbean Windward Islands of St Vincent, St Lucia, Dominica, and Grenada listen anxiously to the weather reports. For this is hurricane season, and their livelihoods are at stake. If one happens to strike, they are in grave danger of losing their banana crop. The almost rootless banana tree, mainstay of the islands' economies, has little chance of surviving winds that sometimes reach 140 miles per hour and regularly lash these rugged little islands.

In some years the farmers are lucky, but 1989 was a bad year. That September Hurricane Hugo swept through the islands, knocking out most of their banana crops. A week after the storm, Ingort Jab Jacob sat in his small off-licence on the edge of the dusty pot-holed road that winds its way through the mountainous island of Dominica, reflecting on his good fortune. For although Hugo had destroyed 75 per cent of his banana crop, it had left unharmed his yam, dasheen, and other root crops, referred to as 'ground provisions' in the Caribbean. He also had his off-licence, a wise investment following a good banana harvest one year. He and his family would be able to survive the nine months or so that it takes for a new banana crop to produce fruit.[1]

But not everyone was so fortunate. The devastation caused by Hugo meant that Oxfam became involved in a major relief operation to provide shelter, food, and medical assistance to victims of the hurricane, and help with the longer-term work of crop rehabilitation. Relief operations of this nature are almost seasonal occurrences in the Eastern Caribbean. But despite this, Ingort was in little doubt about the fact that he would be growing bananas again next year. Hurricanes are an occupational hazard of banana production in the Windward Islands, but they are not a deterrent. More than 5,000 farmers grow bananas in Dominica, and the vast majority of them do so on fewer than five acres of land.[2] The picture is similar on the other islands. Furthermore, bananas contribute substantially to the Windward Islands' economy. Ninety-one per cent of St Lucia's foreign-exchange earnings come from bananas. Dominica relies on bananas for 71 per cent of its foreign-exchange earnings, while St Vincent and Grenada respectively rely on them for 28 and 13 per cent of their earnings.[3]

Such a high degree of dependence on a single crop is entirely due to a special trade arrangement in force between these islands and Britain. Under the European Community's Lomé Convention, bananas from former British colonies have preferential access to the UK market. So long as they can deliver agreed quantities of the fruit, farmers such as Ingort are paid a guaranteed and fixed price.

THE HISTORY OF THE LOMÉ CONVENTION

Sixty-nine Third World countries from Africa, the Caribbean, and the Pacific, known as the ACP Group, have special trade links with the European Community through the Lomé Convention. Nearly all these countries are former colonies of the EC countries, mainly France and Britain. Lomé could be seen, therefore, as the concrete expression of Europe's responsibility to its former colonies.

When the Treaty of Rome was signed in 1957, establishing the European Economic Community (EEC) of six (Belgium, France, Federal Republic of Germany, Luxembourg, Italy, and the Netherlands), Europe's relations with the Third World were of a distinctly unilateral nature – that of colony and colonial power. The Treaty provided for existing trade and aid links with these countries to be maintained.

During the 1960s many of these colonies were granted independence. Not wanting to lose their ties with the Community, but indeed to extend them, 18 countries, nearly all former French colonies and all on the African continent apart from Madagascar, formed the AASM (Association of African States and Madagascar). In 1963 they formalised their continued relationship with the European group of six through the Yaoundé Convention. The convention was to last for five years. Its provisions included preferential trade agreements, notably access for raw materials to Europe, as well as financial and technical assistance to be financed by the European Development Fund. A second Yaoundé Convention was signed in 1969, for a further five years.

In 1973 Britain, Denmark, and Ireland were granted membership of the European Community. Britain already had its own trade preferences, with twenty Commonwealth countries, which extended beyond Africa to the Caribbean and Pacific. Provision was made for these preferences to be continued when Britain joined the Community, and the same opportunity was offered to other independent African states. These countries, together with the AASM countries, formed themselves into one group: the African, Caribbean, and Pacific (ACP) Group. When the second Yaoundé Convention expired in January 1975, it was replaced by the first Lomé Convention (Lomé I), as an agreement between the ACP group of 44 countries, and the newly expanded European Community of nine countries.[4]

The Convention was signed in a mood of optimism among the ACP countries and pessimism in the industrialised countries. It was signed just after the first 'oil shock' in 1973/74, and the subsequent rise of OPEC as a major commodity cartel. The industrialised countries feared that the same could be done for other commodities. Many commodity prices were high, and the South seemed to be on the brink of wielding some economic power. As a result, Lomé I was seen by some to be the nearest any North-South agreement had ever been to a partnership of equals.[5] However, the bubble soon burst. Between 1961 and 1973 per capita GDP in sub-Saharan Africa, which had been growing, fell on average by 0.1 per cent a year.[6] Then came the second 'oil shock' in 1979, and commodity prices began to tumble. As they did, Lomé II was negotiated, and came into effect in January 1980 for five years. Lomé III (1985) was also for five years, while Lomé IV (1990) was signed for a ten-year period. By 1990 the ACP group had grown to 69 countries.

Membership of the ACP group and the European Community

Between them, the inhabitants of the 69 ACP States and the 12 member states of the European Community account for 14.1 per cent of the world's population. The total population of the EC member states is 324.7 million; that of the ACP States, 439 million. The composition of the ACP group is as follows:

Africa

Angola	Gambia
Benin	Ghana
Botswana	Guinea
Burkina Faso	Guinea Bissau
Burundi	Kenya
Cameroon	Lesotho
Cape Verde	Liberia
Central African Republic	Madagascar
Chad	Malawi
Comoros	Mali
Congo	Mauritania
Côte d'Ivoire	Mauritius
Djibouti	Mozambique
Equatorial Guinea	Namibia
Ethiopia	Niger
Gabon	Nigeria

Rwanda
São Tome and Principe
Senegal
Seychelles
Sierra Leone
Somalia
Sudan

Swaziland
Tanzania
Togo
Uganda
Zaire
Zambia
Zimbabwe

Caribbean

Antigua and Barbuda
Bahamas
Barbados
Belize
Dominica
Dominican Republic
Grenada
Guyana

Haiti
Jamaica
St Christopher and Nevis
St Lucia
St Vincent and The Grenadines
Suriname
Trinidad and Tobago

Pacific

Fiji
Kiribati
Papua New Guinea
Solomon Islands

Western Samoa
Tonga
Tuvalu
Vanuatu

The European Community is composed as follows:

Belgium
Denmark
France
Germany
Greece
Ireland

Italy
Luxembourg
Netherlands
Portugal
Spain
United Kingdom

LOMÉ'S TRADE PROVISIONS

Lomé's central trade provision is the granting of duty-free access to the EC market for most ACP exports. As a permitted exception to the GATT rule of reciprocity, the ACP countries are not required to grant corresponding preferences to the European countries. However, there are two main limitations. The first is that agricultural products which compete with EC products falling under the Community's Common Agricultural Policy are not granted free access to the Community. In these cases the ACP countries have preferential access over non-ACP countries, but not uncontrolled access. Sugar, for example, is catered for by a special protocol under which ACP countries (and India) have guaranteed duty-free access for specified quantities. In the case of beef, sales by ACP exporting countries are controlled by quota.

The second limitation is that ACP exports are subject to 'rules of origin' criteria. These establish the minimum local content requirement. This means that products are allowed duty-free access to the Community only if one third of their value originates from an ACP country. These rules are designed to prevent non-ACP countries from diverting their exports to the EC so that they can take advantage of the duty free-access afforded to the ACP countries. But this raises a number of problems for the ACP countries. First it inhibits them from establishing simple export-oriented assembly operations, if the goods to be assembled come from non-ACP countries. Secondly, in the case of textiles EC rules stipulate that although the yarn may come from non-ACP sources, the cloth must, which pre-supposes the prior existence of a substantial textile industry of the type which does not exist in most ACP countries.[7]

Critics of Lomé have blamed these limitations on its failure to achieve one of its main stated aims: to promote the performance of ACP countries in EC markets.[8] Since 1975 the share of ACP exports to the EC has fallen. In 1989 they accounted for 3.8 per cent of the Community's imports, down from 8 per cent in 1975. This even compares unfavourably with the fall experienced by developing countries as a whole, down to 14 per cent, from 20 per cent.[9] Other critics point out that exports are concentrated among a small number of beneficiaries. Coffee, copper, and cocoa account for 40 per cent of all non-oil exports to the EC from the ACP countries. Of this, 30 per cent of the coffee is exported by Côte d'Ivoire, nearly all the copper comes from Zaire and Zambia, and 80 per cent of cocoa comes from Côte d'Ivoire, Ghana, and Nigeria.[10] The picture is similar with sugar. Although 17 countries have import quotas under the Sugar Protocol, the sizes of the quotas are unevenly spread, with the result that only five countries, Mauritius, Fiji, Guyana, Jamaica, and Swaziland, account for 80 per cent of the total quota, while Mauritius alone supplies more than one third of the ACP's export allowance to the EC.[11]

In part due, perhaps, to its rather marginal trade concessions and uneven application, Lomé has been unsuccessful in shielding the ACP countries from the negative external environment of the 1980s: falling commodity prices, rising interest rates, and the slump in investment. Economic growth and living standards in many ACP countries have deteriorated, and many people are poorer than they were in the mid-1970s. Not one ACP country has joined the ranks of the newly industrialising countries, and some are even more dependent on primary commodities than they were in 1975. Yet for all its inadequacies and inconsistencies, as a contractual agreement between developed and developing countries, based more on dialogue than dictate, Lomé remains a unique and important instrument of trade and development cooperation.

Lomé trade preferences will be affected by both the outcome of the Uruguay Round and the completion of the Single European Market. The ACP countries fear an erosion of their trade preferences once the Uruguay Round has been completed, because it is likely to result in a widespread reduction in GSP rates. The EC has stressed that the Lomé Convention will have to adapt to the post-Uruguay multilateral trade regime. However, detailed studies have shown that the impact of reduced GSP rates is likely to be marginal.[12] Of much greater concern is the impact of the European single market, which does carry very distinct dangers for the ACP countries.

BANANAS, LOMÉ, AND EUROPE 1992

Bananas are grown for export in a number of ACP countries. Under Lomé they are allowed into the EC duty-free. Taking advantage of old colonial ties, the Windward Islands and Suriname supply the UK market. Somalia exports its bananas to Italy, while Cameroon and Côte d'Ivoire send theirs to France. In all, these countries supply the EC with around 20 per cent of its bananas. The EC also has a number of domestic banana producers. Bananas grown on the Greek island of Crete are given preferential access to the Greek market. Likewise bananas grown in Madeira and the Canary Islands have preferential access to the Portuguese and Spanish markets respectively, while those grown in the French Overseas Departments, of Martinique and Guadeloupe, rely on the French market.

Together, ACP and domestic bananas meet only about half the EC's requirements. The other half is met by producers in Central and South American countries, mainly Colombia, Costa Rica, and Honduras. Their bananas are known as 'dollar bananas', and face a common external tariff of 20 per cent unless they are destined for West Germany. If they are, they are allowed in duty-free, under a special protocol of the Treaty of Rome.[13] All this will have to change once Europe has completed the formation of its single market at the end of 1992.

The goal of the Single European Market is to create 'an area without internal frontiers in which the free movement of goods, persons, services and capital is ensured'.[14] What this means is that ACP suppliers and domestic banana producers will lose the preferential access they have enjoyed in their traditional markets. Instead they will have to compete for EC markets with the dollar bananas. The problem with this is that the production costs of both the ACP and the domestic suppliers are much higher than those of the Central and South American suppliers.

ROSHINI KEMPADOO/OXFAM

St Vincent: harvesting bananas.

Here bananas are grown on large plantations, spread over relatively flat land with good soil and a high degree of mechanisation. Most of them are owned or indirectly controlled by three giant US transnationals: United Brands, Standard Fruit, and Del Monte. While trades unions in many of these countries have managed to negotiate improved pay and conditions, wages on many plantations remain low.

The banana trade in the Windward Islands is also under multinational control, in this instance the British company Geest. But, unlike countries in Latin America, bananas here tend to be grown by farmers such as Ingort Jab Jacobs, on small plots of land. Their reliance on bananas is a direct result of UK policy to help to build up their industries so that they could supply the British market. As a result, these small islands are overwhelmingly dependent on bananas for export earnings, yet their production costs are between 30 and 50 per cent higher than in Latin America.[15]

Studies have shown that due to these higher production costs, completely free trade in bananas within the European Community could result in the ACP and domestic suppliers losing as much as half their current share of the EC market. Even if they maintain their tariff preference, many of them will not be able to compete with the cheaper dollar bananas, and their exports to the EC will decline by an estimated 28 per cent.[16] This is particularly worrying for the Windward Islands, because of their high production costs and heavy reliance on bananas. The problems that they would face as a result have prompted European Commission officials and member-state politicians to make repeated commitments to maintain preferential access for the traditional suppliers after 1992. Mr David Curry MP stated in the UK Parliament in April 1991: 'We are making it clear to the Commission and other member states that any new arrangements [for bananas] must fulfil our commitments to Commonwealth Caribbean suppliers ...'.[17] How this will be done is not yet clear, as the shape of the arrangements for bananas after 1992 is still under discussion. However, what is clear is that the present system will not continue indefinitely. It would be a derogation from the Single European Act, which will lay the legal basis for the Single European Market, and will therefore be subject to legal challenge.[18] The task for the EC member states is, therefore, to design measures which will enable banana producers, such as Ingort Jab Jacobs, to make a decent living for themselves and their families. Unless they do, there will be major economic upheavals, with political and social implications.

In the view of the World Bank, it would be better to remove all market preferences and replace them with direct aid payments. The aid money could then be used either to improve the long-term efficiency of the banana industries or to diversify their economies.[19] Oxfam has been supporting diversification efforts in the Windward Islands for some years. The Chateaubelair Multi-Purpose Co-op, which was established in 1986, has been encouraging its farmer members on the island of St Vincent to plant some of their banana land out to vegetables, with the help of a revolving loan.[20]

While farmers are happy to be involved in this type of small-scale diversification, mainly for domestic production, they are resistant to more ambitious diversification plans. In November 1990 Oxfam helped to fund a symposium for the Windward Islands' Farmers' Association (WINFA). It was to provide a forum in which farmers could discuss their options for the post-1992 period. At the symposium the farmers made it clear that while they are aware of their need to diversify, they are reluctant to switch to alternative crops until alternative markets have been found. Many remember a time when they were advised to grow turmeric as an alternative to bananas. But then the turmeric market collapsed, and they were unable to sell their harvest. In their view bananas remain their safest option.[21] There is little doubt that opportunities for diversification are very limited in that region. Tourism is the most obvious alternative but, for social and political reasons, there is a reluctance to replace dependence on bananas with dependence on tourism.

BEYOND BANANAS: EUROPE 1992 AND DEVELOPING COUNTRIES

In one sense 'Europe 1992' is a less dramatic enterprise than is sometimes portrayed. In a nutshell, all that the members have committed themselves to do is to take steps towards the creation of a customs union – steps that the original group of six had promised to take 35 years before, when signing the Treaty of Rome. However, the outcome will be the creation of a very large trade bloc. It will consist of an internal market of some 320 million people, with an annual GDP of US$2.7 trillion, exports worth US$860 billion, and imports of US$708 billion.[22] The sheer size and economic strength of this market has raised fears that Europe post-1992 will become a 'fortress' – and that countries outside will find it increasingly difficult to do business with the Community.

Community officials have gone to great lengths to reassure countries outside the EC that they have no intention of creating a fortress. Indeed, they maintain that the effect of creating a single market will increase opportunities for trade, as it will stimulate economic activity within the Community. GDP is expected to increase between 4.5 to 7 per cent, which will increase demand for imports, particularly of primary products, while the removal of internal barriers will make it easier for third-party exporters to exploit the full potential of European demand.[23]

However, there is another side to this. It has also been argued that the creation of more efficient production units within Europe will tend to increase the competitiveness of domestic supplies relative to imports. So the share of the EC market supplied by imports may decline. Whether or not the absolute level of imports falls depends on whether this trade-diverting effect is larger or smaller than the trade-creation effect of predicted faster economic growth within the EC.[24] Numerous studies have been carried out in an effort to gauge the impact of 1992 on external trade. The analysis is normally of the 'on the one hand' and 'on the other hand' type. While there is broad agreement that there will be changes, the precise nature of these changes, and their impact on individual countries, or categories of exports, is generally inconclusive, with a few exceptions.

The case of bananas is one such exception. Bananas have assumed particular prominence, because of the severe effect that the Single European Market will have on certain countries. But it also illustrates how decisions taken in the 1992 context could undermine the EC's existing agreements with the South. On this score the ACP countries have a particular worry about 1992. It arises from the fact that their present pattern of exports to the EC, of bananas and other products, is determined by market regulation with individual members of the community. Once internal barriers have been removed, they will have to compete within the much larger European market. This may, as in the case of bananas, result in their exports being substituted by exports from other developing countries. In the view of one OECD official: 'However one turns it, the ACP countries stand to lose. There will be trade diversion away from them.' [25]

Non-ACP developing countries also have their concerns about the completion of the Single European Market. Countries which export textiles to the EC, under the Multi-Fibre Arrangement (MFA), may also be affected by the removal of internal barriers to trade. Under the MFA the EC regulates its textile imports to protect domestic producers. But the Community's MFA is particularly complex, because Community quotas are sub-divided into member states' sub-quotas. With the establishment of the single market, these will have to be dismantled. It has been argued that this may lead to increased opportunities for developing countries' textile exporters, as some of the sub-quotas are under-utilised. Under the present arrangements these cannot be redistributed to countries that fill their quotas, but after 1992 it will be possible for exporters to exploit the full EC quota.[26]

However, all this depends on discussions taking place in the Uruguay Round on the future of the MFA. As already seen, there is a commitment to phase it out. However, this is unlikely to result in free trade in textiles, as the main importing countries will still demand restrictions. Whether or not the new measures will be more or less liberal than the current MFA has yet to be seen. It is likely that those countries within the Community which are heavily dependent on their own textile industries, such as Portugal and Greece, will lobby hard to restrict imports into the Community as a whole.

All developing countries will be affected by the harmonisation of technical standards under Europe 1992. Some fear that this will restrict their exports, because the new EC standards may be higher than those currently in force in member states. The main product groups which could be affected are plants, fish, meat, and toys. In the case of plants, each consignment cleared at the EC border will be issued with a 'plant passport', which will guarantee free circulation throughout the Community. For meat products, slaughterhouses and processing plants will have to be licensed by EC inspectors before their products enter the Community. Likewise fish and fish products will have to meet certain standards, through the compulsory licensing of fishing vessels and processing plants, before they are allowed to export to the Community. Toys, which mainly come to the Community from South-East Asia, will have to meet harmonised EC standards of toy safety.[27] In addition to these health, sanitary, and safety standards, it is likely that environmental standards will be set on a range of developing countries' exports.

There is little doubt that it will be the poorer countries that suffer most from any raising, or extension, of technical standards. They are likely to lack the investment required to up-grade standards. Concern has also been expressed that these measures could be used as a veiled form of protectionism. It is often hard to define where the legitimacy of standards ends and protectionism sets in.[28]

But for all this, there could be some good news for some developing countries too, provided that the EC pushes ahead with its plans to abolish excise duties on coffee, tea, and cocoa. In some member states these are substantial. In West Germany, for example, excise duties on coffee and tea are more than 50 per cent. The effect of the abolition will be to make the products cheaper. It has been suggested that this could raise consumer demand and result in an increase in world imports of coffee, by 3.8 per cent in value terms, and 1.9 per cent in volume. As standards of living in the Community are expected to rise overall it has also been suggested that this will increase the demand for higher quality, mild 'arabica' coffee. Therefore the main gain from this increase in consumption will be for the arabica-producing countries, such as the Central American producers, Kenya, Rwanda, and Tanzania, at the expense of the 'robusta' producers such as Zaire, Cameroon, and

Uganda. Cocoa and tea would also benefit. It has been estimated that volumes of EC cocoa imports would rise by 1.4 per cent, benefiting Côte d'Ivoire, Nigeria, Cameroon, Ghana, and Malaysia. Tea imports would increase by 0.2 per cent and benefit Kenya, India, and Sri Lanka.[29]

The effects of 1992 are difficult to identify, and even more difficult to measure. There is no consensus among economists on the impact of the single European market on developing countries. Some say it will bring overall benefits.[30] Others say its impact will be negative.[31] Some studies show that the Newly Industrialising Countries will stand to gain most from Europe 1992 and that the poorer countries will lose out. Others maintain the opposite to be true. In truth, no one knows, except in very specific cases, such as bananas.

Clearly the EC will have to monitor the impact of its single market on developing countries carefully, and assist where the effects are negative. Direct aid disbursements could be used, for example, to help poorer countries to meet more stringent technical standards. Aid could also be used where product-displacement occurs, such as in the case of bananas. Whatever shape the banana regime takes after 1992, the EC will have to ensure that there are funds available for the Windward Islands either to diversify away from bananas, or to upgrade production.

There are other factors, apart from the completion of the internal market, which could affect the position of developing countries in the EC market. The most important of these is competition, both for markets and investment, with Eastern European countries. With the emergence of these countries from the socialist bloc, there is much talk of enlarging the Community to include them. Whether or not they actually become integrated into the Community, there is little doubt that they will be helped by EC funds to adapt their industrial structures, and by EC trade regimes to improve their trade performance. Both could easily happen at the expense of developing countries.

FREE TRADE IN NORTH AMERICA

Zenaida Ochoa's home is a small hut, pieced together out of bits of wood and cardboard. There are many others like it in the shanty town where she lives, a ramshackle collection of makeshift shelters just outside Mexico's northern-most town, Tijuana. Tijuana lies on the shores of the Pacific Ocean, bordering the USA at the top of the southern Californian Peninsula. Head north up the coast from Tijuana, and you reach San Diego. Keep going, and you will find yourself in Los Angeles and, eventually, San Francisco.

Zenaida will probably never get that far. She has already travelled some distance north to reach Tijuana. Her family are farmers. She is the eldest of six children and wanted to escape her life of rural poverty. She needed a job, so set off for Tijuana, where she had heard that there was plenty of well-paid work in the *maquilas*, or assembly plants. Tijuana was not quite the glamorous city she had expected. A cloud of yellow smog hung over the town, and the busy roads were little more than dust tracks. But undeterred, she signed up for work in a clothing factory, where she discovered that she would earn the equivalent of US$60 a week for working a nine-hour day. It was more than many people get paid (most workers only earn the Mexican peso equivalent of $6.50 a day), and seemed like a small fortune to Zenaida, even though a chicken in Mexico costs a tenth of that.

Six months later she was wondering how long she could carry on in her job. Her health was beginning to suffer from the effects of being hunched over a sewing machine all day in the tin-roofed *maquila*, which sizzles in the summer sunshine. She was plagued by back pain and was having trouble with her eyesight. She had a long walk there and back, and shanty-town living was much worse than conditions on the farm she had left. Each morning she picked her way through raw sewage on the journey to work, and on her return she faced the daily task of fetching water from one of the few taps that served the area. She could see little prospect for improvement. A fellow worker had tried to organise a union to get better pay and conditions, but had been sacked. Her friends in the shanty town had told her that conditions in the other *maquilas* were just as bad. Either she stuck with it, or returned to unemployment and her family farm. Either way her dreams of prosperity had been shattered.[32]

Zenaida is one of around half a million people, Mexicans and other Central American migrant labourers, who work in the *maquiladora* sector. *Maquiladoras* are assembly plants. There are about 1500 of them, mostly US-owned, ranged along the 1,550 mile Mexico-USA border. They import nearly all their raw materials from the USA, assemble them, using cheap Mexican labour, and export them back to the USA. The finished products range from sun-glasses to car-parts. All the border transactions are duty-free, under special arrangements negotiated in the mid-1960s. Apart from creating jobs, the sector has also made a substantial contribution to the Mexican economy. Having tripled output in the last ten years, *maquiladoras* now rival tourism and remittances from émigré workers as Mexico's biggest hard-currency earner, after oil.[33]

As the US and Mexican governments negotiate a free-trade agreement, both advocates and opponents of the proposed treaty look to the *maquiladora* sector as the best indication of its potential for economic growth and abuse, alike. Under the proposed North American Free Trade Agreement (NAFTA), Mexico will be absorbed into the existing USA–Canada Free Trade Agreement, effectively creating a free-trade zone 25 per cent larger than the European Community.[34] The NAFTA trade bloc will be of a very different nature from that of the single European market. The major distinction between the two is that while negotiations in Europe have been based on the idea of creating a community of equal status, the attraction of the NAFTA, to both US and Mexican governments, is that their economies are very different.

For Mexico it offers an opportunity to attract new investment, and speed up the process of export-oriented industrialisation. Economic stagnation in the 1980s and the debt crisis have discredited old models of import substitution, and the Mexican government is now committed to developing new export industries as an alternative strategy. Attracting foreign investment is vital, particularly as the banks are reluctant to lend directly to the government, which is still burdened by debt.[35]

For US corporate interests, the main attraction is a ready supply of unskilled or semi-skilled labour. Slow population growth in the USA, combined with an increasingly service-oriented economy, means that its diminishing labour force will be drawn into the highly-skilled service jobs, leaving a dearth of unskilled labour for its manufacturing sector.[36] Furthermore, Mexican labour is cheap, and un-unionised. The average hourly wage is only US$0.98, one tenth of that paid in the USA.[37]

Advocates of the proposed treaty point to the booming *maquiladora* sector to prove their point. So do the opponents. They argue that the very success of the sector has turned much of the border region into a cesspit of abysmal living conditions and environmental degradation, and that such costs are simply too high.

Cheap, unorganised labour is only part of the attraction of Mexico to US corporate interests. By moving south, they also escape compliance with US environmental and workplace safety standards. Similar laws exist in Mexico, but enforcement is weak, with the result that the border area has been described as an 'environmental calamity'.[38] By law Mexican companies are supposed to ship their toxic waste back across the border to the USA. But the heavily polluted local rivers and contaminated water supplies are powerful evidence that many are not doing so. Air pollution is as bad. Cars lack air-pollution control devices and travel on unmade-up roads, throwing dust into the atmosphere. Added to this is industrial pollution, some of it coming from US furniture makers who fled Los Angeles to escape new restrictions on the emission of solvents. Still more comes from local residents who, in the absence of any other way of getting rid of it, burn their rubbish.[39]

The irony is that pollution does not respect national boundaries. Miles of some of California's most beautiful beaches south of San Diego are closed because of the pollution that flows into the Pacific from Tijuana. Water supplies in Arizona are being contaminated by the river that flows across the border, bringing a particularly stubborn strain of hepatitis-A. In El Paso, the rates for gastro-intestinal diseases are four times higher than in other parts of the USA, due to the lack of a good water supply.[40]

But it is not only the environment that is affected. In the USA workers fear a further loss of jobs as industries move south. Thousands have already been lost to the *maquiladoras*. Some predictions put further losses as high as 40 per cent in key industries as a result of the proposed NAFTA.[41] Yet there are also hopes that a free-trade pact would create jobs inside Mexico and stop the cross-border flow of illegal migrant workers. An estimated 9 million Mexicans work illegally in the USA.[42]

The impact of the NAFTA will be felt in all sectors of Mexico's economy, and nowhere more so than in agriculture. Advocates of the pact, especially in the USA, argue that free trade in farm produce between the USA and Mexico will bring benefits to both sides. They point to the large US market for Mexican tomatoes, avocados, and other fruits and vegetables, and to the vast quantities of cheap US maize which could be exported to Mexico if existing trade restrictions were lifted. Mexico, the argument runs, could most efficiently feed its population with American maize purchased with foreign exchange earned from its vegetable exports.

The problem with this argument is essentially a distributional one. There are over 2.25 million farmers in Mexico, farming fragile soils with limited capital resources. They are protected from US maize imports by a government minimum-price programme and a 70 per cent border tariff. Under free-market conditions, there can be little doubt that they would be swept aside and forced from their land, because Mexican maize farmers are six times less productive than their US counterparts.[43] Their choices would be stark: migration to Mexico City, unemployment and poverty, or illegal migration to the USA. Conversely, the benefits from the boom in vegetable exports will be based in relatively few hands. This is a large-scale, capital-intensive sector dominated by Mexican big business and US TNCs. While agro-exports will generate the dollars which *could* import food, they are more likely to be used to import luxury goods. Even where they are used to import food, there is little prospect of that food finding its way to those who need it (such as the displaced maize farmers). Once again, the real question which agencies like Oxfam have to ask is, 'Who benefits from trade?'

Getting it right
Mexico already depends on the USA for 75 per cent of its trade, so it has been argued that the NAFTA will merely formalise, and speed up, a process of integration which is already well underway.[44] The key issues concern the basis on which the agreement is made. A pact that helps US

industry to evade US labour and environmental law and assigns Mexico to the status of permanent supplier of low-cost labour to the US market is clearly in no one's long-term interests.

In the USA, opposition to the pact has come from a powerful coalition of environmentalists, consumer groups, unions, small businesses, and civil rights campaigners. As a result, Congress is now under pressure to include a Social Charter in the agreement which would address issues such as labour rights and health and environmental standards.[45] The stakes are high. An agreement that fails to deal fully with these issues will serve to exacerbate regional inequalities and deepen the North-South divide. An agreement that does could serve Mexico well and promote genuine development for its people, setting the stage for a fairer continental partnership.

Whatever shape the agreement finally takes could set the pattern for similar agreements between the USA and other Latin American countries. In June 1990 President Bush announced his plan to extend the free-trade area, dubbed his 'Enterprise for the Americas' initiative, 'from Alaska to Argentina'. This is a long way from becoming a reality, but within the region it has sparked a series of initiatives aimed at removing trade barriers and promoting intra-regional trade.

The Andean Pact countries (Bolivia, Colombia, Ecuador, Peru, and Venezuela) are seeking to revive their agreement, reduce tariffs, and increase regional trade. Mexico and Chile are planning a bilateral free-trade agreement, while Mexico, Colombia, and Venezuela plan to establish a three-way free-trade zone by mid-1994. The Southern Cone countries, Brazil, Argentina, Paraguay, and Uruguay, have formed a new alliance, 'Mercosur', to promote regional trade, while similar initiatives are being taken by the Central American countries. The flame of free trade gives every appearance of sweeping through the continent.

Free trade in Asia

President Bush's 'Enterprise for the Americas' initiative has been interpreted as a response to the emergence of the more integrated trade bloc that Europe 1992 will produce, and a reflection of his dissatisfaction with progress in the Uruguay Round. A similar interpretation was offered for plans for a third regional free-trade initiative, this time in Asia.

Following the breakdown of the GATT talks at the end of 1990, Mr Mahathir Mohamad, Malaysia's Prime Minister, proposed plans for an East Asian Economic Grouping (EAEG). On the assumption that all hopes for resuscitating the Round were gone, he argued that an East Asian free-trade arrangement, to stretch from China to New Zealand, would act as an insurance policy against future trade hostilities.[46]

However, the idea was spurned by the USA and treated with indifference by Japan, and has languished as a result.

More recently members of the Association of South East Asia Nations (ASEAN) (Brunei, Philippines, Singapore, Malaysia, Thailand, and Indonesia) have put forward proposals for an ASEAN Free Trade Area. But this will be difficult to adopt for a number of reasons, not least because, with the exception of Singapore, they all depend heavily on commodities, especially crude oil, palm oil, rubber, and tin. ASEAN members, therefore, all compete heavily with one another for the same export markets. They also compete for capital investment and technology from the same sources: Japan, Europe, and the USA and, more recently, Taiwan and Hong Kong.[47]

A tri-polar world

The conjunction of the European single market and the USA–Canada Free Trade Agreement has created an expectation that the world trading system is moving towards regional blocs, as distinct from GATT-wide multilateralism. However, the two were prompted by wholly different motivations. For the USA, a free-trade agreement with Canada, and subsequently with Mexico, is a wholly trade-expanding operation. Europe 1992, on the other hand, was prompted by the goal of making the Common Market commoner, taking the last and most difficult steps towards the unification that the Treaty of Rome had already adopted as its objective.

The fact that they are happening at the same time is coincidence, yet has tended to produce a sense that the world is fragmenting into trade blocs. As if to fulfil this prophecy, yet in fact to defend itself against its consequences, Asia has responded by producing plans for its own trade bloc. This has simply served to heighten fears of a tri-polar world trading system, with three impregnable trade blocs centring round Japan, the EC, and the USA. The implications for weaker economies excluded from those blocs, particularly African states, are worrying.

To counter these fears it is essential that the USA, EC, and Japan strengthen their commitment to multilateralism through the GATT. Yet perhaps the most potent force against the threat of a bloc-infested world are transnational corporations. In the last few decades their operations have become truly globalised, with their investments criss-crossing countries throughout the world. A more protected world trading system would threaten these investments – a situation they would be unlikely to tolerate.

The main problem of the trade bloc phenomenon is the impact that it could have on weaker countries. With NAFTA, there are very real dangers of high social and environmental costs, a further marginalisation of the poor, and a deepening of the North-South divide. The inclusion of a strong Social Charter in the Agreement will be essential for ensuring more equitable development. With Europe 1992, the concern is the way in which this alliance of strong economies will affect weaker trading partners. There will be a need for constant monitoring of trade or investment diversion from these countries, combined with generous aid disbursements to assist restructuring where necessary.

11

CHILE:
The costs of an economic miracle

Humanity has the ability to make development sustainable – to ensure that it meets the needs of the present without compromising the ability of future generations to meet their own needs.[1]

Oxfam began working in Chile in 1974. It was the year following the coup that toppled the socialist government of President Allende and marked the beginning of a military dictatorship, led by General Pinochet, which was to last for sixteen years. At that time the aim of Oxfam's programme was to help to mitigate the terrible consequences of the human rights violations associated with the new regime.

Eighteen years later, Oxfam is still working in Chile. Yet the country has returned to democracy and undergone an economic transformation which is often referred to as a 'miracle'. Unlike many other developing countries, for which the 1980s was a 'lost decade', Chile experienced steady economic growth for much of that time. In contrast to many of its Latin American neighbours, inflation was kept under control, averaging 20.8 per cent between 1980 and 1988 – a fraction of that in Brazil (188.7 per cent), Argentina (290.5 per cent), or Bolivia (482.8 per cent).[2] Furthermore, Chile has made considerable progress in dealing with its international debt. In short, it entered the 1990s in comparatively robust economic health – a miracle indeed.

Why, then, the need for Oxfam? Over the years Oxfam's programme in Chile has been gradually responding to the profound changes that have been taking place in the country. As a result, the emphasis of the programme is no longer on alleviating the effects of human rights violations. Instead it is on the social and environmental costs of Chile's economic transformation. In the words of one Oxfam field worker, 'While the emphasis of the programme has changed, the need for Oxfam support is greater than ever.'[3]

The World Bank and IMF believe that Chile's economic success is, in large part, due to the neo-liberal, export-oriented policies adopted by the military government in 1973 and pursued to the present. These are policies based on the underlying principle of free trade and comparative advantage, which underpin the rationale of the GATT and the international trading system. However, as this chapter shows, a development model such as that employed in Chile, which has a narrow focus on economic growth, is likely to incur social and environmental costs which may make it unsustainable. This chapter focuses on the three economic sectors where the export drive has been most intense, and where Oxfam supports a number of projects to assist the poor and disadvantaged: the fishing, forestry, and fruit industries.

THE ECONOMIC MIRACLE

For the European visitor the area around Chile's capital city is reminiscent of the southern Mediterranean, with similar vegetation and climate. In late summer, bougainvillaea scrambles over whitewashed houses, while sturdy oleander bushes, resplendent with pink or white flowers, line the straight, paved highways. Santiago itself is an elegant city, its centre a mix of graceful old Spanish-style colonial buildings and smart new shopping malls, complete with coffee shops and fountains. There are wide, tree-lined streets and well-tended parks, chic restaurants and high-quality clothes shops, museums, theatres, and art galleries. The streets bustle with activity, giving the appearance and feel of a modern, dynamic, and cultured city. It could just as well be Paris, Madrid, or New York. From here Chile's economic success is evident.

Until 1973 Chile, like many other Latin American countries, had pursued a path of economic development which attempted to decrease the economy's dependence on the export of a few primary commodities. In Chile these were copper and nitrates. Influenced by the ideas of Raul Prebisch and others at the Economic Commission for Latin America (ECLA), governments in many Latin American countries believed that the only way that they could escape from the periphery of the world economy as suppliers of food and raw materials was through a strategy of industrialisation.[4] They did this by developing local industries to produce the many manufactured consumer goods – clothes, shoes, and processed foods as well as durables like electrical equipment – which had always been imported.[5] Such a policy affected trade, because the government gave less support to the traditional export sector, and instead invested in the new import-substituting industries. It also imposed taxes on imported consumer goods, to discourage people from buying foreign goods in preference to locally produced ones, effectively protecting the new industries.

The World Bank and the IMF have been critical of such policies. They argue that countries which have adopted a protectionist trade policy in order to promote industrialisation through import-substitution have industrialised less quickly than those countries which have adopted an outward-oriented or free-trade strategy. The reasons given for this are that a protectionist strategy promotes the inefficient allocation of resources, because countries end up producing goods which they could import more cheaply. In addition, such a strategy requires a costly administrative system to enforce taxes on trade and other trade barriers, and this system often becomes corrupt. The Bank also argues that protected industries are less efficient, because they are not exposed to the discipline of international competition, and they show little interest in adopting new technologies.[6] Protectionism also prevents an economy from diversifying along lines determined by its 'comparative advantage' in the world economy.

Free-market ideology guided the development of economic policy in Chile after the coup in 1973. Trade barriers were dismantled, and the exchange rate devalued, in an effort to shift the economy from protectionism to an outward-oriented strategy. Markets were 'liberalised', and government price controls and subsidies removed. The result of this shift in the structure of the economy, which occurred very rapidly, was great hardship for many Chileans. Many manufacturing firms in the import-substituting sector were shut down, which led to massive job losses.[7] The repression of all forms of trade union activity meant that protest was impossible.

The government's economic policy-makers believed that this hardship was a necessary, if painful, short-term sacrifice, which would be followed by the development of new export industries as productive resources and investment shifted to sectors in which Chile had a comparative advantage in production. These would provide new jobs and bring a lasting dynamism to the economy. By the end of the 1980s there seemed to be much reason for optimism. The country's export base had changed. Its dependence on copper, which in 1973 accounted for 82 per cent of export earnings, had declined to only 47 per cent in 1990. Three new export industries had emerged – fishing, fruit, and forestry – and were providing Chile with 30 per cent of its foreign-exchange earnings.[8] There has also been an impressive growth in manufactured exports linked to these sectors, particularly in paper, wood, cellulose, and fishmeal. In 1988 manufactures accounted for 32 per cent of export earnings, compared to only 12 per cent in 1971.

The success of Chile's export policy is clear from Figure 8, which compares the total value of exports from Chile and Bolivia between 1970 and 1989. While exports in Chile have displayed an upward trend, particularly in the second half of the 1980s as the new export industries have started to contribute significantly to export earnings, Bolivian exports have shown a steady decline.

Figure 8: Export values for Chile and Bolivia, in US$m, 1970–1989

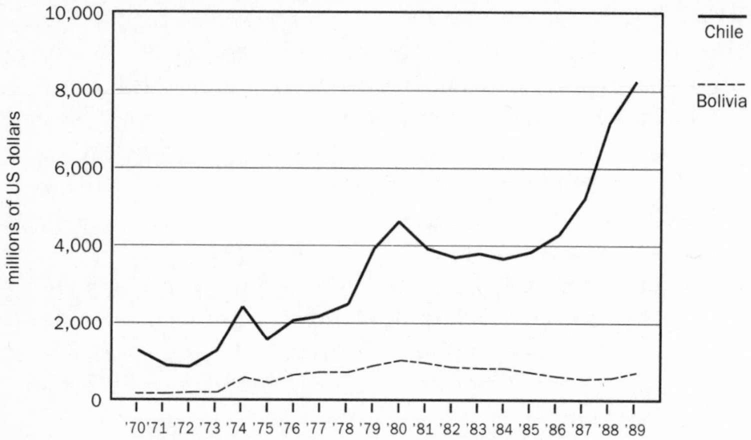

(Source: *UNCTAD Commodity Yearbooks*, 1986, 1989, and 1990, New York: United Nations)

The greatest success story among the new export industries has been the fruit industry. The central valleys around Santiago are almost entirely devoted to fruit production. The Mediterranean-type climate and easy access to the ports are natural advantages favouring fruit production, but the availability of cheap labour has been crucially important too. Apples and grapes are the two largest exports, but plums, apricots, peaches, lemons, oranges, avocados, pears, and kiwi fruit are also grown.

The highway that cuts through the middle of Chile acts as the industry's central nervous system, along which the boxed-up fruit is transported for export. Orchards and vineyards fan out from it, interspersed with huge packing houses, many of them foreign-owned, with the big US companies, United Fruit and Dole, very much in evidence. Production is increasing each year, as newly planted areas become productive. There is enormous potential for continued increases: a further 300,000 hectares of land could be allocated to fruit farming.

The forestry industry has also thrived. Chile's extensive forest reserves are among the most important in Latin America. The country has 7.6 million hectares of natural forest, including larch, native pine, soapwood, and tamarugo. Following a change in the law in 1974 designed to encourage tree planting, Chile now has 1.3 million hectares of planted forest, 87 per cent of which is radiata pine and 4.8 per cent eucalyptus.[9] Forest plantations are projected to reach 2 million hectares by the mid-1990s.[10] Chile boasts considerable comparative advantage in its forestry industry, because its climatic and soil conditions yield high growth rates. Combined with low labour costs, this makes Chile one of the world's lowest-cost timber producers, and means that it is poised to become one of the world's top exporters of forestry products in the 1990s.

Before 1973 the forestry industry was largely state-owned and geared principally around meeting the needs of the national market. Since then it has been privatised. Foreign investment has been successfully encouraged, and the export of forestry products promoted. In terms of value, only about 30 per cent of exports take the form of logs or sawn wood. Nearly half comes from cellulose. There is also expansion in the export of forestry products with a higher value-added content, such as newsprint and wood panels. Sales of wood products were estimated at US$762 million in 1989, up from US$231 million in 1981.[11] The Director of the National Forestry Corporation (CONAF) predicts exports of US$1.2 billion by 1993.[12]

A similar policy prescription has produced comparable results in Chile's fishing industry. Once again, with 6,435 km of coastline at its disposal, Chile has considerable comparative advantage in this industry. The foreign fishing fleets moved in in the late 1970s, together with foreign investment in the processing industry. More recently Chile has traded shares in the national fishing industry to private companies, in return for reductions in the national debt; this is known as a 'debt equity swap'. Such changes have massively boosted production.

Unilever is among a number of companies which have invested heavily in Chile's fishing industry. Unilever has three companies engaged in fishmeal processing, the seaweed industry, and salmon farming. Today Chile is the world's largest exporter of fishmeal (which represents about two thirds of total fisheries output), ranks third among salmon exporters, is the sixth-largest producer of seaweed, and accounted for 6 per cent of the world's fish catch in 1988. Revenues from sea products have soared from just US$22 million in 1973 to US$900 million in 1989, making it the country's third-largest export earner after copper and agriculture.[13]

The USA is Chile's most important trading partner. Japan and West Germany are also significant markets for Chilean exports, with Britain taking up fifth position, after Brazil (see Table 10 on the following page). Imports of Chilean products into the United Kingdom amounted to £1,796 million in 1988, mainly copper, wood products, animal feed (fishmeal) and fruit.[14]

Table 10: Chile's main trading partners (% of total value)

Exports to:	1985	1990	Imports from:	1985	1990
USA	25.5	17.1	USA	21.8	18.9
Japan	11.5	16.2	Japan	6.2	7.8
West Germany	10.8	11.0	Brazil	8.3	7.8
Brazil	6.1	5.7	West Germany	7.0	7.2
UK	7.5	6.5	Argentina	3.5	6.9
Italy	5.8	4.7	France	2.6	4.1
France	4.2	4.7	Venezuela	8.9	2.6
Total (inc. others)	100.0	100.0	Total (inc. others)	100.0	100.0

(Source: The Economist Intelligence Unit: *Chile Country Report No.4, 1991*, London: Business International Ltd.)

THE SOCIAL COSTS OF THE ECONOMIC 'MIRACLE'

One concern expressed by a number of Oxfam's project partners is that nutritional levels have declined among the poorer and more vulnerable sectors of Chilean society. Various statistical surveys show that, on average, people are eating much less than they were at the beginning of the 1970s. The per capita consumption of animal protein is estimated to have fallen by between 15 and 25 per cent, while calorific intake has fallen by between 10 and 22 per cent.[15] This is a worrying trend, and there is considerable evidence to link it with the priority that has been given to export production rather than food production, since 1973. The trend has been most visible in the fishing communities:

> In the Calbuco area we talked to inshore fishermen who used to be involved in collecting shellfish. They described how there used to be abundant supplies of shellfish, which formed an important part of the local diet. Then the big companies moved in and started to sell to foreign markets. Now all of the banks of shellfish in the area are cleaned out and the shellfish gatherers have moved into fishing. But the same thing is happening to fish. Now there is a scarcity of fish in the local markets, or the fish that is available is too expensive for local people to buy. As a result they are eating less protein. The local diet now mainly consists of bread, noodles and potatoes.[16]

Because of Chile's long coastline, fish and seafood have always been an important source of protein in the national diet. However, from 1973 the per capita consumption of fish and seafood fell by a third; from 6.3 kg per capita in 1973 to 4.4 kg in 1986, at a time when the fishing industry was expanding rapidly.[17] The major reason given for this is that 97 per cent of production is exported.[18] It is this decline in seafood consumption that is most responsible for the overall decline in protein consumption.

The export orientation of agricultural production has had a similar impact. Investment has been concentrated on large-scale production for export. Peasant producers supplying local markets with traditional staples like beans have received very little support, and many have been forced to sell their land to the fruit exporters. The result has been a fall in the production of basic foods relative to export agricultural production, even in absolute terms in some years.[19] This shortfall in production has not been matched by a corresponding increase in food imports. These, too, have declined since 1973.[20]

On the positive side, Ministry of Health Statistics show a consistent decline in rates of infant malnutrition between 1975 and 1989, apart from a slight rise in the mid-1980s.[21] Several studies suggest that this has been achieved as a result of government nutrition programmes that have targeted babies and young children, and pregnant and lactating women.[22] However, what the statistics do not show is what is happening to the health of other sectors of the population, for example school children, adolescents, men and non-nursing women, and the elderly.

Poor employment practices
Chile is, and always has been, a very legalistic society. It has a labour code dating back to 1978/9 which, if it were followed, would go some way to ensuring workers' rights. Yet in the experience of Oxfam's project partners, Chile's economic 'miracle' has been achieved at the expense of good employment practices, and even the minimum standards laid out in the labour code have been flouted. Concern is greatest in the areas where the export drive has been most intense: the fruit, fishing, and forestry industries.

In 1988 official figures showed Chile's unemployment rate to be 12 per cent.[23] A survey carried out in areas of Greater Santiago showed unemployment to be more like 30 per cent. The inconsistency between these two figures can probably be explained by high levels of under-employment, which has grown alongside the expansion of the fruit industry over the course of the last fifteen years. In 1990 it was estimated that the fruit industry, which stretches the length of Chile's fertile central valley, requires a workforce of around one million during harvest. A staggering 80 per cent of these are needed only for the harvest, leaving a mere 20 per cent on permanent contracts.[24] These seasonal workers can expect employment for anything between two and six months of the year, depending on how mobile they can be. To get longer periods of work, some of them turn themselves into migrant workers, following the season as it works its way down the central valley, living in temporary camps that they set up on the edge of the vineyards or orchards.

Clarita is one Chile's seasonal fruit workers. She lives in a small village in the heart of the Aconcagua Valley, a major fruit-growing region north of Santiago. She has eight children and several grandchildren. Not all of them live with her. Two of the eldest girls have left home to join the industry's migrant workforce. The small plot of land on which Clarita's family built their house is the property of a local landowner. Clarita pays her rent by working as a domestic for him. The landlord also controls their supply of water and electricity, which they have to pay for separately. If they do not, he cuts them off. Their water supply comes from a single tap, situated about 100 metres from the house, and is shared with 17 other households.

Clarita has been working in the fruit industry for nearly thirty years. She used to be able to work all the year round. When the grape harvest was over, a nearby factory, which canned a variety of locally grown fruit and vegetables destined for the home market – tomatoes, olives, peaches, and beans – would pick up the employment slack. The factory closed down soon after the 1973 coup. Since then people living in the area have had to rely for work on an increasing monoculture of fruit. Nowadays there is hardly anyone in the area in full-time employment, and many people are forced to migrate south with the harvest.

Clarita normally expects about four months' work a year in the local fruit farm. At this time she usually works a twelve-hour day in the packing house, cleaning and packing the grapes. Most of the workers are women, and they get paid by the number of boxes they fill. In July or August she is sometimes able to get work doing maintenance on the vines, such as pruning, and in October there is a brief spell of work picking the leaves off the plants to let the sun get to the ripening grapes. Field work is paid at a daily rate of 1,000 pesos (equivalent to US$3.20). All the workers suffer from time to time from the effects of the chemicals used on the grapes. According to Clarita, skin and digestive problems are the most common.[25]

Business has been bad in the last couple of years. Traces of cyanide found in Chilean grapes exported to the USA in early 1989 led to a slump in the market. Prices fell, so the owner of the fruit farm cut back on his workforce by taking his grapes to a different packing house for processing. He also refused their demands for an annual pay rise.

While the seasonal nature of work in the fruit industry brings its own special set of problems, conditions of employment in the fishing and forestry industries are also very poor. In the fishing industry, which employs around 90,000 people, the main concerns are lack of safety provisions and the long hours of work.

About 30 per cent of the workforce in the fishing industry work onshore in the fish-processing plants, where health and safety conditions are particularly poor. In canning factories workers often have to use acid compounds. Many of them are not provided with protective clothing or, if they are, it is of poor quality. Burns and skin problems are common. The extreme cold in the factories leads to bronchial diseases for many of the workers, and they often suffer cuts from the knives they use to cut up the fish. Attempts by employees to enforce the labour code, which stipulates that companies must have an inspection committee to monitor workers' safety, are frequently undermined by the company, which threatens these workers with dismissal.

The off-shore fishing industry carries its own risks. According to one Oxfam project partner, the industry with the highest death rate in Chile is in-shore fishing, where around fifty people a year are lost over-board.[26] Because the waters have been fished so intensively, the small fishermen are having to go much farther out to sea than is safe for the size of their boats or the amount of equipment they carry. The risks are so great that insurance companies are no longer prepared to cover them, and bereaved families are often left destitute.

The problem is similar in the forestry industry. One trade union leader described the working conditions:

> The work is for people with no other options. They work with no tools. If it is raining they might stop, but they have no special clothes and they still get soaked. If you are piling wood, then you have to move 4,500 kilos of it in a day. If you are working a circular saw, then you might lift 70 logs to it in a day, and each one weighs 60 kilos, lifted on your shoulder. What machinery there is is dangerous, like chainsaws. If a worker is injured, then there is no proper means of transport to hospital: they have to go in the same lorry which carries the wood. So most accidents are fatal.[27]

The hours worked in all three industries were well above those stipulated by the Labour Code, which states that no more than 48 hours should be worked in any one week, and no more than ten hours in any one day. In the fruit industry workers put up with very long hours, because of the seasonal nature of the work. But in the fishing industry this is not the case. Some factories expect workers to do a seven-day week, others have them on ten-hour shifts, or more.

Where union organising has been successful, there tends to be a dramatic improvement in pay and conditions. In 1973 30 per cent of the labour force was unionised. Union membership was effectively outlawed in the first phase of the military dictatorship, and the unions' national Congress, federations, and confederations had their assets seized. The new labour code of 1978/9 allowed for a restricted form of union organising, with the result that around 12 per cent of the Chilean workforce is currently unionised.[28]

In the fruit industry the figure is considerably less, with only 3 per cent in unions.[29] One of the reasons for this is that under Chilean labour law a union cannot be formed unless there are fifteen, or more, permanent employees. In many packing plants there are fewer than fifteen permanent workers on the payroll. The vast majority are temporary, or seasonal, workers. This in itself is a problem. Organising seasonal workers into trades unions has obvious difficulties, especially when many of them move around the country, following the work. But their needs are particularly great as they are more vulnerable to exploitation than regular employees. This view is supported by Oxfam's project partner, ICAR (Training and Rural Support Unit), which provides a programme of training and advice for temporary agricultural workers, particularly women and shanty-town migrants. ICAR believes that the only way to improve their working and living conditions is by helping them to organise to demand their basic rights.

Union organisation is at a more advanced stage of development in the fishing industry, where in some areas a high proportion of fish-processing plants have union representation, and a high proportion of members are women. A typical figure would be around 26 per cent of employees. Union officials in the Concepcion area say that it has been a long struggle to get this far, and that their main objectives now are to increase membership and greatly improve conditions of work.[30] Organising in the forestry industry is more difficult, as work is often contracted out, and people are moved from company to company.

THE ENVIRONMENTAL CONSEQUENCES OF THE ECONOMIC MIRACLE

While there is much concern in Chile today about poor employment practices and the growing numbers of migrant labourers, there is also widespread and growing concern about the ecologically unsustainable nature of the 'miracle'. The expansion of exports has, by and large, been based on production that exploits natural resources. Copper, fishing, and forestry together account for about 65 per cent of Chile's export earnings.[31] There is also concern about pollution caused by the dumping of mineral wastes from the mines, chemicals from the cellulose industry, and the widespread use of pesticides in the fruit industry.

Forestry
The vast majority of Chile's timber exports are from plantations, with only about 10 per cent coming from natural forests. Despite this, there is growing concern about the destruction of natural forests.[32] A number of

Oxfam's project partners have been instrumental in publicising the loss of 500,000 hectares of natural forests and the threat of further destruction.[33] This has occurred in two ways. First, the government gives generous subsidies for the cost of initially setting up and subsequently maintaining plantations. But in order to qualify for the subsidies, the forestry companies have cleared the natural forest, often by burning it, and then turned it into plantations. One study shows that between 1978 and 1987 in two regions alone, 9 per cent, or 50,000 hectares, of natural forest was destroyed in this way.[34]

Secondly, although the forestry industry takes only 10 per cent of its timber from the natural forest, the timber that it does take is being used in the fastest-growing sector: woodchip. Valuable hardwoods such as beech and oak are being turned into woodchip. Woodchip exports in 1989 were 1.8 million tonnes, a fourteen-fold increase in only three years.[35] Half of this comes from the area around Puerto Montt, a small town in the south of Chile.[36]

> Puerto Montt, as its name suggests, is on the coast, and the Humbolt current which arrives there directly from the Antarctic creates a climate similar to that of Scotland. Like many small towns there is not much to see in Puerto Montt, although the skyline does feature two volcanoes. However, it is a mountain of another sort that people are keen to show visitors. Puerto Montt is currently famous for its mountain of woodchip. There are actually two of them at the port, side by side, waiting to leave for Japan. The local community worker who showed them to us was a little disappointed. He said they were smaller than usual, because a shipful of woodchip had left a couple of days ago. But to us they seemed big, towering over the two-storey houses on the other side of the barbed-wire fence which encloses the port. They dwarf the lorries which arrive in a slow but steady stream to disgorge more of Chile's natural forests, now reduced to bits a couple of inches square.[37]

As local people watched the woodchip piles grow in their midst, they became increasingly concerned about the seemingly uncontrolled plundering of the natural resource base on which they so heavily depend. It is easy to see why they are worried. In Puerto Montt everything is made from wood. Their houses and furniture are made of wood. Wood is their only source of fuel, for heating and cooking. They sought the assistance of CODEFF (*Comite Nacional Pro Defensa de la Fauna y Flora*), an environmental pressure group supported by Oxfam, to monitor the environmental impact of the forestry industry in their area. CODEFF describe how permission was granted to a Japanese company,

IAIN GRAY/OXFAM

A hardwood tree from the natural forest of southern Chile ends its life in a timber yard at Puerto Montt.

Marubeni, and its Chilean partners to turn 120,000 hectares of natural forest into woodchip. They claim that 2.5 million hectares of natural forest, 33 per cent of all Chile's forests, are now under threat.[38]

The forestry industry gives rise to other concerns for the environment. The flora and fauna of the native woods are destroyed in the process of establishing plantations, and the clearing operations frequently cause soil erosion. Heavy doses of rabbit poison are laid, which kill the larger flesh-eating mammals and birds as well as the rabbits. Then once established, the pine plantation contributes to a rapid increase in soil acidity, destroying many native plants and micro-organisms in the soil.[39]

The replacement of natural forest with pine monoculture is also altering the hydrological cycle, leaching water and nutrients from the soil, reducing water supply to the valleys, eroding soil and thereby contaminating rivers. Other flora which grow beneath deciduous forest cannot survive in pine plantations. The forestry industry also uses contaminants such as mercury and various bleaches in the cellulose plants, and they are now found in rivers near plants.[40] Mercury has been found in concentrations up to seven times the normal maximum dosage permissible for the human body in the river Bio-Bio, the largest river in Chile and source of drinking water for Concepcion and Talcahuano.[41]

The fishing industry

In the fishing industry concern for the environment is focused on two problems. One is the extent of over-fishing, generally by foreign fishing fleets. The other is the pollution caused by the fish-processing industries.

It is now apparent that the fish stocks along Chile's coast are being depleted faster than they are able to reproduce. According to one processing-plant worker, 'When the industry first started, a normal mackerel being processed was 60 cm long. Now the majority going through the factory are 15 to 25 cm long, and sometimes not even that, while the minimum reproductive size is 30 cm.'[42] This is also having an effect on local inshore fishermen, who are having to spend much longer at sea to catch the same amount. As the president of one of the local fishermen's unions explained: 'A few years ago we would go out each day with that day's paper and fresh bread and be back by three or four in the afternoon with a full catch. Now we have to go out for as much as two or three days to get the same amount.'[43]

The other concern is the complete lack of controls on the pollution created by the fish-processing plants. One Oxfam worker described it:

Organic wastes from the fish-processing industry, both liquid and solid, have actually contaminated the whole bay of San Vincente and Coronel. The waters are dead. Nothing lives in them any more. The wastes from the fish processing are pumped into rivers and the sea, and as a result of these wastes, chemicals such as mercury and a fungicide – pentachlorophenol – have been absorbed by the shell-fish and fish at levels that are dangerous for human consumption.

The organic waste from processing plants in some areas is being directly bulldozed into the sea by the Japanese, who are building new processing plants. In these areas we were told that the coast-line is now devoid of shellfish. The whole process has been going on for eight to ten years and is getting worse. One hopeful development is that companies like Indus Lever (a subsidiary of Unilever) are buying fish wastes for processing into salmon food.

The air around the processing plants is foul. The processing gives off a noxious gas which permeates every waking moment for the people who live in the area. These gases could be easily burned off, but they have so far failed to invest the money needed to do so.

The unions predict that the fishing industry in the Puerto Montt area will soon collapse.[44] Figures for catches of 'merluza del sur' (hake), a principal fish for export, show a decline of between 25 to 35 per cent from 1988 to 1990.[45] Other studies indicate that 60 per cent of the resources in the fishing industry show signs of over-exploitation.[46]

Despite this, investment, much of it by foreign companies, is proceeding at a tremendous rate. By 1988 the industry had a catch capacity of 18.5 million tons. However, the actual catch that year, of only 5.3 million tons, was clear evidence of the extent of over-exploitation.[47] The fears of local people were summed up by one union leader: 'We know that when the foreign investment is gone, the fish will be gone, and what we will be left with is a desert sea.'[48]

The fruit industry

Every year around four million kilos of pesticides, three kilos per person in Chile, are routinely dumped on the 220,000 hectares of land that are devoted to fruit production for the export market.[49] Many of these chemicals are highly toxic. Among them are nine of the twelve most toxic pesticides in the world.[50] The twelve are collectively known as 'The Dirty Dozen' by international campaigning organisations which have been trying to get them banned, or at least tightly controlled, for a number of years. Some of them are banned in Chile, but continue to be used. Among these are Folidol, one of the most toxic. A single teaspoon on the skin is reputed to be enough to kill an adult.[51]

Oxfam has been concerned about the effects of the use of harmful pesticides in Third World countries since the early 1980s. In 1982 an Oxfam report highlighted their dangers to both health and the environment. In Third World countries these problems are particularly acute, because a lack of controls on their application often results in their heavy and sometimes indiscriminate use.[52]

Agra, a partner organisation in Chile, has been trying to monitor the use of pesticides in the fruit industry, and publicise their effects.[53] It laments the lack of official records kept on accidents, poisonings, and chronic health problems caused by pesticides. Through information given to Agra by its own extensive network of contacts with workers in the industry, it is aware that the problem is very serious indeed. Isolated incidents of pesticide poisonings are reported in the Chilean press, revealing what AGRA believes to be the tip of an iceberg. For example, in January 1988, 26 grape pickers were poisoned in Mapocho, when fumigators were ordered to spray fields of grapes while they were working in them. All needed hospital treatment. They were refused compensation, or even pay, for the days of work lost as a result.[54] A month later it was reported that 90 workers were poisoned in a seed factory in Colina, when they were accidentally exposed to a mixture of toxic pesticides. Only the rapid response of the emergency services prevented the accident ending in tragedy.[55] There are also reports of poisonings, many of them fatal, among children. These typically occur when parents, unable to read warning labels, have unwittingly exposed their children to high levels of pesticides, believing them, for example, to be effective for controlling lice and other parasites.[56]

Accidents and acute poisonings are only part of the danger of the uncontrolled use of pesticides. Long-term exposure to pesticides is also believed to cause chronic health problems. Here again AGRA laments the lack of record keeping. Doctors, its researchers say, are not trained to link certain health problems with pesticide poisonings. This means that there is a lack of medical data in Chile linking chronic health problems experienced by farmworkers to pesticide exposure. However, there is no shortage of scientific data elsewhere on the subject. Exposure to pesticides has been linked to cancer, birth defects, and neuro-behavioural, reproductive, and fertility problems.[57] Numerous studies of workers exposed to high levels of pesticides confirm these results. In India women agricultural workers were found to carry an increased risk of spontaneous abortion, stillbirth, and sterility.[58] In the USA men working in a pesticide-producing factory experienced higher than average rates of sterility. The pesticide paraquat, which has been widely used in Chile, has been associated with damage to the nervous system and muscular weakness, sometimes leading to paralysis. In Colombia workers exposed to this chemical have reported chronic skin lesions and the loss of finger nails.[59] A study of farmers working with pesticides in the Philippines found that 55 per cent of them displayed abnormalities in the eyes, 41 per cent abnormalities in the lungs, and 54 per cent abnormalities in the cardiovascular system.[60]

There is much concern in the fruit-growing areas of Chile about the long-term impact of intensive pesticide use on health. Oxfam Canada is funding a project on the health and environmental impacts of chemical use in the Aconcagua Valley. Doctors in the area are shocked by the increase in children born with genetic deformities over the last ten years. Further research will tell if this is connected to the use of pesticides.[61]

The intensive use of pesticides also takes its toll on the environment. People living in the fruit-growing areas have noticed a decrease in flora and fauna. Studies in the USA have linked chlordane, endrin, and hepta-chlor, all in use in Chile, to the elimination of bees and earthworms.[62] There are also reports of water contamination by toxic chemicals.[63]

SUSTAINING THE MIRACLE

When the fish stocks run out and the foreign companies move on, the people of Puerto Montt will be left high and dry. Their traditional way of life, and their livelihoods, will have been destroyed. This will be not only a local tragedy but, in terms of lost foreign exchange, a national catastrophe. It underlines the fragile basis of Chile's economic 'miracle', and raises questions about how long it can be sustained.

Many organisations in Chile, including a number of Oxfam's project partners, take a pragmatic view. They accept that the new export industries are now a vital part of the Chilean economy, but believe that they must be developed in a way that is sustainable. This will involve substantial changes and a far more active role for the government in regulating industry and directing investment. The return to democracy offers the opportunity for this change. Many universities and research institutions in Chile have put forward programmes for the alternative development of Chile's new industries under democratic government. The government has also acknowledged the very considerable environmental costs to date, and is seeking the assistance of non-government organisations in designing new policies. One way it has done this is by establishing an Environmental Commission to study the problems. CODEFF has been invited to participate.

CODEFF has produced its own proposals for the fishing industry. These are based on the twin principles of the sustainable use of natural resources and meeting the needs of the Chilean people. It proposes government credit policies favouring the small-scale fishing sector. As this sector supplies domestic markets and is more labour-intensive, CODEFF believes greater investment will lead to more fish for Chileans to buy, and more jobs. CODEFF sees an important role for the government in regulating the activities of the fishing industry, both to protect the natural resource base and to set standards for conditions of employment. It believes that the government should be responsible for carrying out research into conservation and management of the sea, and into the development of new products for the domestic market and for export. The contribution that exports can make to economic growth is set within the context of integrated and sustainable national development.[64]

CODEFF has also produced proposals for the development of the country's forests. These stress the importance of developing Chile's natural forests in a sustainable way, reversing the policies of the military government which provided significant subsidies to the plantation sector, while allowing the native forests to decline. They believe that a well-managed forestry policy could yield a permanent harvest of wood and other forest products.[65] It has also been proposed that the government should nationalise ownership of the plantations, to enable access to a large number of small producers and businesses.[66]

The future development of agriculture is now being debated. AGRA is involved in educating workers about pesticides and campaigning for stricter regulations on their use. It would like to see the future development of the agricultural industry directed away from exports towards meeting the needs of the Chilean people.[67] Credit policies favouring small-scale peasant producers growing basic food crops for local markets have been proposed as a way of increasing domestic food production and employment.[68]

The challenge that faces the democratically-elected government is to ensure a balance between economic growth and sustainable development. The establishment of tight environmental controls and the setting of acceptable minimal health standards will be vital for achieving this. It will need to regulate companies, especially those operating in the new industries, to ensure that environmental and labour standards are respected. This will not be an easy task, but it is a crucial one if economic growth is to be sustained, and the lives of ordinary Chileans improved.

12

SHRIMPS FOR SALE:
Diversification in Bangladesh

The key to Chile's economic transformation has been the successful diversification of its export base. By prioritising the expansion of its fruit, fishing, and forestry industries, the government has managed to reduce the country's dependence on copper. The need for Third World countries to diversify their export base is a recurring theme of this book. As we have seen, reliance on a narrow range of primary commodities leaves countries highly vulnerable to fluctuations in world market prices or changes in market-access arrangements, such as those currently facing the banana producers of the Windward Islands.

The need for diversification is widely recognised by policy makers. It is a key objective of most IMF and World Bank economic restructuring programmes. It is also one of the stated aims of the Lomé Convention's compensatory financing scheme, STABEX, and a principal objective of the second account of UNCTAD's Common Fund for Commodities. A recent United Nations report on Africa's commodity problems stressed the urgent need for African countries to diversify their export base. It said that African governments should:

> Continue to give high priority to efforts to diversify within the commodity sector, seeking to develop new products and to search for markets for such products; encourage the further processing in Africa of agricultural and non-agricultural commodities; and expand the process of industrialisation, including a strengthening of the necessary infrastructure and developing the skills required.[1]

This is, of course, easier said than done. As the UN report implies, successful diversification relies on there being a secure niche in the market-place for the new product. It must also be possible for the government to attract the necessary investment, technology, and training required to establish the venture and ensure that it does not interfere with broader development objectives, such as sustainability or food security.

In recent years Bangladesh, one of the poorest and most densely populated countries in the world, developed a new export industry: shrimps. The industry is now well established, and is making a significant contribution to country's foreign-exchange earnings. However, as with the new industries in Chile, its development has entailed both social and environmental costs.

THE STORY OF ROHINA KHATOON

Rohina Khatoon and her family live in one of Bangladesh's many *bustee*, or shanty town, areas. Their bustee, called Notun Bazaar, is situated on the outskirts of Khulna city, inland from the Bay of Bengal. Like many shanty towns in Bangladesh, it sits on a river bank, which floods every monsoon.

Notun Bazaar, an area of about one square mile, is densely populated by its 16,000 inhabitants. It has no water, electricity, or health facilities and the houses are crudely constructed out of bamboo, rushes, and, in some cases, cardboard. All it boasts in terms of basic services is a small primary school, constructed and run by a local Oxfam-supported community project, Gono Shahajjo Sangstha (GSS), which takes two hundred children in two daily shifts.[2]

Just outside the bustee there is an open shed. It has been constructed by a local entrepreneur for shrimp processing, and represents one of the very few employment opportunities for the people of Notun Bazaar. Occasionally Rohina is able to secure herself a few days' employment in the shed during the annual three-month shrimp-harvest season, although competition is fierce. Everyone in Notun Bazaar wants a job. When she is hired, she spends ten to twelve hours a day perched on a small stool, crammed in with the other women workers. Their job is to clean and shell the shrimps and lay them out for freezing. She takes her two youngest children with her to work, as they are not old enough to attend the primary school, but they have to amuse themselves on an open piece of ground next to the shed, which is always a worry to her. Long hours on the stool mean that her back is permanently sore. De-shelling the shrimps in unhygienic conditions inevitably produces ulcers on her hands. The owner of the processing shed ignores the Bangladeshi factory regulation which requires ointment to be provided for their prevention. Instead Rohina is laid off work until they heal. There is always a ready supply of labour to replace her in Notun Bazaar.[3]

The seafood El Dorado

Bangladesh is sometimes referred to as the 'land of rivers', since much of the country is built on the delta formed by the Ganges, Meghna, and Brahmaputra rivers. Given that it has 1.58 million hectares of permanent water, 2.83 million hectares of seasonal inland waters, and 480 km of coastline, it is hardly surprising to find that the fishing industry is of considerable significance to this small country.[4] Over 5 million people depend on it for a living, fish supply 80 per cent of the nation's animal protein, and it is now providing the country with much-needed foreign exchange.[5]

Rohina Khatoon is working in one of Bangladesh's newest and most profitable export industries. In 1988/89 12 per cent of the nation's foreign-exchange earnings came from fisheries products, of which the vast majority, more than 80 per cent, came from the export of shrimps and prawns (see Table 11). Britain alone imported fish products worth more than £11 million from Bangladesh in 1988, three quarters of which were shrimps.[6]

Shrimps are now big business in Bangladesh. They rank as the country's third-largest export earner, after garments and jute manufactures, but they are also a relatively new export for the country. While fishing, and shrimp production, have always been an important artisanal activity, and fish a crucial part of the local diet, industrialised processing of fish products, mainly shrimps, for export began only in the early 1980s.

The industry is split geographically and financially. The geographical divide is determined to a large extent by the environmental requirements of the two types of shrimps that Bangladesh exports. Along the south eastern coast, between the city of Chittagong and the village of Teknaf at the southernmost tip of Bangladesh, a salt-water variety of shrimp, known as the black tiger shrimp, is farmed in coastal, fully tidal ponds. This is where shrimp production is being developed on a large-scale commercial basis. The International Development Agency (IDA), an affiliate of the World Bank, has established a large demonstration hatchery in the area. So has Lever Brothers Bangladesh, a

---

Table 11: Bangladesh: exports of fisheries products
(Taka mn, current prices, f.o.b.)

	Fish	Prawns/ shrimps	Frogs' legs	Total export value	% of total
1985/6	29	205	26	260	9
1986/7	511	3,417	306	4,234	13
1987/8	476	3,612	424	4,512	11
1988/9	456	3,821	438	4,715	12

(Average exchange rate 1989: $1 = Tk 32.27)

(Source: Economist Intelligence Unit: *Bangladesh Country Profile* 1991–92, London: Business International Ltd., p. 25)

Bangladesh: a member of a shrimp cooperative in South Khulna netting shrimps.

Unilever subsidiary, which is engaged in a joint venture with the Bangladeshi government, on a 61/39 per cent ratio. Beximco, a Bangladeshi import/export firm and one of the country's largest conglomerates, also has a major investment in shrimp culture at Cox's Bazaar, where its turnover in 1988 from shrimp exports was £8 million.[7]

In south western Bangladesh, on the other side of the Bay of Bengal in the Khulna district, a different variety of shrimp is being produced for export. Here, with the ponds much farther inland but still on a coastal plain, a variety of brackish water shrimp is being produced in the less saline water. In this district it is mainly Bangladeshi businesses which have invested in the industry, on a much more modest scale than the investments in the Chittagong area. By the end of the 1980s an estimated 25,000 hectares in this area had been turned over to shrimp cultivation.[8] Most shrimp farms are between 5 and 50 acres in size, and much of the acreage given over to shrimp production has been rented from small farmers who previously used the land to grow rice and some jute.[9]

SHRIMPS AND THE BANGLADESHI ECONOMY

Most of Bangladesh's huge population of 115 million people, packed into an area only a little over half the size of Britain, relies on agriculture or fishing for a livelihood, often operating outside the money economy. Adverse weather, usually in the form of heavy flooding, regularly wreaks havoc on Bangladesh's people and economy as it destroys food and export crops alike.

Bangladesh is overwhelmingly dependent on aid. Since its liberation from Pakistan in 1971, the amount of aid entering the country has steadily increased. By the mid-1980s it had received a total of US$21 billion in foreign economic assistance.[10] In the financial year 1989/90, one source recorded that 99 per cent of all development expenditure had been met by external sources.[11] One of the reasons for Bangladesh's dependence on aid is its very poor and narrow resource base, which leaves it heavily dependent on imports. It has no minerals, and its forest resources have been severely exploited over the years. The one resource that does exist in large quantities is natural gas, but none of it is exported, and the country still runs up a substantial bill for fuel imports.

Traditionally its main export is jute. Although jute was always grown in Bengal for local use, it did not become a major export crop until rapidly-industrialising Britain found a use for it in the nineteenth century. As a colonial power, it ensured a ready supply of the raw material for processing, mainly in the Scottish town of Dundee. The hot, wet, humid climate proved ideal for its cultivation, and Bengal's economy rapidly became dependent on jute. Bangladesh still provides more than 70 per cent of the world's jute exports.[12] Jute, both raw and manufactured, continues to play a key role in the country's economy, contributing nearly 30 per cent of export earnings (see Table 12).

Such a heavy dependence on a single crop would not necessarily be a problem, were it not for the very weak position of jute in the international market place. On the demand side, jute's main use, as a packaging material, is constantly challenged by more durable competitively-priced synthetic packaging materials, predominantly polypropylene. On the supply side, with production so heavily concentrated in Bangladesh, floods or droughts resulting in crop losses tend to have a dramatic effect on world prices. Jute prices are, therefore, subject to wild fluctuations, but tend to be low. The hope for the future is that for environmental reasons the use of jute will be encouraged over that of synthetics. Unlike its competitors jute is both biodegradable and pollution-free.

Table 12: Major exports of Bangladesh, 1988/89

	(Taka mn)	% of total
Garments	14,274	33.4
Jute manufactures	9,259	21.7
Fisheries products	5,239	12.3
Leather	4,526	10.6
Raw jute	2,813	6.6
Tea	1,214	2.8
Fertiliser	1,543	3.6
Refined petroleum products	520	1.2
Total (inc. others)	42,686	100.0

(Source: Economist Intelligence Unit: *Bangladesh Country Profile* 1991–92, London: Business International Ltd., 1991, p. 44)

But even if jute's position in the international marketplace strengthens, there is still a need for Bangladesh to diversify its economy away from its traditional exports – principally jute, but also hides and tea, which also suffer from unstable international market prices. Successful diversification has taken place into garments manufacture, which overtook jute as the country's principal export earner in 1987/88. Foreign-exchange receipts for garment exports have leapt from only US$7 million in 1982 to over US$700 million in 1991.[13] The other successful area of diversification has been shrimps.

A small fish in a big sea

Unfortunately for Bangladesh, it was not the only country which diversified its economy into shrimp production during the 1980s. Shrimp production in Asia increased by more than 700 per cent between 1980 and 1988 – from a total of 57.2 thousand tonnes to 441.5 thousand tonnes.[14] Bangladesh's industry, which increased production from 2.7 thousand to 25.0 thousand tonnes during that period, turns out to be only a very small fish in a very large sea. Other major Asian producers which have similarly boosted yields and exports during the 1980s are China, India, Indonesia, the Philippines, Taiwan, Thailand, and Vietnam, all of whom produce more than Bangladesh.

If the 1980s was a 'lost decade' for much of the Third World, it was also the decade of the shrimp for much of Asia. The remarkable growth of the Asian shrimp industry can be attributed to three factors. Firstly, new production technologies, which were pioneered in Taiwan but quickly spread across Asia, had a dramatic impact on yields. The technologies were based on refinements in the production of the baby shrimps sold to farmers for rearing, and on the development of compound feeds. They were focused on the intensive cultivation of the *penaeus monodon*, the black tiger shrimp, yields of which were boosted from 284 kg per hectare to 7.7 tonnes per hectare.

But equally important was the second factor: marketing. Again Taiwan led the way, by successfully promoting the black tiger shrimp in the most obvious and lucrative Asian market, Japan, and thus challenging the traditional dominance of white shrimps. The third, inter-related, factor also concerned the Japanese market. During the 1980s the shrimp made the jump from being a restaurant food to being used in home cooking. It was thus transformed from a luxury food to a relatively low-cost, steadily supplied commodity. In three years, between 1984 and 1987, just as forecasters were predicting that Japanese consumption had peaked, annual per capita consumption of shrimps rose from 2.5 kg a year to more than 3 kg.[15] This was good news for the Asian producers who rely overwhelmingly on the Japanese market. Consumption in the other major developed-country markets, the USA and EC, is much lower, at 1 kg and 300 g respectively, and Asian producers cannot easily compete with Central and Latin American producers for the US market, because of their much higher transport costs.

But by the end of the decade the shrimp boom looked as if it was over, as export prices plunged by 40 to 50 per cent. Asian shrimp exporters blame this on the protracted illness and death of the late Japanese emperor, Hirohito. Respect for the Emperor is said to have curbed Japanese appetites, resulting in fewer shrimps being eaten and stocks mounting.[16] Since then the market has picked up, but not at the same rate as before. The price slump marked a sea change in the business, from being production-driven to being market-driven. Meanwhile the search for new markets and cheaper production methods is on. Shrimps are still a profitable business, but with the market becoming more competitive, it is only a matter of time before the less efficient producers, often the ones with the least resources and the most need, are pushed off the export map.

A profitable business

But meanwhile the profits to be made from shrimps are considerable. In the Khulna District of Bangladesh a one-acre pond yields around 400 lbs of shrimps. The pond operator will sell them in Khulna to a fish processor for the equivalent of about £400. Allowing for his stocking costs, he will make a profit of about £350 per acre for the seven-month production cycle. At the other end of the chain, those shrimps may end up in Oxford market in the UK, where in May 1989 the same species was selling for £7 a pound. The shrimps would have lost some weight through the cleaning and shelling process – 400 lbs would be reduced to around 360 lbs – but at £7 a pound these same shrimps, the yield of the one-acre Khulna pond, would finally be sold for a staggering £2,520.[17]

In between, the shrimps would have been processed: cleaned and shelled in a processing shed such as the one outside Notun Bazaar, by women such as Rohina Khatoon. This would not add much to their cost of production, as Rohina is paid only 15 taka (£0.30) for a day's work.[18] The shrimps are then frozen, stored, and transported to their Northern market. With such high profit margins, impressive as the export figures are, it does not seem that the Bangladeshi economy is gaining all that it could from this highly lucrative industry.

The Philippines also records high profits from its shrimp industry. Following the collapse of the sugar industry in the mid-1980s, wealthy landlords on the sugar-producing island of Negros thought they had found a way out of the slump in sugar prices. Catering to the expanding Japanese market, they found that through shrimp farming they could make profits of at least 20,000 pesos (US$896) per hectare, nearly four times the profit of 5,000 pesos per hectare from sugar production. The problem came later when prices on the Japanese market fell, and they once again confronted the dangers of relying on a single market.[19]

Food for export: land and shrimp cultivation

The export of a luxury protein from a country that is unable to feed its own population, is massively dependent on imports of food aid, and is so prone to climatic disaster as Bangladesh has to be questioned. The main issue is the impact of shrimp cultivation on people's access to food, which could be affected through their access to land or employment.

The land in the Khulna area that is devoted to shrimp cultivation has mostly been leased from the owners of small or medium-sized landholdings by local businesses. The shrimp production cycle, from stocking the ponds to harvest, takes seven or eight months. The land is then returned to its owner who, in the remaining months of the year, is able to devote the land to rice production. However, there are two main problems with the practical application of this land-share arrangement. First, the acquisition of land is often attended by considerable corruption, so that a new type of 'landlessness' is being created; and secondly, it is reducing rice yields.

An estimated 25,000 acres of land around the Khulna area are currently under shrimp production. Apart from 3,000 acres of it, which are farmed cooperatively, this land is under the control of rich, urban businessmen. Their corrupt techniques of land acquisition are all too familiar to the people who live in the area. According to local sources, one method commonly used in acquiring land for shrimp production in the Khulna area involves gaining control of the local government-owned waterways. The key to shrimp production is a ready supply of saline water. The shrimp entrepreneurs gain control of these vital rivers and canals by renting them from corrupt local officials, sometimes by bidding at rigged auctions which are not publicly advertised. Once the entrepreneur has them, he will make lucrative offers to rent the land that is next to the waterways, and then flood it to a degree that also floods the land of other small-scale cultivators in the same area. The increased salinity that occurs as a result reduces their rice crop by about two-thirds. Their land becomes of much less value to them, and they are left with little choice other than to rent it out at rock-bottom prices.[20]

Rice yields in the area, under the land-share agreement, have been reduced. Peasant farmers who have leased their land claim that the increase in salinity required for shrimp cultivation has reduced rice yields from one and three quarter tons to around half a ton per acre. They also say that it will take many years to restore the land's fertility.[21]

Employment and shrimp cultivation

Shrimp production creates seasonal landlessness. For the seven or eight months that it takes to produce the shrimps, peasant farmers who have leased out their land join the ranks of the landless labourers. Shrimp production not only takes up land and increases the labour pool. It also reduces employment opportunities.

By its very nature, shrimp production is capital-intensive, rather than labour-intensive. Labour is initially required to build up the ponds and, occasionally, repair the dykes. But for the rest of the time, apart from guarding the ponds, there is no employment. Where the same land hitherto provided employment opportunities for landless labourers year round on rice or jute production, it now not only fails to do that, but actually *adds* to the labour pool. According to an Oxfam project partner in the Khulna area, there is now an out-migration of landless labourers to the slums of Khulna city.[22]

Those landless people who have stayed in the villages have sometimes turned to illegal means to keep their families fed. Mohammed Hassan of Agerhat village in the South Khulna area is one such case. He lost his one-acre plot of land to a money lender in the mid-1980s. He had put up the land as collateral for a loan to buy seeds and fertiliser. The area was then hit by a cyclone which wiped out his crop. He had no option other than to surrender his land over to the money lender and join the ranks of landless labourers.

For several years Hassan survived by working as a seasonal agricultural labourer. Then a wealthy Dhaka businessman managed to acquire all the land in the area, and turned it over to shrimp cultivation. Hassan's only means of livelihood disappeared overnight. He is now one of a growing number of landless labourers in the South Khulna area who steal shrimps for a living. He goes to the ponds at night, often encountering, and usually outwitting, the private army employed by the pond operator to protect his property. Hassan then sells his haul to middlemen, who in turn sell it on to the processing plants around Khulna city. Hassan gets much less than the market value for his shrimps, but at least he manages to feed himself and his family.[23]

Fighting back

Institutionalised theft is not the only way that the peasant farmers have fought back. More than a thousand of them in the South Khulna area have successfully reclaimed the land they rented out to the local businessmen, and are now using it themselves for shrimp production. In 1986 they formed a shrimp cooperative with the assistance of the Khulna-based development agency, Gono Shahajjo Sangstha (GSS), which also runs literacy and education programmes in the area, supported by Oxfam. Regaining their land has been a difficult and painful process. The businessmen have often resorted to bullying tactics and violence, through their private armies, to try to terrorise the peasant farmers into leaving the land. But the farmers have resisted, and managed to reclaim what is rightfully theirs. They now farm shrimps collectively, having formed themselves into smaller units of production.

The ecological consequences of shrimp production

Shrimp cultivation has also been criticised on ecological grounds. In many Asian countries, including Bangladesh, mangrove swamps have been destroyed to build shrimp facilities. This is particularly evident in the area of the Bay of Bengal known as the Sunderban, where the destruction of mangrove plantations has steadily depleted the region's shrimp resources.[24]

Another concern is the impact of shrimp cultivation on soil salinity. The World Bank claimed that shrimp cultivation would be beneficial in this respect, as the proper construction of dykes required by the industry would stop saline water seepage into agricultural lands.[25] However, in the experience of farmers in the Khulna area, shrimp cultivation is causing soil salinity, and thus harming crop production. There is also some evidence to show that dykes, weakened by cutting to let brackish water on to the land, are then more prone to flooding with saline water.

Diversification and democracy

Diversification is an important policy objective for Third World countries which need to expand their export base. However, the case of the Bangladeshi shrimp industry highlights some of the problems that can arise when economic development is not matched with social and environmental objectives. In this case there is a clear conflict over the use of land for food production, as opposed to export production. The industry has also reduced local employment opportunities and is having an adverse impact on the environment. Its benefits are unevenly distributed, so that while considerable financial gains are being made by the local entrepreneurs, many other people are actually poorer as a result.

Many of these problems could be overcome, if initiatives such as the shrimp cooperative were actively encouraged, both by the government and by multilateral agencies investing in the industry, such as the World Bank. It underlines the importance of popular participation and democratic accountability, not only at government level, but also at local level, in developing such initiatives. People-centred development is at the heart of the trade model employed by the alternative trading movement and, as the following chapter shows, can bring considerable benefits to small-scale producers.

13

BRIDGING THE GAP:
Alternative trading

Oxfam was founded in 1942 as a relief agency to help hungry civilians in occupied Greece. It is still a relief agency, responding to disasters all over the world, but since the 1960s the emphasis of its work has shifted to long-term development. The transition occurred with the growing realisation that poverty and suffering cannot be effectively relieved without also identifying and tackling their root causes.

It was no coincidence that Oxfam's 'Bridge' programme started at this time. The idea was first mooted in 1964 when, according to an early history of the organisation, 'Oxfam workers, visiting the scenes of disasters abroad, were shown some goods people had made and wanted to sell to regain their self-respect.' It was suggested that the products could be sold in the chain of Oxfam shops, selling mostly donated second-hand goods, which were by now well established throughout Britain; and thus the idea of the Bridge scheme was born.[1] Bridge, the major part of Oxfam Trading, is an Alternative Trading Organisation (ATO). Established by Oxfam in 1965,[2] it operates from offices attached to a warehouse on an industrial estate outside Bicester, a market town in the centre of England. Its trading principles are summarised as follows:

> Through buying crafts and foodstuffs from trading partners committed to economic and social justice, Bridge aims to help poor people in developing countries improve their standard of living.[3]

Oxfam saw that by providing a market for Third World products, paying prices judged to be fair in the local economy, and buying through organisations which ensured that the bulk of the price reached the actual producers, it could begin to attack one root cause of poverty: the dependence of small-scale producers on local traders, who pay them low prices. As a further measure of solidarity, Bridge returns its profits to support the growth of small businesses in producer countries.

The Bridge display room in the basement of the warehouse is an Aladdin's cave of Third World crafts. Panama hats, Peruvian wall hangings, Sri Lankan bangles, Kenyan baskets, Indian candlesticks,

Bolivian knitwear, and candlesticks from the Philippines cram the shelves and cover the floor, each one representing a group of hopeful producers. Many will be disappointed. The majority never reach the shops or the mail-order catalogue. Standards have to be high, and colours and design must suit contemporary British taste. However, there are limits to the numbers of Hegelong guitars from the T'Boli tribe of the southern Philippines, or foot massagers from Java, that the UK market can absorb.

ALTERNATIVE TRADE IN HANDICRAFTS

Ninety three per cent of the goods sold through the Bridge scheme are handicrafts. Poor communities derive a number of advantages from the handicraft trade. Production provides vital income for women, whose usual work is often unpaid. This is of major importance, for it is now widely recognised that paying women directly is the best way of ensuring that children are fed, clothed, and schooled. Handicrafts add value to local materials such as jute, cotton, or wool. Production can often take place at home, during the quieter times of the year, for example after harvest, and therefore need not interfere with other activities such as food production. Illustrating these advantages is one of Bridge's longest-established handicraft trading partners, the Bangladeshi organisation, CORR – The Jute Works.

CORR – The Jute Works

The Jute Works came into existence in 1973 as a project originally funded by a number of development agencies, including Oxfam. It started as Bangladesh's post-liberation efforts were coming to an end. Many men had died in the fighting, leaving widows and children without any source of income, and dependent on relief aid. The Jute Works was set up to provide some of these destitute women with an opportunity to earn some money.

Women in the jute-growing regions of Bangladesh have traditionally used jute to make a range of functional household items. At that time jute was still Bangladesh's main export, but demand for it on the international market had flagged, owing to the increasing use of synthetics. Although prices were low, it was still widely grown, in rotation with rice, as most farmers' only hope of a cash income. Domestic demand for locally produced jute goods was low, but some of the aid agencies working in Bangladesh felt that there could be a market abroad for some of these attractive products if they were traded through the Alternative Trade Organisations. The Dhaka-based nuns who founded The Jute Works believed that there could be a fruitful coincidence between this perceived Western demand for 'ethnic' goods, the ready supply of jute, and the desperate need of so many women for an income. They were right. The best-known Jute Works export, the 'sika', a hanging basket which is used for storage in Bangladesh, has found its way into homes all over the world, usually as a container for houseplants. It is commonly featured in the Oxfam Trading catalogue. Richard Adams, founder of another British ATO, Traidcraft, describes his first big purchase from the Jute Works in Dhaka in 1974:

> My first call the next morning was to the Jute Works. Information about my visit had failed to reach the people there, but they recognised me as one of their overseas customers, even though my order had been a small one. I explained that I hoped to buy enough handicrafts to fill up a large cargo plane. Disbelief turned to amazement and then to jubilant enthusiasm. The Jute Works took on the atmosphere of Santa's Workshop, with eager helpers rushing to fill up my sleigh! They would not have enough from their own stock: people would be sent to the village production centres and asked to send all they could. Would I take seconds? Would I take palm leaf mats, crochet work and embroidery? Would I take bamboo furniture, cane baskets and sweeping brushes? Yes, I said, I would take almost anything that might sell in Britain, providing that it did not come to more than fifteen tonnes and one hundred cubic metres or £10,000 altogether.[4]

Bangladesh: Making a sika for sale through the Jute Works cooperative. Rahima supports her family with her monthly income of 250 taka (appoximately £5.00). So far she has saved 250 taka, and has borrowed money to buy a goat.

The Jute Works is now entirely self-financing. Currently over 7,000 women are making goods for it. They are organised into small producer groups who buy their jute locally, or grow their own. The Jute Works gives them orders. It works with the women on design and quality control, as well as encouraging functional literacy classes. Its Group Development Fund encourages and assists with other forms of income generation including calf, goat and poultry rearing, sewing, rice cultivation, and fish farming. There is also a producers' provident security fund and a small credit project.[5]

The average earnings of a producer are about 150 taka a month, for what is very much part-time work. The Jute Works is realistic in acknowledging that handicrafts can never be the economic solution to poor women's problems, but can provide a useful supplementary income, and can be an entry point into education and awareness-raising.[6] The story of Kazuli illustrates the impact of such a project on the life of one woman:

Kazuli and her husband Bishu live with their five children in two small rooms, constructed of mud with a flat tin roof. There are no windows in these rooms, or furniture. The family sleep on grass mats on the mud floor. In the summer months they are warm and dry, but plagued by insects and mosquitoes. In the winter the floor becomes damp and cold and they frequently suffer from bronchitis or pneumonia.

Both Kazuli and Bishu, whose marriage was arranged by their families when Kazuli was only sixteen, have known better times. Kazuli came from the family of a respectable land-owning farmer. Bishu's family also owned land, but latterly lost it through flood and erosion. The couple now own little more than the land their home stands on, and rely entirely on Bishu's earnings as a casual labourer working in the fields of local landowners. His earnings are pitifully low. During the planting and harvesting season he is normally able to work throughout the week. At other times of the year the best he can hope for is two or three days' work a week. For a ten-hour day he can expect to bring home between Tk25.00 and Tk30.00, enough to buy one and a half kilos of rice, a quarter of a kilo of wheat flour, and a few spices. Kazuli is sometimes able to supplement their meagre diet with green leaves or vegetables that she has managed to collect. Very often they have only a few left-overs from the day before to eat.

In the early days of their marriage Kazuli worked as a domestic to supplement their income. But Bishu soon forbade her to do that. It hurt his pride that a woman in his family should have to work outside the home. So for the sake of her marriage and her family she had little choice other than to abandon her job and watch her husband toil to try and feed them.

Kazuli then came into contact with other village women, and through them heard of a scheme whereby a group from the city (Dhaka) were training women in handicrafts and functional literacy. These women were earning between Tk60 and Tk100 a month, and had acquired status and respect from their families and their community. She decided to join the group, the Kathalia Mothers' Club, one of the Jute Works' producer groups consisting of 26 women. Three years later Kazuli was one of the group's most skilled workers, earning up to Tk200 a month. She had also started a rice-husking scheme. With the financial backing of the group she had taken out a loan to buy the equipment needed to turn paddy into rice, which she could then sell in the market. Her husband had joined in the scheme and together they were managing to repay the loan. She was earning enough to send two of her children to school and was planning to send a third in the near future. But for Kazuli the greatest gain of her association with the Jute Works is that she is now able to ensure that her children have regular meals.[7]

ALTERNATIVE TRADE IN COMMODITIES

Around 7 per cent of Bridge's sales come from food products, such as coffee, tea, nuts, honey, and spices. Since early 1990 cocoa has also been in many of Oxfam's high street shops. For the price-conscious shopper this is not the place to go. The Oxfam cocoa, attractively packaged in a red canister, retails at a few pence more than most commercial brands. The higher price is justified by claims that it provides a better quality of life for the producer. This is unambiguously stated on the packaging:

> This cocoa comes from 'El Ceibo', a cooperative of peasant farmers in northern Bolivia. The co-op takes its name from a local tree which shelters the vulnerable cocoa plant from the sun. Similarly, 'El Ceibo' acts as an umbrella organisation to its 1,000 members. It pays them a higher price for their cocoa beans and provides technical advice, transport and education. It also runs a small processing factory in La Paz, enabling the farmers to bypass large processors.

El Ceibo

In a meeting room in Sapecho, a small village in northern Bolivia, 40 or 50 cacao farmers – men, women, and children – are about to experience their first taste of chocolate. Chocolate in every conceivable shape, size, and form is stacked on a table: chocolate rabbits, eggs, and bars, each piece tastefully and expensively wrapped, the finest quality Swiss confectionery from the smart shops of Zurich and Geneva. The farmers are all too familiar with the yellow-brown cacao pods that they labour to harvest, but today, for the first time, they are being introduced to the end product.

They belong to a peasants' cooperative, and are taking part in a seminar on organic cacao production, led by Joachim, a European volunteer aid worker. Joachim, who has had a long association with the cooperative, is working with the farmers to promote organic production. 'It's all about markets,' he explains. Several years ago he was approached by a German company which was looking for supplies of organic cocoa to process into chocolate in its Swiss factory. 'We are responding to their response to the growing demand for greener products in Germany, although it also makes economic and ecological sense for the producers here.' He hopes that El Ceibo will soon be exporting organic cocoa, although they must still await verification that their products are truly organic – and international standards are tough. Once they have been verified, new market opportunities could open up for the cooperative.[8]

El Ceibo is the umbrella organisation for its 36 member cooperatives. These are spread over a large area. Some are as far as 50 km from Sapecho, the village where the El Ceibo cooperative centre is situated, but all are in Bolivia's Alto Beni (High Jungle) region. Sapecho is 372 metres above sea level, on the edge of the Amazonian rainforest, with a sub-tropical climate that is ideal for cacao production. The village is only 240 km (149 miles) from Bolivia's capital city, La Paz, but the journey, on a good day, takes at least twelve hours. The road, which is little more than a mud track in places and is frequently cut off by land slides during the rainy season, drops from an altitude of 3,636 metres, twisting down through the appropriately named Yungas, or 'Hanging Valleys'. In places it narrows so that there is just enough room for a truck to pass, with sheer drops of several hundred feet on one side, and overhanging cliff face on the other. Casualties are not uncommon: the remains of vehicles can sometimes be seen littering the bottom of the ravines. Yet this is the lifeline of the Alto Beni. All produce, bound either for the home market or export, must pass along this hazardous route through to La Paz.

It is the head of household who joins El Ceibo as a cooperative member. This means that most members are men, although, as the cooperative committee explains, there are also women members who, as widows or single women, qualify as heads of household. They are at pains to explain that women receive equal recognition with men in the cooperative and that the family of any member has automatic access to the cooperative.[9] In reality the men play a dominant role, reinforced by the tradition that cash-crop production is their responsibility, while the women take care of the food crops.

Don Pedro, as head of his family, has belonged to the El Ceibo cooperative since it began in the mid-1970s. Like many of the farmers in that region, he was part of the government's 'colonisation' programme which took place during the 1960s and 1970s. In an attempt to shift people off the high plains and mining areas around La Paz and move them into the very under-populated Alto Beni region, the government handed out parcels of land to anyone who would agree to move. Many did move. Some could not survive the tropical climate of the area and moved back to the highlands. Others, like Don Pedro, have managed to settle. Don Pedro farms a ten-hectare plot of land just outside Sapecho. It is reached by a narrow track up through the forest which opens up into a small clearing and a thatched hut which is home to him, his wife, and their four children. The track leads on into the forest and Don Pedro's cacao trees.

When Don Pedro was allocated his land, he probably felt that he had been unlucky. Most of his ten hectares range over a steeply sloping hillside. He has fruit trees growing in between his cacao which provide shade for the cacao and food for the family, but it would be hard to grow vegetables or rice on such a gradient. Two years ago, with the help of the cooperative, Don Pedro began farming organically. He is pleased with the results. Rather than frequent applications of expensive fertilisers, which in the ten years that he had been using them seemed to be depleting the quality of his cacao, he now uses a nitrogen-fixing leguminous plant known locally as 'kudzu'. Kudzu grows prolifically. It acts as ground cover, holding the top soil in place, and saving Don Pedro the trouble of having to dig it back around the trees after a heavy rainfall. He says that his trees are healthier and yields are improving as a result.

The only problem is that organic production is very labour-intensive. He constantly has to check his trees for pests, remove diseased fruit, and cut unwanted growth – work previously made unnecessary by chemical applications. The extra work involved means that he is probably no better off financially. The gain from the improved yields, lower input costs, and the higher prices paid for organically grown cacao is off-set by the extra labour involved. Cacao production now absorbs all his time, which means that he has had to cut back on all other forms of income generation or food production.[10]

Don Pedro sells his cacao beans to his local cooperative, which, in turn, sell them on to the centre, where there are facilities for drying the

BELINDA COOTE/OXFAM

Bolivia: Don Pedro Bernebe grows cacao organically on his smallholding near Sapecho, 150 miles north of La Paz. He sells the beans to the El Ceibo cooperative, which processes them. Cocoa from El Ceibo is exported to Alternative Trading Organisations in Europe, like Oxfam Trading.

beans. The cooperatives which are farther away dry the beans themselves and then sell them to the centre. The centre transports the beans to La Paz, to the small processing factory run by El Ceibo. The factory employs about ten people to process and package the cocoa. Each year the cooperative exports around 200 tonnes to OS3, an Alternative Trading Organisation in Switzerland. The price that OS3 pays for the cocoa is worked out annually with the cooperative, and is based on production costs. This protects El Ceibo from the vagaries of the world market, where prices for cocoa, as for other commodities, have been unstable and generally very low in recent years. OS3 pays for transport costs from the Chilean port of Arica to the Netherlands, and then sells the cocoa on to other ATOs, such as Traidcraft, for retailing. Oxfam used to purchase from OS3, but now buys direct from El Ceibo. Profits go towards the running costs of the cooperative and are shared out among members.[11]

In the days before the El Ceibo cooperative was formed, the Alto Beni producers had only one option for marketing their cocoa. They sold it through a middleman who had monopoly control over cocoa marketing in the region, and was paying very low prices for their produce. The farmers decided to try to get round this by marketing cooperatively. Assisted by foreign funding, the organisation grew from there, and is currently marketing around 35 per cent of the region's cocoa.

As a player on the international cocoa market, Bolivia is just one of many countries that export a very small quantity of cocoa. The market is dominated by a handful of large producers. In 1988 for example, Côte d'Ivoire, Malaysia, Ghana, Nigeria, Brazil, and Cameroon accounted for 75 per cent of all cocoa-bean exports.[12] The market is also over-supplied. In 1988 total world consumption of cocoa (beans equivalent) was 2,015,100 metric tons, while the combined exports of cocoa beans and cocoa products (beans equivalent) amounted to 24,605,000 metric tons. Such an imbalance, even given that some of the cocoa products would be re-exports, would account for the low world market prices.

Trading through the ATO network ensures that the El Ceibo producers, such as Don Pedro, benefit from a relatively stable market, and steady prices based on their production costs. At the other end of the chain the consumer can relax with a cup of cocoa in the knowledge that a much a greater margin of the price paid in the shop has benefited the Bolivian producer, and that Don Pedro and others like him also benefit from advice about improved production techniques.

Increasing food sales

Handicrafts will probably always be the main marketing concern of Bridge. Apart from the gains to producers, they lend themselves well to promotion through Oxfam's shops and mail-order catalogue. Establishing a market for foods presents a new set of challenges: 'There are many more problems to be overcome in importing food products,' said Bridge's manager for Latin America and Africa, Edward Millard. 'They have to conform to strict health regulations. For example, honey has to be stored at correct temperatures in transit otherwise the HMV content will rise above permitted levels.[13] Another difficulty is distribution. If we don't pack the honey jars properly, then our shops open the box to find a sticky mess and broken glass. But the biggest problem of all is keeping it in stock 365 days a year. If customers come in for our coffee and tea and we are out of stock, they go back to the supermarkets to buy. Yet sometimes we cannot avoid delays in the arrival of shipments.'

But in the last few years Edward and others like him in the ATO world have become committed to acquiring the skills necessary for importing, processing and packaging food products, as they have witnessed the increase in rural poverty in the Third World. 'The collapse in prices of commodities on the international markets has had dire consequences for producers. Coffee growers, for example, can no longer cover their costs of production. I cannot travel around countries like Bolivia ignoring their desperate need for markets, just because handicrafts are easier to import!'

Bridge has been responding to this need in a number of ways. First, by increasing its range of food products like cocoa from El Ceibo, which was one of the first products in this new range. Second, by repackaging theproducts, to draw customers' attention to the situation of producers. And third by joining a new coffee-marketing initiative. Until recently the marketing of coffee by ATOs in Britain was closely related to campaigns based on specific countries. Its purpose was as much to offer consumers an opportunity to show solidarity with a campaign as to provide producers with a market for their coffee. Examples of these have been coffee from the African Frontline States, as a part of the Anti-Apartheid campaign, and coffee from Nicaragua and Tanzania, whose governments were committed to progressive development policies. After the election victory of UNO Presidential Candidate Violeta Barrios de Chamorro in Nicaragua at the beginning of 1990, the US embargo against Nicaraguan exports was lifted. This meant that Nicaraguan coffee producers were suddenly in the same situation as other coffee producers. Although they no longer suffer from the damaging effects of the trade embargo, they still have to face hopelessly low world market prices for coffee.

Bridge is one of four Alternative Trading Organisations which have, for the first time, joined forces to market coffee.[14] The new brand, 'Cafédirect', was launched in October 1991. As its name suggests, the coffee is purchased direct from small farmers' organisations. First purchases came from Central and South American producers. It is hoped there will also be an African blend of Cafédirect in the future. The price paid to producers for their coffee is based on the International Coffee Organisation's floor price, which, at the time of the launch, was US$1.20 per lb. This compared favourably with the world market price of around 85 cents per lb. The ICO floor price is worked out between producer and consumer members of the agreement and relates, as far as possible, to production costs. It is judged to be the minimum that growers need to be able to cover their costs and make a small profit on their harvest. If the world market price rises above the ICO floor price, then Cafédirect suppliers are paid the world price. In addition, producers are part-paid in advance. This is to tide them over between harvest and sale, a time when many coffee growers are forced to borrow from money lenders.

The ATOs hope that it will soon be possible to market Cafédirect through a wider range of retail outlets. For this purpose, a proportion of the price agreed with producers is being kept in a marketing fund. For the meantime it will be sold through their own distribution networks. In the case of Bridge, this is through some of the 625 Oxfam shops which sell crafts and foodstuffs, and through its mail-order catalogues.

A DROP IN THE OCEAN

Bridge is just one of more than fifty Alternative Trading Organisations in the North. (There are many more in the South which export for producers.) While these Northern ATOs all differ in the way they operate and the goods that they trade in, they basically share three core aims: to cooperate with small-scale producers to help to improve their living conditions through fairer trade; to educate consumers about the problems that small-scale producers face as a result of unfair trading practices; and to campaign for fairer trading conditions in the world.

In recent years these organisations have begun to realise the importance of organising themselves into a more cohesive force to achieve their trading, educational, and campaigning aims. In May 1989 some thirty ATOs, including Bridge, formed the International Federation of Alternative Trade (IFAT). IFAT's office in Amsterdam performs the function of negotiator and importer on behalf of affiliated organisations. Before the formation of IFAT, ten European ATOs had been meeting regularly to exchange ideas and to give one another mutual support. Their decision to formalise this group led to the creation of the European Fair Trade Association. Some EFTA members are also members of IFAT.

Bridge is among four of the largest ATOs. In the financial year 1990/91 Oxfam Trading sold around £8.5 million worth of Bridge products, an increase from £2.5 million in 1985/86. While combined ATO turnover has probably more than doubled in the last five years, it is estimated to be, at most, £250 million a year.[15] This is a mere drop in the ocean when compared with that of a moderate-sized company such as the British sugar traders, Tate and Lyle, whose turnover in 1990 was £3,431.9 million.[16]

While alternative trading is undoubtedly growing, there is no disguising the fact that alternatively traded products remain firmly on the margins of consumerism. Even within the Oxfam shops, Bridge goods have to compete with the donated goods, which are more profitable (for Oxfam), and are frequently relegated to the rear of the shop, the basement, or upstairs. The catalogues are an important sales point, but reach only a very small minority of consumers. Alternatively traded foods can sometimes be found in specialist wholefood shops or health shops, but again these are frequented by only a small minority of consumers.

However, alternative trading demonstrates how world trade could be organised, based on a more equal relationship between North and South. While in this respect it has undoubtedly achieved quality, and has played an important role in educating a significant minority of the public, it has failed to achieve quantity. It has brought real benefits to some producers, such as the women contracted by CORR – The Jute

Works and the El Ceibo cocoa farmers, but their numbers are small. With a share of no more than a fraction of world trade, alternative trade presents neither a threat to the world trading system, nor any serious alternative for the vast majority of producers.[17]

As the 1980s drew to a close, it became apparent that the decade had, indeed, been 'lost' for many developing countries and that poverty was on the increase. Low commodity prices and shrinking world markets for some products, combined with debt and rising interest rates, has hit many countries hard. Yet the poorer they become, the more difficult it is for them to attract the investment and technology required to diversify or up-grade production and earn their way out of debt. They are well and truly caught in the trade trap. The need for fairer world trade has never been greater. The challenge of the 1990s is to apply the alternative model more widely, and to promote fairer trade as a part of mainstream commercial activity.

14

FROM THE MARGINS TO THE MAINSTREAM:
Fairer trade initiatives

Oxfam and a number of other organisations concerned with Third World development share a vision of the supermarket of the future. On the coffee shelves, there will be the familiar array of products to choose from: filter coffee, expresso coffee, coffee for percolators, coffee from Colombia, Jamaican Blue Mountain coffee, continental coffee, instant coffee, coffee beans, and more. There are different brand names to choose from, and decaffeinated versions of some. Two-thirds of them carry a small but distinctive logo. It tells the shopper that the coffee has been produced under fair conditions. The coffee growers have been paid a price for their coffee which ensures that they can cover their production costs and make a living. That price may well have been above the world market price. Some of the payment has been made before delivery, so that the producers do not have to borrow from moneylenders. They have also been ensured reasonable security on future orders.

On the tea shelves, there is the usual array of products and brands: loose tea, tea bags, decaffeinated tea, instant tea, tea from Darjeeling, Lapsang Souchong tea and more. But one of the well-known brands has the same logo displayed on its distinctive packaging, and a number of 'own label' products also carry it. It guarantees that the tea pickers are paid decent wages, that housing conditions on their estate are good, that the workers are free to form unions, and have access to basic services such as health and education.

This is the supermarket of the near future, if the dream can be realised. For every product originating from the Third World there is one brand, or more, carrying the logo. For consumers concerned with fairness in the Third World, their shopping baskets can become a powerful statement of their commitment to the poor – a commitment which they have been able to put to practical effect.

Some marketing analysts claim that it will not be long before this new form of product labelling is a common sight in high street shops. Their prediction is based on marketing logic. In their view, this is the only direction left for product labelling. It develops naturally out of the first three waves of product labelling. In Britain the first wave concerned, in marketing terms, the 'post-purchase consumer experience', and produced, among others, the Kitemark. This guarantees that the product bearing it conforms to certain standards of safety. For example, in buying a toaster the consumer wants to be assured that it will not blow up on first use. Then came the second wave of labelling. This was the 'green' wave, designed to assure consumers that in using the product they would not harm the environment: that their washing-up liquid would not pollute the water table, or aerosol cans deplete the ozone layer. The third wave came as an extension to this. Consumers now wanted to make sure that the product they wanted to buy had not already caused environmental damage: were dolphins slaughtered in the fishing nets or was the tuna caught by line? Did the wood come from the Brazilian rainforest or from a more readily renewable source?

So, the argument goes, there is only one direction left for product labelling: 'So far, a key factor in each wave has been concern about the individuals on the *receiving* end of the product. But once you start to look at how a product is grown, processed, or manufactured, it can't be long before you become aware of the individuals on the *production* end.'[1]

MAX HAVELAAR

It was concern for individuals on the production end that inspired the Dutch 'Max Havelaar' scheme, the first experiment in 'fourth wave' labelling. The Max Havelaar Quality Mark, a scheme to promote fairer trade in coffee, was launched in November 1988. The name 'Max Havelaar' is taken from a novel written by a Dutch civil servant who worked in the former Dutch East Indies, now Indonesia, in the nineteenth century. While there, he could not reconcile himself to the policies of the colonial government, which forced local farmers to work on the Dutch coffee plantations, with the result that they neglected food production and there was famine. On his return to Holland he decided to write a book about it. *Max Havelaar, or the Coffee Auctions of the Dutch Trading-Society*, by Eduard Douwes Dekker, has become a Dutch classic.

The project was launched on 15 November 1988. The initiative came from a group of small coffee producers in Mexico and was taken up by a wide coalition of sympathetic Dutch organisations representing consumers, development agencies, religious groups, and trading organisations. According to the Max Havelaar Foundation it is based on

... a very widely accepted – although less widely practised – approach to development cooperation. The Third World needs basic price and income guarantees for sound agricultural development. Similar guarantees have been the cornerstones of integrated agricultural development policies in Europe and the United States, not only as a result of pressure from farmers but also arising out of self interest. Even if it ultimately becomes necessary to eliminate these protectionist measures because of their cost, it is widely recognised that certain levels of protectionism have been essential for equilibrated and rapid development.[2]

They decided to work through the Dutch coffee roasters, who were invited to participate in the scheme, provided that they met certain criteria. The coffee that they buy must be purchased from democratically-run organisations of small coffee producers identified by the Max Havelaar Foundation. The roasters would be required to sign long-term contracts with these groups, and to pay 60 per cent of the agreed price in advance of the harvest. The agreed price would be the world market price for coffee, plus a margin. The lower the world price, the higher the margin, and vice versa. The price differential would be reflected in the retail price. In return, the coffee would be accredited by the Max Havelaar Foundation with the Foundation's own seal of approval. As a general principle, Max Havelaar only buys up to 30 per cent of any one organisation's harvest, to avoid creating dependency.

The scheme has been successful. By mid-1991 more than 300,000 coffee farmers were selling through the Max Havelaar scheme, and it is making a very real difference to their lives. Rufino Herrera and the Federation of Coffee Growers in the Dominican Republic, already mentioned in Chapter 1, have a contract through the Max Havelaar scheme. For the coffee that they sell through this scheme they are able to make a profit of between US$10 and US$15 per quintal, rather than the loss they make on the international market. But it is not only the price that helps. According to Rufino, the access to credit that the scheme gives them is also enormously important, as it means that they do not have to resort to borrowing from money lenders.[3]

The Max Havelaar Foundation says that it receives requests for access to the scheme from all over the world, and that they are unable to meet more than a fraction of the demand. But they are optimistic that the scheme is having a knock-on effect. There is evidence to show that in those areas where farmers are selling through Max Havelaar, the existing middlemen are beginning to pay higher prices to prevent farmers from selling all their best beans to Max Havelaar.[4]

On the consumer side, Max Havelaar coffee is now available in more than 6,000 supermarkets throughout the Netherlands, instead of being restricted to the 230 alternative trading shops. In the scheme's first two and a half year period it gained a 2.3 per cent market share, compared with the 0.2 per cent of coffee sold through alternative traders before the launch of the scheme. Just as important is the educational function of the scheme. Market research findings show that 73 per cent of the general public in Holland are now aware of the scheme and what it is trying to achieve.

The Foundation is now exploring the possibility of adapting the scheme to other commodities. Cocoa, textiles, and tea are among the candidates. They have also launched a Max Havelaar scheme in Belgium, and plans are in progress to launch a similar initiative in France. Since October 1991 Max Havelaar coffee has been the official coffee of the European Parliament. But perhaps their greatest achievement is to have become a model and inspiration to like-minded organisations in other countries.

THE FLAME OF FAIR TRADE

In August 1989 representatives from fourteen organisations met in Gateshead, England, at the offices of Traidcraft. They were a mixture of Alternative Trading Organisations and development agencies who, inspired by the success of Max Havelaar, had decided to get together to see if something on similar lines could be established in Britain.

The meeting was taking place at a time when 'green consumerism' was at its height. A variety of environmental problems, such as depletion of the ozone layer, global warming, and water pollution, had led consumers to demand assurances that their purchases would not add to the damage. For the manufacturers and retailers this spelt market opportunity, a new way to add value to a product. They responded by filling the shelves of shops and supermarkets up and down the country with 'eco friendly' products in all forms. Anxious not to be left off the green bandwagon, commercial companies were soon claiming their product to be greener than the next. Some were bringing out new 'environment-friendly' lines. Others were simply claiming new standards for existing products. While arguments raged over the authenticity of some of these claims, one thing was clear: green issues were now firmly established in the marketplace. This was partly the cause and partly the effect of making the environment a mainstream concern.

If 'friendly to the environment', why not 'friendly to the producer'? That was the question on the minds of the participants at the Gateshead meeting. Indeed, for some the question was not *if*, but *when* the market would go down the 'development-friendly' road. They were persuaded by the marketing analysis of product labelling which made the 'fourth wave' an inevitable next step. This analysis, combined with the stark realities facing Third World producers as a result of rock-bottom commodity prices and unjust global trading systems, gave birth to the

Fairtrade Mark. While inspired by the Max Havelaar scheme, the Fairtrade Mark is designed to encompass a wider market.

> The specific objective of the project is to ensure a fairer deal for Third World producers in international trade. The Fairtrade Mark will seek to do this by influencing changes in mainstream commercial practices and in consumer attitudes, so that consumer demand in the UK for a greater availability of more equitably traded products can be both stimulated and met. It is hoped that resources may be available to fulfil a contingent objective, which is to encourage discussion and action on fair trade issues among manufacturer, retailers, and the public.[5]

In theory any manufacturer marketing a product that originates from the developing world, such as tea, textiles, coffee, cocoa, or bananas can apply to the Fairtrade Foundation for its seal of approval – the Fairtrade Mark – to be carried on the product. But to qualify for the seal of approval, the company involved has to provide proof that certain criteria have been met. The criteria are similar to those being used by the Max Havelaar scheme. The producer must have been paid a price which reflects the costs of production and the quality of the product, plus a reasonable margin for investment and development, and to cover future production uncertainties. Financial credit should have been made available to the producer where necessary, to reduce pre-sale uncertainties and to protect the producer against financial exploitation. Purchasing should be from producer organisations whose interests are aligned with those of the producers and accountable to the producers. The trading relationship should be established on the basis of quality, continuity, and mutual support.[6]

Using these broad criteria as guidelines, more detailed criteria will be set for each product. For example, in considering awarding the Fairtrade Mark for products grown on plantations, the Fairtrade Foundation will look for evidence that workers are free to unionise and negotiate; that standards of housing and other basic services are good; that wages are above the national minimum. It will need to be satisfied that men and women are paid equal rates for work of equal value; that health and safety regulations are met; and that production is environmentally sustainable.

There is nothing new about these criteria. Those on labour standards are closely aligned to existing standards laid down by the International Labour Organisation. Those regarding price and purchasing contracts closely reflect the aims of most International Commodity Agreements, many of which also carry social clauses which stipulate minimum fair-labour standards. As such, fair trade schemes, such as Max Havelaar and the Fairtrade Mark, are simply attempting to ensure that the aims of these international codes are met by manufacturers. In doing so, they are directly challenging the corporate world to ensure a better deal for producers. One key to the success of the Fairtrade Mark is the consumer. If the demand is there for more fairly traded products, they will be provided. This much has been learnt from the 'green' movement.

While the reality of the 'fourth wave' on the supermarket shelves is still some way off, the flame of fair trade has been lit. Assisted by this new era of closer collaboration between alternative trading organisations, other schemes in other parts of the world are being discussed, including one by the European Fair Trade Association for a European-wide fair trade initiative. These schemes allow us a vision of a future where fair trade is an integral part of global economic relations.

15

ACTION FOR FAIRER TRADE:
Summary and recommendations

SUMMARY

Oxfam's overriding concern is to reduce poverty and suffering. The nature and causes of poverty vary significantly from one country to another. Yet the interlinked problems of heavy dependence on commodities and declining terms of trade are shared by many of the developing countries in which Oxfam works.

The collapse in the real prices of commodities since the beginning of the 1980s has been disastrous for the poorer developing countries which rely overwhelmingly on commodities for their export earnings. Falling prices have had a severe impact, contributing substantially to the increase in Third World poverty and to the widening gap between rich and poor countries. Surprisingly, perhaps, while the debt burden has been extensively discussed, and solutions sought, comparable attention has not been paid by the international community to the underlying problem of the long-term decline in commodity prices that faces many developing countries.

Hardest hit by the fall in commodity prices are the producers. The collapse in tin prices that took place in the mid-1980s sealed the fate of Bolivia's tin industry, with the result that thousands of miners lost their jobs. Many felt that they had no option other than to try making a living from the illegal drugs trade. Others have joined the swelling ranks of the unemployed in the sprawling urban shanty towns. A similar fate was faced by sugar workers on the Philippines island of Negros, who faced starvation when international sugar prices collapsed. Small coffee producers in many parts of Latin America found that they could no longer even cover their production costs when the price of coffee collapsed. In common with poor farmers in many parts of the developing world, they also have to contend with inadequate or unfair access to credit, lack of storage facilities, and difficulties in marketing and transporting their produce. Many are landless, or are forced by the pressure on land to over-exploit marginal areas, further degrading the fertility of the soil.

The future development of these commodity-dependent Third World countries depends crucially on their ability to generate resources. To do this they need a substantial improvement in their export earnings – which can be achieved only if commodity prices increase and their economies are diversified.

On the question of improving commodity prices, there are complexities on both sides of the demand and supply equation. On the supply side there is a tendency to increase production irrespective of demand. This has been influenced by a range of factors, including the need for developing countries to pay off their debts. On the demand side there is a long-term tendency towards relative decreases in consumption. In addition, increasing protectionism in industrial countries means that developing countries are often denied access to Northern markets.

On the question of diversifying their economies, developing countries face many difficulties. They lack capital for investment, and find that tariff structures and non-tariff barriers block their efforts to find markets for their new exports. Those countries which have managed to diversify successfully, such as Chile, have done so at high social and environmental costs.

Neither of the existing international trade organisations – GATT and UNCTAD – has been able to deal with the formidable problems facing most developing countries. Successive rounds of GATT negotiations have largely failed to control the growth in bilateral and unilateral protectionism. From a Southern perspective, GATT is an undemocratic and closed institution, dominated by a small number of developed countries which promote the interests of Northern multinational corporations. It treats trade in isolation from other financial considerations which are of crucial importance to the developing world, such as the debt crisis and high interest rates.

Third World development issues are central to UNCTAD's negotiations. However, especially in recent years, the North has shown little willingness to negotiate measures that might redress the inequities of the global economic system in favour of developing countries. For this reason, although its secretariat acts as an important think-tank for developing countries, UNCTAD is now little more than a North/South debating forum.

The 1990s present a number of new challenges for developing countries, offering both threats and opportunities. The completion of the European Single Market, and the economic growth expected to arise from it, could result in increased export opportunities for some countries, but will divert trade from others. Likewise, the North American Free Trade Agreement could be an opportunity for Mexico to enhance its development prospects, but there is a risk of high social and environmental costs. The emergence of these blocs and a possible third (in East Asia) could threaten the interests of the poorer developing countries, particularly in Africa.

A further dimension relates to the global environmental crisis. All too often export-oriented development strategies are failing to value non-renewable environmental resources or to meet social needs adequately. The rapid deforestation and overfishing that can result are threatening the livelihoods of poor people. At the same time, increased poverty and marginalisation, coupled with rapid population growth, are forcing poor people to degrade the environment still further to survive. There is a growing recognition that poverty in the South and over-consumption of energy in the North are putting intolerable pressure on the global environment.

An increasing number of consumers in the North have responded to the environmental crisis by demanding environment-friendly products. While the 1980s were undoubtedly the decade in which green consumerism came to the fore, there are signs that the 1990s may become the decade of 'development-friendly' consumerism. A number of schemes have already been established to promote fair trade in Third World products by giving a seal of approval to products (such as tea, coffee, and cocoa) to show that manufacturers have met certain criteria which ensure a better deal for poor producers.

Oxfam has direct experience of the poverty and suffering of small producers in Africa, Asia, and Latin America. Our overseas programme attempts to tackle some of these problems by supporting the self-empowerment of local communities. This experience has taught us that poverty can be effectively alleviated only if initiatives at grassroots level are complemented by policy change at the national and international level.

The fundamental changes that are required depend on political will in both the North and the South. Throughout the South, popular pressure for democratically accountable government is leading to change. This is beginning to shift the major obstacle to implementing development in which poor people themselves participate, and share decision-making. The need now is for governments in the South to prioritise poverty reduction when restructuring their economies. At the same time, the onus is on governments in the North to respond to the positive changes that are happening in the South. To preserve fragile democracies in the South, Northern governments must make a serious effort to redress the inequities in North/South economic relations. In this, public opinion is crucial, as is the power of Northern consumers to make fairer trade a reality.

RECOMMENDATIONS

Drawing on its 50 years of overseas experience, Oxfam concludes that there is a range of issues which must be seriously considered in order to create fairer trade and help poor producers in the South.

Governments in the South

Real progress could be made if governments of developing countries committed themselves to:

Reducing poverty and responding to popular demands for more democratic and accountable government by:

— Respecting human rights and giving the poor a greater say in their societies.

— Tackling the massive inequalities in the distribution of wealth, for example by implementing agrarian reform programmes designed to ensure more equitable access to land and other resources.

— Pursuing economic reform aimed at achieving socially and environmentally sustainable development.

— Meeting the basic needs of poor people for food, shelter, education, employment, and health care.

Assisting producers by:

— Encouraging the payment of reasonable wages.

— Improving prices paid to producers.

— Improving marketing and credit facilities.

Taking steps to promote self-sufficiency in food by:

— Supporting the production of basic food crops.

— Encouraging the marketing of locally produced agricultural products.

Adopting measures to control the supply of commodities, which would help to stabilise prices, by:

— Cooperating with other developing countries to manage and control the supply of commodities, for example by joining and adhering to the rules of International Commodity Agreements (as detailed in Chapter 4).

These recommendations, although fewer in number than those for governments in the North to consider, imply major structural change and redistribution of resources to ensure equity alongside economic growth.

Governments in the North

Governments of industrialised nations could commit themselves to:

Helping developing countries to achieve food security and sustainable development by:

— Unambiguously recognising their right to protect and stimulate agricultural production, in order to promote food self-sufficiency within the framework of the GATT (see Chapter 9). This right should not be restricted or undermined by other negotiations, for example by structural adjustment programmes.

— Ensuring that environmental costs are included in the pricing of products based on natural resources (see Chapter 9).

Securing and improving markets for developing-country exporters by:

— Preserving multilateralism in world trade (Chapters 9 and 10).

— Implementing policies designed to stop the dumping of subsidised agricultural exports on world markets in unfair competition with Third World produce. This would include measures such as phasing out the European Community's system of export subsidies (Chapters 8 and 9).

— Progressively removing tariff and non-tariff barriers on products from the South (see Chapter 8).

— Upgrading Generalised System of Preference schemes so that they are easier to use and their product range is extended to goods such as textiles, agricultural products, and minerals (see Chapter 9).

— Assisting those countries which suffer losses as a result of their agreement to end export 'dumping', remove tariff and non-tariff barriers, and up-grade GSP schemes. These include the poorer food-importing countries, which would face higher bills for food imports, and the ACP group of countries, which may suffer losses as a result of the erosion of their preferential status in the European market. In this respect the European Community has a special responsibility to the ACP group of countries (see Chapter 10). The EC could compensate these ACP countries in a number of ways, including:

– relaxing the Rules of Origin in the Lomé Agreement to assist the development of export-oriented manufacturing industries in the ACP countries (see Chapter 10);

– granting additional finance and encouraging investment to help the ACP countries either to be able to compete more effectively (through up-grading production, and improved marketing and infrastructural development), or to diversify into other areas of economic activity (see Chapter 10);

– setting up a new mechanism to monitor the 'trade diversion' effects of Europe's Single Market on developing countries, particularly the ACP countries (see Chapter 10); where such countries do lose markets, transitional arrangements should be made and aid granted to assist diversification and/or the up-grading of production;

– ending the Multi-Fibre Arrangement and ensuring that no further barriers are imposed on imports of textiles and clothing from the developing world. This will need to be accompanied by measures to assist the restructuring of textile industries in the North to alleviate the social costs incurred in the dismantling of the Multi-Fibre Arrangement (see Chapter 8).

Taking measures that will help to improve and stabilise international commodity prices by:

— Ensuring that funds are made available for the financing of buffer stocks for those commodities that are of most importance to developing countries, for example the ten 'core' commodities identified by UNCTAD in its Integrated Programme for Commodities (see Chapter 4).

— Substantially reducing the debt burden of developing countries, to alleviate the pressure on them to pay off their debts by increasing the supply of commodities (see Chapter 3). Debtor countries should not be expected to pay more to service their debts than they can afford without damaging their economic development. As a development of the British government's Trinidad Terms initiative, all creditor governments could agree to early implementation of significant debt reduction for the poorest, most indebted developing countries. Creditor governments, when requiring debtor nations to conform with structural adjustment programmes, should not insist on rigid adherence to IMF-approved schemes if the debtor nations can devise alternative programmes that prioritise social and environmental needs alongside economic growth. Similar terms for official debt reduction could be extended to other indebted Third World countries, together with more significant reduction of commercial debt, and action to ease the burden of debt service on loans from multilateral institutions.

— Reviewing World Bank and IMF policies designed to increase commodity exports as part of structural adjustment programmes. Great care needs to be taken to avoid planning for increased exports of products for which markets are already saturated (see Chapter 3).

— Strengthening the EC Stabex system by means of flexible additions to the fund when it is exhausted. The IMF compensation facility could be made more accessible to poorer developing countries by incorporating more flexible conditions for loans from the Fund (see Chapter 4).

— Making funds available to developing countries through the World Bank so that they can trade in futures (see Chapter 5).

Supporting developing countries in their efforts to diversify their exports by:

— Making funds available for diversification programmes in the South, for example through the second 'window' of the Common Fund. Priority should be given to those countries which are most highly dependent on a narrow range of primary commodities (see Chapter 4).

— Progressively removing escalating tariffs on tropical products, to encourage processing to take place in the producer countries themselves.

Supporting the creation of a new International Trade Organisation:

— Serious consideration could be given to the South's proposals for the establishment of a new International Trade Organisation, in which GATT and UNCTAD would merge, and in which broader economic considerations would be fully taken into account. A pre-condition for this merger would be that the current mandate of UNCTAD should form an integral part of the new organisation. In addition to those areas currently dealt with by GATT, the new ITO would have among its objectives the protection of the global environment, improved technology transfer to developing countries, and the control of transnational corporations (see Chapter 9).

Consumers in the North

Consumers in industrialised countries could help by:

Whenever possible buying products that are fairly traded, such as:

— those that carry a 'fair trade' seal of approval, such as the Max Havelaar stamp or the UK's Fairtrade Mark (see Chapter 14);

— products that are sold through alternative trading outlets, such as Oxfam shops (see Chapter 13).

CONCLUSION

These recommendations are indeed far-reaching, and will cost a great deal to implement, in both the North and the South. However, as the previous chapters show, they are underpinned by Oxfam's direct experience of working with poor producers in many parts of the developing world, and they reflect the magnitude and complexities of the problems that confront the poor. These recommendations are made as a contribution to a vital public debate, because – if they were implemented – they would, in our belief, benefit those communities which Oxfam exists to serve.

NOTES

CHAPTER 1

1 Interview with researcher Francis Rolt, Shinyanga, August 1988.

2 One kanga weighs about 225 gm, so accounting for a high wastage in ginning, spinning, and weaving, the 912 kg that she harvested that year would produce over 720 kangas.

3 *Africa's Commodity Problems: Towards a Solution*, a report by the United Nations Secretary General's Expert Group on Africa's Commodity Problems, UNCTAD/EDM/ATF/1, Table 2.

4 UNCTAD *Commodity Yearbook 1989*, Table 2.31.3, New York: United Nations, 1990.

5 *Africa's Commodity Problems*, op. cit.

6 While fuel exports are important to a few of the countries in which Oxfam works, analysis of the oil markets has been excluded from this study. The influences upon the supply and demand for oil are complex, and depend on factors which are, to a large extent, unique to the oil market. However, sudden price changes in the oil markets can have a profound impact on developing countries. The impact of the Gulf Crisis on Less Developed Countries was outlined in a report prepared for Oxfam by the Overseas Development Institute, London in February 1991. It shows how many poor countries were severely affected by the high oil prices that lasted from August 1990 to January 1991. Furthermore, there were several countries whose economies were hit by a combination of other associated events such as loss of remittances, loss of export markets, and loss of tourism revenues.

7 *The ACP – EC Courier*, No. 116, July–August 1989, p. 59.

8 A. Powell: 'Commodity and developing country terms of trade – what does the long run show?', *Economic Journal*, November 1991.

9 UNICEF: 'The Social Consequences of Adjustment and Dependency on Primary Commodities in sub-Saharan Africa', paper presented to the ACC Inter-Agency Expert Meeting on Commodities, organised by UNCTAD, 1–3 May 1989, Geneva.

10 *Primary Commodities – Market Developments and Outlook*, by the Commodities Division of the Research Department, International Monetary Fund, Washington DC, July 1990 (Appendix, Table 1).

11 Especially Raul Prebisch and Hans Singer, who developed the Prebisch-Singer hypothesis.

12 H.W. Singer: 'The relationship between debt pressures, adjustment policies and deterioration of terms of trade for developing countries (with special reference to Latin America)', *Working Paper Series No. 59*, The Hague: Institute of Social Studies.

13 UNCTAD: *The Least Developed Countries 1989 Report*, New York: United Nations, 1990.

14 These are Mauritania, Rwanda, Niger, Burundi, Uganda, Somalia, Malawi, Ethiopia, Burkina Faso, Sudan, Mali, Togo, Guinea Bissau, Mozambique, Chad, Sierra Leone, Gambia, Lesotho, Myanmar, Bangladesh, Nepal, Afghanistan,

Bhutan, Haiti, and Yemen Arab Republic. (ibid.)

15 ibid, p. 22.

16 World Bank: *Global Economic Prospects and the Developing Countries,* Washington DC: World Bank, 1991, p.12.

17 ibid.,p.10.

18 ibid., p.25.

19 ibid., p.15.

20 'A new world order', *The Economist,* 28 September–4 October 1991.

21 Annual Review of Cotton, 1987, Marketing Development Bureau, Dar Es Salaam.

22 Information on Tanzania's cotton industry provided by researcher Francis Rolt, Shinyanga, August 1988 and by Oxfam Country Representative for Tanzania, Alfred Sakafu, interviewed in Oxford, July 1991.

23 Oxfam Country Representative, Alfred Sakafu, June 1991, Oxford.

24 Economist Intelligence Unit: *Dominican Republic Country Profile 1988–89,* London: Business International.

25 Caribbean Tour Report, October/November 1987, by John Clark, Oxford: Oxfam.

26 Rufino Herrera, interviewed by the author, 22 October 1990, Oxford.

27 Rosalinda Pineda–Ofreneo: *The Philippines – Debt and Poverty,* Oxford: Oxfam, 1991.

28 See especially Oxfam projects PHL 137 – FESIN: Federation of Small Fisherfolk in Negros; PHL 124 – NAFCAR: National Coalition of Fisherfolks for Aquatic Reform; PHL 149 – National Consultative Assembly for Fisherfolk Empowerment.

CHAPTER 2

1 Research visit by the author, Siglo Veinte, March 1990.

2 John Crabtree *et al.*: *The Great Tin Crash – Bolivia and the World Market,* London: Latin America Bureau, 1987.

3 ibid., p.4.

4 Stefan Wagstyl: 'The crisis no one is ready to resolve', *Financial Times,* 1 November 1985.

5 Extract from a report written by Ken Duncan in application for the funding of Hospital Coposa, 14 June 1979. Filed under BOL 33, Volume II – Oxfam Archives.

6 Doña Zenobia Reynaga de Chavarria, interviewed by the author, Llallagua, Bolivia, March 1990.

7 Crabtree, op. cit, p.80.

8 Extract from Oxfam project file, BOL 88.

9 Economist Intelligence Unit: *Bolivia Country Profile 1991–92,* London: Business International.

10 ibid.

11 'Bolivia – where the nuts come from', *Financial Times,* 18 July 1991.

12 ibid.

13 Economist Intelligence Unit, op. cit.

14 'A war that is far from being won', *Financial Times,* 18 June 1991.

15 'Poverty thwarts drugs fight in Bolivia', *Financial Times,* 18 July 1991.

16 'US drug force faces inquiry in Bolivia', *The Independent*, 8 July 1991.

17 NACLA: 'Coca: the real green revolution', *NACLA Report on the Americas*, Vol. XXII No. 6, March 1989, page 26, New York: North American Congress on Latin America.

18 'Poverty thwarts drugs fight in Bolivia', *Financial Times*, 18 July 1991.

19 Interview with Jose Maria Herrera Penaloza of QUANA – Centro de Education Popular, Irupana, 16 March 1990.

20 In a meeting with members of ACCOPCA (Association Central de Comunidades Productores de Cafe), Coripata, 17 March 1990.

21 Interview with the author, Coripata, Bolivia, 17 March 1990.

22 Amando Supo, CORACA sub-manager for marketing, interviewed by the author, 17 March 1990, Irupani.

CHAPTER 3

1 UNCTAD: *Handbook of International Trade and Development Statistics, 1989*, New York: United Nations, 1990 (Table 3.2 – 1987).

2 See, for example, IMF Reports *Primary Commodities and Market Developments* for 1986, 1987, and 1988; and the ODI Briefing Paper 'Commodity Prices: Investing in Decline?', London: Overseas Development Institute, March 1988.

3 IMF: *International Financial Statistics – Supplement on Trade Statistics*, Washington DC: International Monetary Fund, 1988, p. XV.

4 IMF: *Primary Commodities – Market Developments and Outlook*, Washington DC: International Monetary Fund, 1986, p.6.

5 IMF: *IMF Survey*, Washington DC: International Monetary Fund, 29 April 1991.

6 'World recovery not assured', *Financial Times*, 11 June 1991.

7 John Peterson: 'International trade in services: the Uruguay Round and cultural and information services', National Westminster Bank, *Quarterly Review*, August 1989.

8 Statistics supplied by the Central Statistical Office, Newport, Gwent, August 1989.

9 Central Statistics Office, Dublin.

10 Central Statistical Office, Newport, Gwent.

11 UNCTAD: *Impact of Technological Change on Patterns of International Trade*, UNCTAD/ITP/16/TEC/3, New York: United Nations, 19 May 1989.

12 UNCTAD: 'Impact of New and Emerging Technologies on Trade and Development' (A Review of the UNCTAD Secretariat's Research Findings), TD/B/C.6/136, p.48, New York: United Nations, 1986.

13 Roskill: 'The Economics of Tin – 1990', sixth edition, London: Roskill Information Services, p. 245, Table 97.

14 ibid., p. 257.

15 UNCTAD 1986, op. cit., p.49.

16 Sartaj Aziz: 'Agricultural Policies for the 1990s', p.46, Paris: OECD, 1990.

17 IOCU Trade Kit: 'Facts sheet: The cost of protectionism', *The Consumer View on GATT and International Trade*, The Hague: IOCU, 1990.

18 M. Kelly *et al.*: 'Issues and Developments in International Trade Policy', Occasional Paper 63, Washington DC: International Monetary Fund, 1988, p.48. In 1986, total support for the dairy industry in the USA worked out at $1,400 per cow (based on August 1991 exchange rate: £1 = ECU 1.42, $1 = ECU 1.17).

19 UNCTAD: *Commodity Yearbook 1990*, Tables 2.9.3 and 2.9.4, New York: United Nations, 1990.

20 Kelly *et al.*, op. cit., p.47.

21 IMF: 'Primary Commodities – Market Developments and Outlook', Tables 43, 45, and 47, Washington DC: International Monetary Fund, 1989.

22 See, for example, the following Oxfam publications: 'Debt and Poverty in Jamaica' (Belinda Coote, 1985); *Zambia: Debt and Poverty* (John Clark, 1989); *The Philippines: Debt and Poverty* (Rosalinda Pineda–Ofreneo, 1991).

23 H.W. Singer: 'The relationship between debt pressures, adjustment policies and deterioration of terms of trade for developing countries (with special reference to Latin America)', *Working Paper Series No 59*, p.4, The Hague: Institute of Social Studies, 1989.

24 ibid, p.10.

25 ibid.

26 Commodities Division of the Research Department, IMF: 'Primary Commodities – Market Developments and Outlook', Table 54, p.78, Washington DC: International Monetary Fund.

27 The World Bank and UNDP: *Africa's Adjustment and Growth in the 1980s*, p.26, Washington DC: World Bank, 1989.

28 Belinda Coote: *The Hunger Crop – Poverty and the Sugar Industry*, pp. 72–6, Oxford: Oxfam, 1987.

29 *Biotechnology and Development Monitor* No. 2, March 1990, joint publication of the Directorate General International Cooperation of the Ministry of Foreign Affairs, The Hague, and the University of Amsterdam, The Netherlands.

30 'Coffee and biotechnology', *Biotechnology and Development Monitor*, No. 4, September 1990.

31 ODI, op. cit.

32 Belinda Coote, op. cit., 1987.

33 Martin W. Holgate *et al.*: 'Climate Change – Meeting the Challenge' (report by a Commonwealth group of experts), p.57, London: Commonwealth Secretariat, September 1989.

CHAPTER 4

1 Economist Intelligence Unit: *Cameroon, Central African Republic, Chad Country Profile 1990–91*, London: Business International Ltd., 1991.

2 Guy de Lusignan: *French-Speaking Africa Since Independence*, London: Pall Mall Press, 1969.

3 Economist Intelligence Unit, op. cit.

4 From case studies prepared by Sarah Westcott, Oxfam Country Representative for Chad, March 1989.

5 Oxfam Project Chad 054 – Savings and Credit Cooperatives, 'CREC'.

6 Based on the conversion rate in June 1991: £1.00 = CFA fr 503.80.

7 Sarah Westcott, op. cit.

8 Fiona Gordon-Ashworth: *International Commodity Control*, London and Canberra: Croom Helm, 1984, p.88.

9 Jock Finlayson and Mark Zacher: *Managing International Markets*, New York: Colombia University Press, 1988, p.285.

10 ibid., p.284.

11 John Jackson: *Restructuring the GATT System*, London: Pinter, 1990, p. 10.

12 Finlayson and Zacher, op.cit.,p.140.

13 Gordon-Ashworth, op. cit., p.82.

14 International Cocoa Agreement, 1986 (as extended), October 1990, Chapter XV, Article 64. International Cocoa Council.

15 Finlayson and Zacher, op. cit., p.31.

16 ibid., pp. 33–7.

17 Gordon-Ashworth, op. cit., p.40.

18 ibid., p.42.

19 ibid, pp. 42–3.

20 The 18 commodities covered by the Integrated Programme are: bananas, cocoa, coffee, cotton and cotton yarn, hard fibres and products, jute and jute manufactures, bovine meat, rubber, sugar, tea, tropical timber, vegetable oils and oilseeds, bauxite, copper, iron ore, manganese, phosphates, and tin. Of these, the ten 'core' commodities, which are mainly exported by developing countries, are cocoa, coffee, cotton and cotton yarn, hard fibres and products, jute and jute manufactures, rubber, sugar, tea, copper, and tin.

21 IMF: *Primary Commodities – Market Developments and Outlook*, Washington DC: International Monetary Fund, 1990.

22 C.L. Gilbert: 'International commodity agreements: design and performance', *World Development*, Vol. 15 No. 5, May 1987.

23 ibid.

24 ibid.

25 Gordon-Ashworth, op. cit., p.45.

26 *UNCTAD Bulletin* No 254, July to August 1989.

27 Information supplied by the United Nations Non-Government Liaison Service, Geneva, August 1991.

28 ibid.

29 Finlayson and Zacher, op. cit., p. 67.

30 A.P. Hewitt: 'Stabex and commodity export compensation schemes: prospects for globalization', *World Development*, Vol. 15 No. 5, May 1987.

31 Pownell and Stuart: 'The IMF's compensatory and contingency financing facility', *Finance and Development*, December 1988.

32 Article 186 of the Fourth ACP–EC Convention, signed in Lomé on 15 December 1989.

33 ibid.

34 Hewitt, op. cit.

35 Data provided by the Department of Trade and Industry, August 1991.

36 Independent Group on British Aid: *Real Aid: What Europe Can Do*, London: IGBA, 1990.

37 Information supplied by the Overseas Development Administration, August 1991.

38 'UK Policy on Compensatory Financing', paper provided by the Overseas Development Administration, London, August 1991.

39 ibid.

40 Information supplied by the Department of Trade and Industry, August 1991.

41 Finlayson and Zacher, op. cit., pp. 235–41.

42 Information supplied by the Department of Trade and Industry, August 1991.

CHAPTER 5

1 Clairmonte and Cavanagh: *Merchants of Drink: Transnational Control of World Beverages*, Penang: Third World Network, 1988, p.72.

2 R.M. Eldridge and R. Maltby: 'On the Existence and Implied Cost of Carry in a Medieval English Forward/Futures Market', University of Leeds.

3 Strictly, it is with a forward contract that no financial flows take place. As is shown later, futures contracts do imply some financial flows at the time of the transaction.

4 *The Concise Oxford Dictionary*, seventh edition, Oxford: Oxford University Press, 1982.

5 From Fact Sheets provided by London Fox and the London Metal Exchange.

6 Extract from 'The tin men', by Alan Rusbridger, *The Guardian*, 12 March, 1986 (reprinted with permission).

7 A. Powell: 'The management of risk in developing country finance', *Oxford Review of Economic Policy*, Vol. V No. 4, Winter 1989, pp. 69–87.

CHAPTER 6

1 *UNCTAD Commodity Yearbook 1989*, New York: United Nations, 1990, Table 2.13.3, p. 169.

2 ibid; and *UNCTAD Statistical Pocketbook*, New York: United Nations, 1984 and 1989.

3 H. Hobhouse: *Seeds of Change: Five Plants that Transformed Mankind*, London: Sidgewick and Jackson, 1985, p.94.

4 International Tea Committee: Annual Bulletin of Statistics, 1988, Table G2, 1984 to 1986. (Figures calculated on the committee's estimate that 1lb of tea constitutes 200–240 cups.)

5 Per capita consumption has declined from a peak of 4.50 kg in 1961 to 2.77 kg in 1984–86, according to *Primary Commodities: Market Developments and Outlook*, by the Commodities Division of the Research Department, International Monetary Fund, Washington DC, July 1989, p.62.

6 'Keynote Report on Hot Drinks', fourth edition, 1988.

7 Research Department, IMF, op. cit., p. 62.

8 International Tea Committee, op. cit., Tables D12 (p.72) and D2 (p. 64).

9 *The Grocer*, 20 July 1991, p.31.

10 Commonwealth Development Corporation Report and Accounts, Project Report, 1986.

11 M. Vije: *Where Serfdom Thrives: The Plantation Tamils of Sri Lanka*, Madras: TIRU, 1987, p.43.

12 Oxfam project Sri Lanka 048.

13 Edinburgh World Development Movement: *Unacceptable Faces of Tea: James Finlay of Glasgow*, 1983.

14 Anwarullah Chowdhury: 'Women Tea Workers in Bangladesh: A Study of Plantation Women Workers of Sylhet', Lecture Series 3, November 1988, Bangladesh: Centre for Women and Development.

15 ibid.

16 In a letter to the author from R.J.K. Muir, Chairman, James Finlay plc, Glasgow, 20 September 1991.

17 P. Roussos: *Zimbabwe: An Introduction to the Economics of Transformation*,

Harare: Baobab Books, 1988, p.172.

18 Roy Trivedy: *Oxfam Action Research Programme, Mulanje, 1987–88*, Oxford: Oxfam, 1990.

19 Project reference: Malawi 072, 'Mulanje Rural Development Programme'.

20 Research Department, IMF, op. cit.

21 ibid.

22 These are Thompson, Lloyd and Ewart; Geo. White and Co; Wilson Smithett and Co; and Haines and Co (London) Ltd. Haines is owned by a subsidiary of Brooke Bond, adding to Brooke Bond's vertical integration into the industry.

23 UNCTAD: *Studies in the Processing, Marketing and Distribution of Commodities*, New York: United Nations, 1984, pp.8–9.

24 Based on a visit to the London Tea Auction in Sir John Lyon House, 2 May 1989.

25 UNCTAD: *Studies in the Processing, Marketing and Distribution of Commodities*, New York: United Nations, 1984, p.12.

26 International Tea Committee, op. cit., pp.60–61.

27 *Financial Times*, 16 October 1984.

28 *The Guardian*, 27 September 1989.

29 *The Telegraph*, 3 October 1989.

30 Hillsdown Holdings plc: Group Profile, 1989.

31 The World Development Movement: *The Tea Trade*, London: WDM, 1979.

32 *The Financial Times*, 20 April 1989.

33 ibid.

34 ibid.

35 Information supplied by the Cooperative Wholesale Society, 14 February 1990.

36 According to Lyons Tetley Market Research Executive, Heather Alderton, in conversation with the author on 14 February 1990.

37 Taken from the 'Student's Broadsheet', produced by The Tea Council, Sir John Lyon House, 5 High Timber Street, London EC4V 3NJ (undated).

38 *The Grocer*, 3 August 1991, p. 6.

39 The Tea Council, op. cit.

40 *The Grocer*, price supplement 1 April 1989.

41 *The Financial Times*, 20 April 1989.

42 With the exception of Brooke Bond Foods, which do not pack any 'own–label' teas, according to Unilever Public Affairs Manager, Chris Bunting in a letter to Oxfam, 17 October 1991.

43 According to D. Pogson, blender packager, Northern Tea Merchants, Chesterfield, interviewed by Duncan Brewer, 19 April 1989.

44 *New Internationalist*, June 1987.

45 'Teatime in Turkey', *Unilever Magazine* No 61, Issue 3, 1986.

46 ibid.

47 International Tea Committee, op. cit.

48 *The Grocer*, price supplement, 1 April 1989, p.68.

49 ibid.

50 In a letter to Oxfam, Unilever, parent company of Brooke Bond, states that 'The overall assumption behind the (Chapter) is the link between poorly paid plantation workers and a highly profitable end product; the implication is that the profit is at the expense of the plantation worker. In fact, the wages of the tea estate workers compare well with those of other agricultural workers in producing countries. In countries where Brooke Bond Group owns, or part owns, tea estates, levels of pay are agreed either between unions and employers (usually with some Government involvement) or they are decided by Government directive. All Brooke Bond tea estate workers are paid these wages and they also benefit in a number of other ways. The introduction of new plucking methods has resulted in additional earning capacity for the pluckers themselves. The (Chapter) also fails to reflect the fact that Brooke Bond Group supplies a range of benefits including education and medical facilities for all its estate workers.' (17 October 1991).

51 Information supplied by Jo Feingold, ex–Secretary General of the International Federation of Agricultural Producers.

52 R.J.K. Muir, op. cit.

CHAPTER 7

1 Philippines Coconut Authority: *Spectrum of Coconut Products*, Quezon City: PCA, undated.

2 Unilever: 'Vegetable Oils and Fats', educational booklet, 1975.

3 *La Lettre de Solagral*, No. 67, Paris: February 1988, pp.8–17.

4 Overseas Development Institute: *Commodity Prices: Investing in Decline?*, London: ODI, 1988.

5 *FAO Trade Yearbook – 1988*, Volume 42, Rome: Food and Agriculture Organisation, 1990.

6 Economist Intelligence Unit: *Philippines Country Profile 1990–91*, London: Business International Ltd.

7 ibid.

8 Based on the average conversion rate for 1987 of pesos 33.71 = £1.00.

9 At the time that this research was carried out (February/March 1987), the minimum daily non–agricultural wage was pesos 37. The minimum daily agricultural wage would have been a few pesos less than this.

10 Department of Agrarian Reform, cited in *Land Reform in the Philippines*, Metro Manila: IBON Databank Philippines, Inc., 1988, p.166.

11 IBON: *IBON Facts and Figures 1988*, Metro Manila: IBON Databank Philippines.

12 Research carried out by Adrian Moyes for Oxfam, February/March 1987.

13 Based on the average peso–sterling conversion rate for the first half of 1991 of pesos 45 to £1.00.

14 Information supplied by Community Crafts Abroad of the Philippines, August 1991.

15 *Philippine Daily Inquirer*, 25 June 1991.

16 United Coconut Association of the Philippines: *UCAP Annual Statistics 1988*, Metro Manila: UCAP, pp.2–25.

17 G. Hawes: *The Philippine State and the Marcos Regime – the Politics of Export*, Ithaca and London: Cornell University Press, 1987, p.57.

18 Research conducted by Adrian Moyes for Oxfam, 1987.

19 United Coconut Association of the Philippines: *Coconut Statistics 1987*, Vol. VI, No. 21, Metro Manila: UCAP, p.107.

20 FAO op. cit., Table 126.

21 Geoffrey Bastin: 'The CAP and the oilseeds economies of the developing countries', in *The CAP and the Third World*, London: Catholic Institute for International Relations, 1986.
22 Unilever Report and Accounts, 1989.
23 *The Financial Times*, 7 March 1991.
24 Rhys Jenkins: *Transnational Corporations and Uneven Development*, London and New York: Methuen, 1987.
25 'Europe's top 500 companies', *The Financial Times*, 11 January 1991.
26 Unilever Annual Accounts, 1989.
27 Figures from Unilever's Annual Report for 1988 and UNCTAD *Handbook of International Trade Statistics 1989*, New York: United Nations, 1990, Table 6.4, calculated on the following rates of exchange relative to £1.00 sterling: Philippines: peso 45; Chad: CFA franc 503; Tanzania: shilling 178.
28 Prediction made by brokers Smith New Court (*Evening Standard*, 2 November 1990).

CHAPTER 8

1 Kirkpatrick Sale: *The Conquest of Paradise*, London: Hodder and Stoughton, 1991, p.124.
2 *The Economist*, 6 July, 1991.
3 Comite para la Defensa de los Barriales (COPADEBA), Oxfam project DMR 036.
4 The term 'Third World' was first used by the French economist Alfred Savry in 1953.
5 UNCTAD: *Uruguay Round – Papers on Selected Issues*, New York: United Nations, 1989, Table 4, p. 349.
6 Economist Intelligence Unit: *Bangladesh Country Profile 1989–90*, London: Business International Ltd.
7 'World trade survey', *The Economist*, 22 September 1990.
8 UNCTAD, op. cit., p.221.
9 Clive Robinson: *Hungry Farmers – World Food Needs and Europe's Response*, London: Christian Aid, 1989, p.27.
10 Discussion Paper 90.6: 'Proposed Strategies for Reducing Agricultural Protection in the GATT Uruguay Round', Canberra: Australian Bureau of Agricultural and Resource Economics.
11 UCAP: 'The Fight of the Philippine Coconut Industry in the US', Manila: United Coconut Association of the Philippines, September 1989.
12 B. Ross: 'The Coconut Industry: An Appropriate Tool for Development in the Philippines?', unpublished MA thesis, 1990, p.28.
13 UCAP: 'Tropical Oils Issue – a Special Report', *Coconuts Today*, Manila: United Coconut Association of the Philippines, 1988, p.8.
14 ibid.
15 UCAP: 'The Fight of the Philippines Coconut Industry in the US', Manila: United Coconut Association of the Philippines, September 1989.
16 UCAP: *Coconut Statistics 1987*, Vol. VI No. 21, Manila: The United Coconut Association of the Philippines, October 1988, pp.1–40.
17 UCAP: *Coconut Industry Kit*, Manila: UCAP Research, June 1989.
18 UCAP: *Coconut Statistics 1987*, Vol. VI No. 21, Manila: The United Coconut

Association of the Philippines, October 1988.
19 *Bantaaw – Economic and Social Indicators of Mindanao*, Vol. 11, No. 3, Davao City, The Philippines.
20 *The Financial Times*, 7 March 1991.
21 European Parliament Working Document A2–205/86, 19 January 1987, drawn up by the Committee on Development and Cooperation on the Community's relations with developing countries with regard to trade and raw materials.
22 The World Bank: *World Development Report 1989*, Oxford: Oxford University Press, 1989, p.15.
23 N. Hopkinson: *The Uruguay Round and Prospects for World Trade*, Wilton Park Papers 21, London: HMSO, 1989.

CHAPTER 9

1 In a model of comparative advantage it does not matter if country A is more efficient at producing all the same products that country B produces. However, it will optimise its economic efficiency by concentrating its productive resources in those sectors where it enjoys the greatest advantage (or least disadvantage).
2 RONGEAD: *GATT Briefing* No 1, June 1990, Lyon: RONGEAD.
3 *Southern African Economist*, February/March 1991.
4 M.J. Finger and A. Olechowski: *The Uruguay Round – A Handbook on the Multilateral Trade Negotiations*, Washington DC: The World Bank, 1987, p.101.
5 Fiona Gordon-Ashworth: *International Commodity Control*, London: Croom Helm, 1984, p.40.
6 Craig MacPhee: 'A Synthesis of the GSP Study Programme', UNCTAD/ITP/19, New York: United Nations, 5 December 1989, para 13.
7 D.K. Brown: 'Trade preferences for developing countries: a survey of results', *The Journal of Development Studies*, Vol. 24 No. 3, p. 347.
8 MacPhee, op. cit., Table 1.
9 ibid. paras 58 and 59.
10 Brown, op. cit., p.350.
11 Lucy Kellaway: 'EC plans better deal for world poor', *The Financial Times*, 25 July 1990.
12 Speaking at a Conference organised by Novib and the Third World Network: 'GATT, Uruguay Round and Development', The Hague, June 1990.
13 John Jackson: *Restructuring the GATT System*, London: Pinter, 1990, p. 38.
14 N. Hopkinson: *The Uruguay Round and Prospects for World Trade*, Wilton Park Papers 21, London: HMSO, 1989.
15 ibid.
16 UNCTAD: *Uruguay Round – Papers on Selected Issues*, New York: United Nations, 1989, p.66.
17 World Bank: *Global Economic Prospects and the Developing Countries 1991*, Washington DC: World Bank, 1991, p.10.
18 Hopkinson, op. cit.
19 ibid.
20 RONGEAD: *GATT Briefing – On Trade-Related Aspects of Intellectual Property Rights* No. 2, July 1990, Lyon: RONGEAD.
21 H. Hobbelink: *Biotechnology and the Future of World Agriculture*, London: Zed

Books, 1991, p.109.

22 C. Raghavan: *Recolonization – GATT, the Uruguay Round and the Third World*, London: Zed Books, 1990, p.87.

23 Hopkinson, op. cit.

24 Within the GATT 'agricultural products' are defined as those products which do not fall within the remit of the negotiating groups on Tropical Products and Natural Resource-Based Products. They are cereals, meat, dairy products, oilseeds/vegetable oils (non–tropical), and sugar. In terms of value, these products account for the bulk of world trade in agricultural products.

25 Kevin Watkins: 'Changing the rules: the GATT farm trade reform and world food security', *GATT Briefing – On Agriculture, Food Security and the Uruguay Round*, No. 4, November 1990, Lyon: RONGEAD.

26 The Cairns Group consists of Argentina, Australia, Brazil, Canada, Chile, Colombia, Fiji, Hungary, Indonesia, Malaysia, New Zealand, the Philippines, Thailand, and Uruguay.

27 'An Integrated Approach to Food Security', prepared by the Food Matters Working Group of the Liaison Committee of Development NGOs to the European Community, adopted February 1991.

28 *The Guardian*, 13 December 1990.

29 Steven Shrybman: 'International Trade and the Environment', Canadian Environmental Law Association, 1989 (unpublished).

30 J. Davidson and D. Myers, with Manab Chakraborty: *No Time to Waste: Poverty and the Environment*, Oxford: Oxfam, forthcoming (April 1992).

31 Kevin Watkins, *The Guardian*, 11 January 1991.

32 GATT Focus, GATT Information Bulletin, December 1990.

33 John Vidal, *The Guardian*, 6 September 1991.

34 HIVOS, NCOS, NIO, Novib: 'The South on the World Market: Preconditions for Sustainable International Trade', The Hague, 1991.

CHAPTER 10

1 Field research by Anna Feuchtwang in the Windward Islands in 1989.

2 Robert Thomson: *Green Gold – Bananas and Dependency in the Eastern Caribbean*, London: Latin America Bureau, 1987.

3 B. Borrell and M–C. Yang: *EC Bananarama 1992*, Working Paper on International Trade WPS 523, Table 2, Washington DC: World Bank, 1990.

4 *The ACP–EC Courier*, No. 120, March–April 1990.

5 Shridath Ramphal: 'Rekindling the spirit of Lomé', *Lomé Briefing* No. 1, Brussels: Liaison Committee of Development NGOs to the European Communities, 1983.

6 *The ACP–EC Courier*, No. 120, March–April 1990.

7 K. Watkins: 'Africa and the European Community: The Lomé Convention', in *Africa South of the Sahara – 1990*, London: Europa.

8 H.E. Leslie Armon–Wilson, Jamaican Ambassador to the EC and ACP member of the Lomé IV negotiating team, speaking at a media briefing sponsored by the World Development Movement, held at the London School of Economics on 19 May 1989.

9 *The Financial Times*, 21 July 1989.

10 Drusilla Brown: 'Trade preferences for developing countries: a survey of results', *The Journal of Development Studies*, Vol. 24 No. 3, 1987, p.344.

11 Belinda Coote: *The Hunger Crop – Poverty and the Sugar Industry*, Oxford: Oxfam, 1987, p.61.

12 Watkins, op. cit.

13 Borrell and Yang, op. cit.

14 M. Davenport: *Europe: 1992 and the Developing World*, London: Overseas Development Institute, 1991, p.1.

15 E. Mayo, 'Beyond 1992', Occasional Paper 1, London: The World Development Movement, 1989.

16 Borrell and Yang, op. cit.

17 Recorded in *Hansard*, 30 April 1991, p.171.

18 Davenport, op. cit.

19 Borrell and Yang, op. cit.

20 Oxfam project STV 505.

21 Information supplied by Oxfam Desk Officer for the Caribbean, Charmaine Arbouin.

22 L.J. Emmerij: 'Europe 1992 and developing countries', *Journal of Common Market Studies*, Vol. XXIX, No. 2.

23 Paolo Cecchini: *The European Challenge: 1992*, London: Gower, 1988.

24 C. Stevens: 'The impact of Europe 1992 on the South', *IDS Bulletin*, Vol. 21 No. 1, University of Sussex: IDS Publications Unit, January 1990.

25 Emmerij, op. cit.

26 *The Developing Countries and 1992*, ODI Briefing Paper, London: Overseas Development Institute, November 1989.

27 Davenport, op. cit., p.60.

28 Emmerij, op. cit.

29 Davenport, op. cit., p.61

30 For example, A. Koekkoek, A. Kuyvenhoven, and W. Molle: 'Europe 1992 and Developing Countries', *Journal of Common Market Studies*, Vol. XXIX, No. 2, December 1990.

31 For example, Emmerij, op. cit.

32 *Wall Street Journal*, 27 September 1989.

33 W. Orme: 'The Sunbelt Moves South', New York: North American Congress on Latin America, May 1991.

34 *Herald Tribune*, 12 November 1991.

35 *The Financial Times*, 3 June 1991.

36 N. Harris: 'Mexico and North American free trade', *Development Policy Review*, Vol.9 No.3, September 1991, London: Overseas Development Institute.

37 *The New York Times*, 14 April 1991.

38 *The Financial Times*, 17 May, 1991.

39 *Wall Street Journal*, 27 September 1989.

40 *The Financial Times*, 17 May 1991.

41 *The Financial Times*, 14 June 1991.

42 World Development Movement: *Spur*, February 1991.

43 *The Financial Times*, 3 July 1991.

44 Orme, op. cit.

45 *The Financial Times*, 30 January 1991.

46 *The Financial Times*, 6 January 1991.

47 *The Financial Times*, 31 July 1991.

CHAPTER 11

1   World Commission on Environment and Development: *Our Common Future*, Oxford: Oxford University Press, 1987.

2   World Bank: *World Development Report 1990*, Oxford: Oxford University Press, Table 1, 1990.

3   Richard Harthill, Oxfam Country Representative in Chile, March 1990.

4   Raul Prebisch: *The Economic Development of Latin America and its Principal Problems*, New York: United Nations, 1950.

5   J. Gatica Barrios: *De–industrialisation in Chile*, London: Westview Special Studies on Latin America and the Caribbean, 1989.

6   World Bank: *World Development Report 1987*, Oxford: Oxford University Press, 1987, pp.87–91.

7   Gatica Barrios, op. cit.

8   Economist Intelligence Unit: *Chile Country Profile 1990–91*, London: Business International.

9   Rudolfo Contreras: *Mas alla del Bosque – la exploitacion forestal en Chile Amerinda*, Santiago, 1989, p. 53.

10 *The Financial Times*, 29 June 1989.

11 Maria Helena Hurtado: 'Careless harvest', *South*, May 1990.

12 *The Financial Times*, 29 June 1989.

13 Hurtado, op. cit.

14 Department of Trade and Industry: Overseas Trade Statistics of the UK, 1988.

15 A. Araya: 'Ese Mar que Tranquilo se Vende', *Informa CODEFF*, July 1989; J. Echenique: 'El Sector Agrario en la Perspectiva Democratica', *Estudios Agrarios Boletin* 24, August 1989, GEA, Universidad Academia de Humanismo Cristiano.

16 Extracts from tour report of Oxfam worker, Sharon Thompson, March 1990.

17 Echenique, op. cit.

18 J.C. Cardenas: 'Pesqueria Chilena y Desarrollo Democratico', preliminary paper for Comite Nacional Pro Defensa de la Fauna y Flora (CODEFF), Chile.

19 D. Hojman: *Neo–liberal Agriculture in Rural Chile*, Basingstoke: Macmillan, 1990, p. 4.

20 Echenique, op. cit.

21 *Anuarios de Atenciones y Recorsos 1975–1989*, Estadisticas e Indicadores de Atenciones Dpto Coordinacion e Informatica, Ministerio de Salud, Chile.

22 S. Valiente, F. Monckeberg, and N. Gonzalez: 'The Political Economy of Nutrition in Chile', Instituto de Nutricion y Tecnologia de los Alimentos, Universidad de Chile, Serie Sisvan Inta 34/85; R. Contreras, S. Duhart, M. Echeverria and H. Lopez: 'Salud Publica, Privada y Solidaria en el Chile Actual', *Documento de Trabajo* no. 44, July 1986, Programa de Economia del Trabajo Academia de Humanismo Cristiano.

23 Economist Intelligence Unit: *Chile Country Profile 1989–90*, London: Business International, p.13.

24 Figures supplied by GEA (Grupo de Estudios Agro–Regionales), Santiago, interviewed on 26 March 1990.

25 Field research by author, March 1990.

26 Direccion General de Territorio Maritimo y de Marina Mercante, quoted in *Quepuca*, December 1988, magazine of OPDEC (Oxfam project Chile 661).

27 Carlos Lopez L., trade union leader, interviewed by Iain Gray in Concepcion, 28 March 1990.

28 Figures supplied by Oxfam project partner Centro de Estudios Sociales, Santiago, in interview with Sharon Thompson, 19 March 1990.

29 Information from Oxfam Project Summary Application Form for CHI 627 B9 (Instituto de Capacitacion y Apoyo Rural).

30 Union officials interviewed by Sharon Thompson in Concepcion, March 1990.

31 Economist Intelligence Unit, op. cit., 1989–90.

32 Contreras, op. cit., p.50.

33 For example: CHI 101 – Servicio de Estudios Regionales; CHI 628 – Aurora; CHI 675 – Comite Nacional pro Defensa de la Fauna y Flora.

34 *South*, May 1990.

35 ibid.

36 Oxfam project CHI 628 – Aurora (1990), 'Antecedentes Generales del Sector Forestal Xa Region, Puerto Montt'.

37 Iain Gray: Oxfam staff tour report, March 1990.

38 CODEFF Magazine, July 1989.

39 Study by CODEFF (Oxfam Project CHI 675) in the Province of Bio Bio, 1983.

40 Rudolfo Contreras, interviewed by Iain Gray on 28 March 1990, Concepcion.

41 Ernst Hajek: 'Problemas Ambientales de Chile', AID and Universidad Catolica de Chile.

42 Processing plant worker interviewed by Iain Gray and Sharon Thompson, Talcahuano, 27 March 1990.

43 President of the Fishermen's Crew Union, Talcahuano, interviewed by Sharon Thompson and Iain Gray, 28 March 1990.

44 Bernard Carillo, president of the Federacion de Trabajadores de la Industria Pesquera de la Zona Sur de Chile, interviewed in March 1990.

45 Anuarios del Servicio Nacional de Pesca, Ministerio de Economia.

46 Cardenas, op. cit.

47 ibid.

48 President of the Fishermen's Crew Union, Talcahuano, interviewed by Sharon Thompson and Iain Gray, 28 March 1990.

49 Information supplied by Oxfam project partner, Agra (CHI 093), in interview with the author, 28 March 1990, Santiago.

50 The nine are Folidol, Pentaclorofenol, Paraquat, Lindane, Aldrin, Deildrin, Heptachlor, DDT, and Endrin ('La Docena Maldita', *Hoja de Divulgacion*, Santiago: AGRA, 1987).

51 Juan Manza Guilano: 'Las Plaguicidas: Una Dependencia Peligrosa', *Documento de Trabajo* No 4, Santiago: AGRA.

52 D. Bull: *A Growing Problem – Pesticides and the Third World Poor*, Oxford: Oxfam, 1982.

53 CHI 093: Agra Limitada, Santiago.

54 *Fortin Mapocho*, Mapucho, 29 January 1988.

55 *Las Ultimas Noticias*, 5 February 1988.

56 *La Tercera*, 26 January 1989.

57 Marion Moses: 'Pesticide-related health problems and farmworkers', *The Pesticide Handbook*, (eds. Sarojini Rengaru and Karen Snyder), 1991.

58 ibid.

59 *The FAO Code: Missing Ingredients*, Pesticide Action Network International, 1989.

60 *New Scientist*, 24 February 1990.

61 *La Epoca*, 5 April 1989.

62 Bull, op. cit.

63 According to Oxfam project partner, ICAR.

64 Cardenas, op. cit.

65 'Consideraciones para una politica forestal en el gobierno de transicion 1990–1994', CODEFF Documentos Serie Forestal 89/11.

66 J.G. Morales: 'El Estado y el Sector Privado en la Industria Forestal', Grupo de Estudios Agro–Regionales, *Boletin* 24, August 1989.

67 Giuliano Manza, op. cit.

68 Hojman, op. cit.

CHAPTER 12

1 United Nations Secretary General's Expert Group on Africa's Commodity Problems: *Africa's Commodity Problems: Towards a Solution*, UNCTAD/EDM/ATF/1, Geneva: UNCTAD, p.70.

2 Oxfam project number Bangladesh 204.

3 Interviewed by Jim Monan in Notun Bazaar, Khulna, April 1989.

4 *Agricultural Information Development Bulletin*, United Nations ESCAP, September 1989, Vol. 11, No. 3, p.18.

5 *New Scientist*, 13 April 1991.

6 UK Department of Trade and Industry Statistics: 1988 UK imports and exports.

7 *The Financial Times*, 15 January 1988.

8 *Environmental Country Strategy Bangladesh*, Danida, December 1988.

9 Interview by Jim Monan with shrimp cooperative, Khulna, April 1989.

10 Government of Bangladesh: *Bangladesh Economic Survey 1988*, Dhaka: Ministry of Finance.

11 Economist Intelligence Unit: *Bangladesh Country Profile 1990–91*, London: Business International, p.8.

12 UNCTAD: *Commodity Yearbook 1990*, New York: United Nations, table 2.32.3.

13 *The Financial Times*, 26 March 1991.

14 Paul Handley: 'Cultured revolution', *Far Eastern Economic Review*, 5 October 1989 (based on figures supplied by the Food and Agriculture Organisation).

15 ibid.

16 ibid.

17 Figures supplied by researcher, Jim Monan, in consultation with the shrimp cooperative, Khulna, April 1989.

18 Interviewed by Jim Monan in Notun Bazaar, Khulna, April 1989.

19 *Far Eastern Economic Review*, 5 October 1989, p.99.

20 From interviews by Jim Monan with fieldworkers of Gono Shahajja Sangstha, April 1989. (Oxfam project Bangladesh 204)

21 Jim Monan: *Bangladesh – The Strength to Succeed*, Oxford: Oxfam, 1990, p.36.

22 Interview by Jim Monan with GSS, Khulna, April 1989.

23 Village interview, South Khulna, by Jim Monan, April 1989.

24 *Far Eastern Economic Review*, 5 October 1989.

25 World Bank: 'Bangladesh Shrimp Culture Project', unpublished report, 1985.

CHAPTER 13

1   Ben Whitaker: *A Bridge of People*, London: Heinemann, 1983, p. 145.

2   Oxfam Trading consists of two parts: trading activities to raise funds for Oxfam's general relief and development work, and 'Bridge', which is an Alternative Trading Organisation. Hence the use of the term 'Bridge', rather than 'Oxfam Trading', throughout this chapter.

3   Bridge policy document, 10 April 1989.

4   Richard Adams: *Who Profits?*, London: Lion, 1989, p.25.

5   Frank Judd (Oxfam Director): 'Notes on a Visit to Bangladesh – 8–15 September 1989'.

6   Ro Cole: memo to Jim Monan, 15 May 1989, Dhaka.

7   Adapted from 'The Living Conditions of Kazuli and a Typical Day in her Life (A Village Producer of CORR–The Jute Works)', unaccredited in Oxfam files.

8   Interview with the author, El Ceibo, Sapecho, 15 March 1990.

9   Author's interview with four El Ceibo administrative members, Sapecho, 15 March 1990.

10   Author's interview with Pedro Bernabe Choque, Sapecho, 15 March 1990.

11   Author's interview with Pascual Quispe Sarco, Vice–President of El Ceibo, and other members of the El Ceibo cooperative, 22 March 1990, El Alto, La Paz.

12   *UNCTAD Commodity Yearbook – 1990*, New York: United Nations.

13   HMV is a substance produced from enzyme activity. EC law allows 40 parts per million. When honey is exposed to heat, the HMV content will rise. If it exceeds the permitted HMV level, it can be sold as a food–manufacturing ingredient, but with difficulty.

14   The four are Oxfam Trading, Twin Trading, Traidcraft, and Equal Exchange.

15   Estimate provided by Bridge staff, September 1991.

16   Tate and Lyle, 1991 interim report.

17   Paper presented at the EUROSTEP meeting by the Max Havelaar Foundation, 30 May 1991, The Hague.

CHAPTER 14

1   Taken from 'The Fairtrade Mark Presentation', a paper prepared by Martin Newman, marketing consultant to the Fairtrade Mark.

2   'Foreseen Developments of the Max Havelaar Initiative on the European Market', Utrecht: Stichting Max Havelaar, 13 May 1991.

3   Rufino Herrera, General Secretary for the Association of Coffee Producers, interviewed by the author on 22 October 1990, Oxford.

4   Paper presented by Max Havelaar Foundation at EUROSTEP meeting, 30 May 1991, The Hague.

5   From 'Moving Ahead', a paper written by the Fairtrade Mark Steering Group, April 1991.

6   The Fair Trade Foundation background information for companies, September 1991.

FURTHER READING

Richard Adams, Jane Carruthers, and Sean Hamil: *Changing Corporate Values – A Guide to Social and Environmental Policy and Practice in Britain's Top Companies*, London: Kogan Page, 1991.

Michael Barratt Brown: *Fair Trade: A Better Deal in the North-South Marketplace*, London: Zed Books (forthcoming).

David Bull: *A Growing Problem – Pesticides and the Third World Poor*, Oxford: Oxfam, 1982.

Frederick Clairmonte and John Cavanagh: *Merchants of Drink – Transnational Control of World Beverages*, Penang: Third World Network, 1988.

Belinda Coote: *The Hunger Crop – Poverty and the Sugar Industry*, Oxford: Oxfam, 1987.

HIVOS/NCOS/NIO/Novib: *The South on the World Market – Preconditions for Sustainable International Trade*, published jointly by HIVOS, NCOS, NIO and Novib, available from Novib, Amaliastraat 7, 2514 JC The Hague, The Netherlands.

Henk Hobbelink: *Biotechnology and the Future of World Agriculture*, London: Zed Books, 1991.

Ben Jackson: *Poverty and the Planet – A Question of Survival*, London: Penguin, 1990.

Rosalinda Pineda–Ofreneo: *The Philippines – Debt and Poverty*, Oxford: Oxfam (in association with the Freedom From Debt Coalition, Manila), 1991.

Clive Robinson: *Hungry Farmers – World Food Needs and Europe's Response*, London: Christian Aid, 1989.

Robert Thomson: *Green Gold – Bananas and Dependency in the Eastern Caribbean*, London: Latin America Bureau, 1987.

Phil Wells and Mandy Jetter: *The Global Consumer – Best Buys to Help the Third World*, London: Gollancz, 1991.

INDEX